Sport and International Development

Global Culture and Sport

Series Editors: **Stephen Wagg** and **David Andrews**

Titles include:

Roger Levermore and Aaron Beacom (*editors*)
SPORT AND INTERNATIONAL DEVELOPMENT

Global Culture and Sport
Series Standing Order ISBN   **978-0-230-57818-0 hardback**
                                   978-0-230-57819-7 paperback
                                   (*outside North America only*)

You can receive future titles in this series as they are published by placing a standing order. Please contact your bookseller or, in case of difficulty, write to us at the address below with your name and address, the title of the series and the ISBN quoted above.

Customer Services Department, Macmillan Distribution Ltd, Houndsmills, Basingstoke, Hampshire RG21 6XS, England

Sport and International Development

Edited By

Roger Levermore
University of Liverpool, UK

Aaron Beacom
University College Plymouth, UK

palgrave
macmillan

First published 2009 by
PALGRAVE MACMILLAN

Palgrave Macmillan in the UK is an imprint of Macmillan Publishers Limited,
registered in England, company number 785998, of Houndmills, Basingstoke,
Hampshire RG21 6XS.

Palgrave Macmillan in the US is a division of St Martin's Press LLC,
175 Fifth Avenue, New York, NY 10010.

Palgrave Macmillan is the global academic imprint of the above companies
and has companies and representatives throughout the world.

Palgrave® and Macmillan® are registered trademarks in the United States,
the United Kingdom, Europe and other countries.

ISBN-13: 978-0-230-54256-3   hardback
ISBN-10: 0-230-54256-5   hardback

This book is printed on paper suitable for recycling and made from fully
managed and sustained forest sources. Logging, pulping and manufacturing
processes are expected to conform to the environmental regulations of the
country of origin.

A catalogue record for this book is available from the British Library.

Library of Congress Cataloging-in-Publication Data

Sport and international development / [edited by] Roger Levermore,
    Aaron Beacom.
        p. cm.
    Includes index.
    ISBN 978-0-230-54256-3 (alk. paper)
        1. Sports–Developing countries. 2. Sports–Economic aspects. 3. Economic
    development. I. Levermore, Roger, 1971– II. Beacom, Aaron, 1960–

    GV689.2.S76 2009
    338.4'7796–dc22   2008029944

10   9   8   7   6   5   4   3   2   1
18 17 16 15 14 13 12 11 10 09

Printed and bound in Great Britain by
CPI Antony Rowe, Chippenham and Eastbourne

Contents

List of Figure and Tables

Figures

Tables

List of Commonly Used Abbreviations

CAF	Confederation of African Football
CSR	Corporate Social Responsibility
EU	European Union
FIFA	Fédération Internationale de Football Association
GDP	Gross Domestic Product
ILO	International Labour Organization
IMF	International Monetary Fund
IOC	International Olympic Committee
MNCs	Multinational corporations
MYSA	Mathare Youth Sports Association
MDGs	Millennium Development Goals
MNCs	Multinational corporations
NGOs	Non Governmental Organizations
OECD	Organization for Economic Co-operation and Development
SCORE	Sport Coaches' Outreach
UEFA	Union of European Football Associations
UN	United Nations
UNICEF	United Nations Children's Fund
UNESCO	United Nations Educational, Scientific and Cultural Organization
WHO	World Health Organization

List of Contributors

Gerard Akindes, has a masters degree in economics and social sciences from the University of Mons-Hainaut and a masters degree in sports administration and African studies from Ohio University. He is currently working on an Interdisciplinary PhD. His research interests lie in African youth sport and development, sports administration in Africa, migration of African footballers, and media in sports. He is co-organizer of the Sports in Africa Conferences and workshops at Ohio University. He is member the editorial board of *Impumelelo*, the Electronic Interdisciplinary Journal of African Sports.

Aaron Beacom, is currently Senior Lecturer (sport policy) and Programme Leader for the MA Applied Sport Development at University College Plymouth, St. Mark & St. John. After six years in sport centre management, Aaron returned to education, teaching on a range of sport and management related programmes. Alongside his teaching, he studied for an MA in European Politics and a PhD in Politics (University of Exeter, 2003). During this period he published two papers in the academic journal *The Sports Historian*. Since completion of this PhD he has developed his research profile in sport and international politics. Most recently, delivery of papers relating to sport in international development at three international conferences was followed by publication of an academic paper in *European Sport Management Quarterly* (March 2007) and co-authoring a chapter on sport in development in the edited book *Management of Sports Development* (editor V. Girginov; publication April 2008).

Jerry Bingham, is the Research & Policy Manager at UK Sport, the body charged by Government with the task of leading sport in the UK to world-class success plus a range of other responsibilities, including developing the UK's sporting influence globally and contributing to the growth of sport in the developing world. Jerry first became involved in sport-in-development issues when he took part in a UNICEF-organized seminar on monitoring and evaluation held in New York at the beginning of 2005, since when he has supported a number of UK Sport's initiatives in this area, including the commissioning of a monitoring and evaluation manual by Professor Fred Coalter of Stirling

University. Jerry was invited to chair the two sessions on sport-in-development that took place at the 2007 International Studies Association Congress in Chicago and which led directly to the production of this book.

Fred Coalter is Professor of Sports Policy at the University of Stirling. His published work includes *A Wider Social Role for Sport: Who's Keeping the Score?* (2007) and *Sport-in-Development: A Monitoring and Evaluation Manual* (UK Sport, UNICEF, 2006) which was based on extensive fieldwork in Africa and India. Currently, he is undertaking a three year study of eight sport-in-development projects in Africa and two in India for Comic Relief and UK Sport. He is also responsible for compiling Sport England/UK Sport's on-line research-based *Value of Sport Monitor*. He is an Honorary Fellow of the Institute for Leisure and Amenity Management, the American Academy of Leisure Sciences and Chief Officers for Culture, Leisure and Community Services in Scotland and a member of the Scientific Advisory Board of the Swiss Academy Development.

Scarlett Cornelissen (PhD, University of Glasgow) is associate professor in Political Science at the University of Stellenbosch. She conducts research on the following topics: changed forms of spatiality and governance, sport and international relations, global tourism and the politics of sport mega-events. A monograph on the political economy of tourism (*The Global Tourism System: Governance, Development and Lessons from South Africa*) appeared in 2005. Aside from the publication of articles in journals such as *Review of International Political Economy* and *Third World Quarterly*, she has also co-edited three books on globalization and international relations. Scarlett is currently regional editor for Africa, of the journal *Leisure Studies*.

Tim Crabbe, is Professor of the Sociology of Sport and Popular Culture at Sheffield Hallam University and a founding member and Chair of Substance, a co-operative social research company based in Manchester, England. He has a specialist interest in the social dimensions of sport and popular culture and a long track record of conducting both 'pure' academic and applied reseach in these fields. His research and writing has focused particularly around the development and analysis of sport and activity based social policy initiatives and publications include, *The Changing Face of Football: Racism, Identity and Multiculture in the English Game; New Perspectives on Sport and 'Deviance';* and *Football and Community in the Global Context*.

Jude Fokwang, holds a PhD in socio-cultural anthropology from the University of Toronto, Canada and an MA in anthropology from the University of Pretoria, South Africa. He is a lecturer in the Department of Social Anthropology at the University of Cape Town, South Africa. Dr Fokwang has conducted fieldwork in Bamenda and Bali in Cameroon and Venda in South Africa focusing on topics such as chieftaincy and democratization, youth identities, citizenship, popular culture and young people's associations. He is the author of several publications on youth identities and politics notably, 'Ambiguous Transitions: Mediating Citizenship among Youth in Cameroon' (*Africa Development* 28 (1&2): 76–104), 'Youth Involvement in Civil Society in Cameroon since 1990' (*Africa Insight* 37(3): 308–326) and co-author with Francis Nyamnjoh of 'Entertaining repression: Music and Politics in Postcolonial Cameroon' (*African Affairs* 104, 251–274). His research interests include the changing dynamics of citizenship in a globalizing world, migration, African diaspora identities, popular culture and urban associations in Africa. He is currently preparing a book on young people's associations in urban Bamenda, Cameroon.

Matthew Kirwin, is doctoral student in the political science department at Michigan State University and a research assistant with the Afrobarometer. He has conducted research on sports and development in Niger and Burkina Faso and has worked in Cote d'Ivoire, Mali and Benin. His other research endeavors have focused on issues such as ethnic identity, political violence and religion and politics. He is the recipient of a West African Research Association Fellowship (2007) and a Fulbright Hays Fellowship (2008–9). He has Masters degrees in political science and African studies from Ohio University. While at Ohio University, he, along with Gerard Akindes, co-founded the Annual Sports and Africa Conference. He speaks French, Hausa and Arabic.

Roger Levermore, is a lecturer in International Development and research manager for the Football Industry Group, at the University of Liverpool Management School. He is co-editor of *Sport and International Relations: An emerging relationship* (2004) and has articles on sport-in-development published in *Progress in Development* and the *Brown Journal of World Affairs*. His research in development has largely concentrated on the region of southern Africa (PhD, University of Plymouth whilst being placed at the South African Institute of International Affairs in Johannesburg) and the latest focus relates to corporate social responsibility on social and economic development.

Sara Nicholls, is a graduate student at the University of Ottawa in the collaborative Sociology of Sport and Women's Studies program. Her work centers on postcolonial feminist analysis of the role of young women in sport for development policy and programs. Sara is the recipient of a Canadian Institute of Health Research ACADRE fellowship and holds an honours degree in Kinesiology focusing on health promotion and gender from the University of Western Ontario. Sara has spent the last 5 years living and working in Southern and Eastern Africa, first with the National Olympic Committee of Zambia and then as the Senior Africa Regional Officer for Commonwealth Games Canada, responsible for programs and partnerships in 10 African nations. Currently, Sara is a Policy Analyst for the Department of Canadian Heritage's International Sport for Development and Peace Unit. Recently named by CAAWS as one of Canada's most influential women in sport in the 'One to Watch' category, Sara is also Canada's Youth Ambassador to the UN for the MDGs.

Lorna Read, is Assistant Vice President Strategy and Planning for the international NGO, Right To Play. She is responsible for oversight of the annual integrated planning process, long term strategies related to restricted donors, and maintaining key relationships with governments, universities, partners, agencies and networks. She holds a Ph.D. in Political Science from Columbia University, New York. Her experience ranges across 17 years of dedication to international development, with a primary focus on Latin America, although her current position has taken her focus to Africa, Asia and the Middle East. Her research has focused on issues related to decentralization, poverty reduction strategies, municipal institution capacity-building and civil society participation in the development process.

Martha Saavedra, Ph.D., is the Associate Director of the Center for African Studies at the University of California, Berkeley. Trained as a Political Scientist, she has taught at St. Mary's College of California, UC Berkeley and Ohio University. Her research has ranged from agrarian politics, development and ethnic conflict in the Nuba Mountains of Sudan to gender and sport in Africa to a new collaborative project on representations of Africa in Chinese popular culture. At the Center, she co-coordinates the Understanding Sudan.org curriculum project, oversees public programs and fellowships, and advocates for the instruction of African languages among other things. She is on the editorial boards of *Soccer and Society*; *Sport in Society;* and *The Interdisciplinary Journal of Sports in Africa*. A veteran of Title IX battles, she has played soccer for over 30 years and is now coaching her sons.

Preface

by Lorna Read (Right to Play) and Jerry Bingham (UK Sport)

This book grew out of two sessions on sport-in-development that took place at the 2007 International Studies Association Congress in Chicago, Illinois, USA. Anyone at that conference who was new to the field would quickly have learnt that, as with other international development interventions and initiatives, sport-in-development is conceived, explained, understood and practised in a variety of different ways. The objective of this book is to put sport-in-development on the map in the development literature, and to position it within the larger international development debates. For a subject that is so rich in analytic potential, and currently so popular, it is surprising that this has not happened before.

Over the last decade, there has been an intensification of initiatives and an increase in the number of organizations that focus on sport-in-development. Included within the international realm of stakeholders are UN organizations, national governments, international sports organizations, NGOs and locally-based community organizations. During the same period, the momentum with respect to the importance of these programmes has grown exponentially. Notably, this translated into the growing interest in and acceptance of sport, as an intervention that both brings its own value, and adds value to a variety of development and humanitarian contexts. Although there is a growing body of research that highlights a relationship between sport, its physical and emotional benefits, and its social and cultural change, it is widely recognized that more needs to be done to understand this relationship and the impact that sport can have. This book presents a timely collection of theoretical debates and case-studies relevant to the advancement of sport-in-development as a pertinent area of research.

Given the number of organizations working at the global, national and local levels, sport-based programmes now exist in practically every country, from Azerbaijan to Zambia. However widespread these programmes might be, the reality is that we are still a very long way from providing access to sport for every child and young person, a level of provision that some (such as the IOC and the UN) argue should be considered as a 'human right' (United Nations Conventions 1979, 1989). The most effective means to ensure an increase in access is through concrete examples of the value of sport-in-development supported by research. Sport-in-development has reached the point where it is critical to leverage the experience and knowledge of organizations operating across a broad range of programmes, countries and issues to build an evidence-base that enables meaningful comparative analysis. The implementation of such a research agenda requires collaboration between researchers, policy makers and partner organizations. As such there is a defined need for further evaluation and research in this field that will produce information that can be disseminated to a variety of stakeholders.

This book addresses a number of significant issues that have arisen alongside the convergence of the international sport community and the international development community as shared goals continue to be articulated. These issues include: (a) definitions of sport; (b) the different levels at which sport intersects with development; (c) sport as an agent that is potentially able to influence the process of social change; (d) ability of sport-in-development to create partnerships from agencies that have quite conflicting agendas; and (e) the ability to sustain micro-level initiatives as well as international sport tournaments. Common understanding is critical with respect to these kinds of issues so that any hurdles to more effective cooperation between the two communities can be overcome. This book represents an important contribution to this end.

As the 'sport' and 'development' sectors continue to collaborate, it is imperative to emphasize that the concept of sport within the context of sport-in-development should be broadly defined such as to include all types of organized physical activity that may serve as a tool for development and peace. Although traditional sports development objectives are often at the heart of sport-in-development projects, what characterizes much of the movement is a perception of sport's capacity to contribute to the achievement of broader social and human development goals, where sport is a means as much as an end. To illustrate this point, there are a number of examples to demonstrate how sport-in-development programmes that emphasize broader goals both complement and are an extension of mainstream sport, such as building of life skills as well as skill building; sport for all as well as sport for elite athletes; reliance on indigenous resources to compensate the need for extensive infrastructure; league-based community based activities; values over and above mere rules; and an emphasis on inclusion that counteracts the perception of sport as often being exclusionary. It would be wrong to imagine that the sport-in-development programmes are homogenous. Rather, it is now widely understood that sport-in-development projects are likely to take one of two broad forms either those that have become known as 'sport plus' and those known as 'plus sport'. These terms are explored in some detail in the introductory chapter. Essentially however, they contrast in that 'sport plus' projects have the major aim of developing sustainable sports organizations to deliver sporting objectives while also addressing one or more social issues, whereas 'plus sport' projects tend to use sport in a more instrumental way as a means of achieving the primarily non-sporting outcomes that are likely to be their main focus. Further, as UK Sport explains in its Sport in Development Monitoring and Evaluation Manual (Coalter, 2006: 2), 'of course, there is a continuum of such programmes and differences are not always clear-cut.' This continuum is, in part, related to the many different contexts in which these programmes take place, which in turn have an effect on the type of outcomes.

The powerful illustrations of the uniqueness of these programmatic interventions include on a broad level the effectiveness with which sport-based programmes have been able to encourage participation and build individual and community capacity. Indeed, there is a growing recognition that, while acknowledging the limitations as well as the opportunities presented by the sport-in-development movement, programmes may provide an additional and valuable intervention to address the MDGs. As the introductory chapter explains in further detail, sport is also widely viewed as offering benefits in the following areas: (1) health promotion and disease prevention; (2) promotion of gender equity and equality; (3) social integration and the development of social capital: (4) peace building and conflict prevention/resolution; (5) post-disaster trauma relief and normalization of life: (6) economic development; and (7) communication and social mobilization.

While much of this book is concerned with a critical analysis of claims such as these, there is significant anecdotal evidence to date which connects sport-in-development programmes to these MDGs and thematic areas. For example, ways in which sport-in-development programmes can contribute to MDG2 (achieve universal primary education) include:

- Sport activities in schools reduce negative attitudes towards school and increase retention.
- Sport activities teach children tolerance, acceptance and the value of inclusion.
- Inclusive extra-curricular sport-in-development programmes foster greater gender equality in schools and contribute to reduced school drop-out rates among girls.
- Quality sport activities improve the relationship between teacher (as a mentor) and child.

On the same basis, ways in which sport-in-development programmes can contribute to MDG3 (promoting gender equality and empowering women) include:

- The inclusion of girls in sport and play activities alongside boys is a powerful means to alter gender stereotypes at the community level.
- Sport activities give women and girls access to public spaces that allow them to gather together, develop social networks and meet with each other in a safe environment.
- Training female teachers as 'coaches' effectively develops and mobilizes female community leaders and role models, and increases community commitment to include girls in sport.

As a final example, ways in which sport-in-development programmes can contribute to MDG6 (combating HIV/AIDS, malaria and other diseases) include:

- Sport as an educational tool can be used to empower children and youth with prevention messages and teach them the skills in early adolescence necessary to establish and sustain healthy behaviour patterns.
- The popularity of sport activities among children and youth provides a forum to bring people together to talk openly about sensitive issues such as safe sex, stigma and discrimination.
- The popularity of sport festivals can provide a powerful communication and mobilization platform for effective vaccination and prevention campaigns that target HIV/AIDS and other infectious diseases such as malaria or measles.

As we indicated earlier, an inevitable part of this book is to engage with the ongoing debate about sport's real effectiveness in addressing these benefits at a community (and individual) level. The nature of the book means that the examination of the role of sport has to be carried out in the relatively unfamiliar milieu of international relations, where motives are invariably complicated and objectives often unclear. To illustrate the point, Levermore's chapter considers the question of power relations as expressed through development (politics), while Kirwin and Akindes discuss the south-to-north movement of athletes from the perspective of dependency theories. The complexity of the development world is such that sports planners and practitioners are having both to re-learn their subject as it relates to a number of very different contexts, and at the same time to find new ways of reassuring funders about the value of their investments.

The contribution of the academic community is vital in this context. To some extent, academics and policy makers are always likely to have different agendas: academics seek to understand the world through some kind of theoretical construct while policy makers are more immediately concerned with what works, or perhaps more correctly, with what can be *shown* to work. However, academics can provide those entangled in the political here-and-now with an important historical perspective on events and they are also uniquely positioned to look across sectors and disciplines, drawing insights from, and applying lessons to, *different* sectors and disciplines. There are numerous examples of such cross-disciplinary involvement in sport itself, where important contributions to policy and practice have variously been made by philosophers, economists, sports scientists, statisticians and others.

Academics can remind us where we've come from and what we've done and they can provide a reality check on overblown ambitions and unsubstantiated claims. They can also help us look into the future in a way that is free from operational or political pressures. Never have these attributes been more needed than in the cross-disciplinary field of sport-in-development, where the coming together of two very different and separate cultures inevitably creates tensions.

While compendia such as this one make an important and necessary contribution to the debate, the published word is not the only medium through which to connect academic, policy and practice communities. All parties should be prepared to meet regularly to share ideas and listen to what others have to say. Policy makers should consider providing researchers with active support and encouragement to develop their research proposals. They may even charge academic experts with developing a sectoral research agenda, potentially generating a range of mutual benefits.

Funding and delivery agencies can – and do – engage academics to go into the field. From academics who work in an applied way, the message gaining currency is that the development task is essentially one of relationship-building – and that, as suggested in the examples above, sport provides one framework in which relationships can be built. Of course, this process does not happen automatically. Sport-based projects have to work to engage often disengaged people and then to keep them engaged. Drawing on his involvement with a number of sport-in-development projects, Coalter's chapter therefore emphasizes that understanding the process of how projects are conceptualized and delivered is at least as important as measuring the outcomes of those projects. In this respect, the academic may act as much as a consultant as an 'inspector', the very process of evaluating projects by understanding and articulating why they operate in a particular way making an important contribution to organizational development and capacity-building.

Another element which is critical to the relative popularity of sport-in-development as compared to other international development initiatives is the engagement of certain aspects of the private domain, such as sport companies, sport teams and athletes. This domain represents access to unique funding sources and an ability to increase awareness among sections of the public to whom other initiatives do not necessarily appeal. As there is an increasing emphasis on global social responsibility, this is an opportune time to engage the private domains (discussed in further detail by Levermore in this publication).

Arguably, Southern sport-in-development projects are throwing into relief many of the issues that Northern planners and researchers have been grappling with for years in terms of evaluating their own domestically-based projects concerned with social development. This is not unrelated to the very rigorous standards of monitoring and evaluation demanded by donors and others – standards that, it has been pointed out, often exceed those they require in their own country. Crabbe's chapter considers the lessons for the wider development community of the UK's Positive Futures programme – one home-based initiative that has been the subject of a comprehensive evaluation exercise. In September 2007, the Positive Futures model was implemented for the first time outside the UK – the Positive Futures Cricket Project in Cape Town is aiming to address issues of gangs, guns, exclusion, education and employment in the area – and it will be instructive to see over time if and how this experience helps inform the continuing development of the UK programme.

Governments and development agencies have engaged relatively recently, with the idea that sport can be used in a systematic way as a development tool. By addressing the subject from a historical and theoretical perspective and by engaging in a range of critical case studies, the book develops an appreciation of contemporary opportunities and challenges facing the movement, as well as suggesting the contours of the sport-in-development landscape.

Bibliography

Coalter, F. (2006) *Sport in Development Monitoring and Evaluation Manual*, UK Sport, 2006.

Millennium Development Goals (2000) *United Nations Millennium Declaration*, September 2000.

United Nations (1979) *Convention on the Elimination of All Forms of Discrimination against Women*, Adopted December 1979, United Nations General Assembly.

United Nations (1989) *Convention on the Rights of the Child*, adopted November 1989, United Nations General Assembly.

1
Sport and Development: Mapping the Field

Roger Levermore and Aaron Beacom

1.1 Introduction

The last decade, and especially since the UN declared 2005 to be its International Year of Sport and Physical Education, has seen a significant expansion in the use of sport (broadly defined) as a tool for initiating social change. Projects involving sport have included attempts to educate young people to appreciate health concerns (such as the dangers of HIV and malaria), engender respect for local communities, discourage anti-social and criminal behaviour, increase gender-awareness, as well as assist with the rehabilitation of people with disabilities and the reconciliation of communities in conflict.

This phenomenon is not new since sport has long been viewed, particularly by governments, as having potential to help induce social order, and to some extent economic development. However, this recent expansion of sport as an actor for social change, especially in what the World Bank classifies as low-income countries (otherwise referred to as the 'Global South'), is partially a result of the recognition that the orthodox policies of 'development' have failed to deliver their objectives. Such policies (advocated strongly by Western Liberal Democracies in the post-war era), emphasize the economic rather than the social environment,[1] yet have often been unsuccessful in enhancing standards of living as absolute poverty remains endemic in many parts of the world (see for example, Black, 2002; Sachs, 2006; The Economist, 2007; Easterly 2007; Calderisi, 2007).

A consequence has been the growing recognition of the need for new strategies, methods and institutions/actors to assist delivery of far-reaching commitments, enshrined for example through the development aspirations presented as the UN MDGs and the UNs Global Compact.[2]

These aspirations highlight two trends. First, the growing emphasis, particularly since the World Commission on Culture and Development Report published in 1995, on culture and vehicles of culture to help deliver social as well as economic development. Second, the increase of institutions such as multinational corporations (MNCs), in the development process.

Among the emerging actors engaged in the development process, are a range of sports institutions/associations (including governing federations and clubs), multinational sports corporations and sports NGOs. It is important to note that many operate in a partnership, whereby a MNC such as Nike or government quango such as UK Sport, will fund a scheme, which is run by an NGO such as Right To Play (Beacom and Levermore, 2008). The NGO may in turn receive additional technical support, networking assistance/ advertising and additional resourcing from sports federations and governments or development agencies. As a result, sport – and these sport-in-development initiatives – has been credited with being a very useful and non-political vehicle to bring disparate and often opposing groups in the development policy-making process together.

The use of sport in international development sits within this broadening of the development focus. For advocates of the sport-in-development movement, the perception that sport can facilitate development because it is not associated with corruption in the development process (like the state has been in many low-income countries) or by the relative failure of previous development policies and institutions, are important factors contributing to its potential.

The benefits of sports' involvement in development processes are slowly being acknowledged by experienced policy makers in the development process for example, work with development agencies, mainstream development NGOs and governments. A number of high-profile statesmen have endorsed the sport/development relationship. This has included most prominently Nelson Mandela and Kofi Annan. The latter has been quoted as saying that sport can improve the lives of communities by tackling obstacles to development (such as conflict, disease and poverty) and contribute to ensuring the successful completion of the MDGs. In the UK, Tessa Jowell, (Minister for Culture, Media and Sport, June 2001–June 2007), commented that 'sport can be used to tackle many of the problems afflicting the developing world', by promoting good health, social development, as well as peace and reconciliation (Jowell, 2005).

Indeed, the UN has been credited with accelerating the sport-in-development movement following the nomination Adolf Ogi (former

President of Switzerland) as Special Adviser on Sport for Development and Peace in 2001. In 2003 the United Nations Inter-Agency Task Force on Sport for Development and Peace concluded that well designed sport-based initiatives that incorporate the best values of sport can be powerful, practical and cost-effective tools to achieve development and peace objectives (United Nations, Inter-Agency Task Force on Sport for Development and Peace, 2003). In November 2003, the General Assembly of the UN adopted a resolution affirming its commitment to sport as a means of promoting education, health, development and peace and to include sport and physical education as a tool that contributes towards achieving the internationally agreed development goals (including the MDGs).[3]

When the UN declared 2005 to be the International Year of Sport and Physical Education, the wide-ranging contribution expected of sport was stated clearly (United Nations, 2005: v):

> The world of sport presents a natural partnership for the United Nations system. By its very nature sport is about participation. It is about inclusion and citizenship. Sport brings individuals and communities together, highlighting commonalties and bridging cultural or ethnic divides. Sport provides a forum to learn skills such as discipline, confidence and leadership and it teaches core principles such as tolerance, cooperation and respect. Sport teaches the value of effort and how to manage victory, as well as defeat. When these positive aspects of sport are emphasized, sport becomes a powerful vehicle through which the United Nations can work towards achieving its goals.

Similarly, a growing number of traditional, mainstream development NGOs are turning to sport to further some of their development goals. For example, the Catholic Agency for Overseas Development (CAFOD) has developed projects that include using football to help integrate former child soldiers back into Liberian society by training them with life and social skills and tracing their families (CAFOD, undated).

Northern governments attempt to harness some of sport's attributes to assist in objectives linked to its international development/relations objectives. The Netherlands, Switzerland, Canada, Norway, and Australia are examples of developed countries that use sport in such a manner. Governments in the Global South are also using sport for macro development purposes. Countries such as Zambia include sport in their national poverty reduction strategy and national development plan to stimulate education, highlight health awareness campaigns and encourage participation in sport.

This book has been written against the backdrop of concern about the ability to deliver development. As noted above, there is a realization among development practitioners, for the need to seek alternative/better methods if substantive progress is to be made. The objective of the book is not to promote sport as an alternative vehicle for development. Other voices have taken up that call and are being met with increasing praise as well as scepticism from policy makers, academics and public alike. It is rather, to identify the potential and the limitations of engagement in activities loosely classified as 'sport' to contribute to the wider development process, particularly in the Global South by enhancing the quality of life in a range of ways.

The introductory chapter addresses the conceptual and contextual issues that form the frame of reference for the debates surrounding so called 'sport-in-development'. It then outlines the rationale and highlights the substance of succeeding chapters.

1.2   Meanings attributed to sport

A distinct and expanding body of literature has emerged over the past three decades, focusing on the characteristics of the physical and cultural phenomenon referred to as 'sport' and how it relates to the societies within which it is located. This literature crosses traditional disciplinary boundaries to include historical works by writers such as Guttmann (1978, 1994), Mandell (1984) and Brailsford (1992) as well as socio-political analyses by a wide range of authors including John Hargreaves (1986, 2002), Jennifer Hargreaves (1994), Cashmore (2005), Bairner (2001) and Maguire (1994, 1999, 2000).

The term 'sport' has been interpreted in a variety of ways. Most emphasize its physical and competitive elements, as well as its cultural determinants. In addition, there is generally reference to the institutionalization of sporting forms[4] and the increasing significance of (largely financial) rewards that extend beyond personal satisfaction as factors that define the contemporary sporting landscape. In this respect, Huizinga in the seminal *Homo Ludens* (1955: 196), refers to the transition of activities, especially in Eurasian countries, from spontaneous 'contest' and 'occasional amusement' to the establishment of 'fixed organization' that was required to facilitate the emergence of a network of team sports and the establishment of teams.

Some commentators, for example Read and Bingham in the preface to this publication, adopt a looser interpretation of where the parameters of sport lie. They use the term to describe a wide spectrum of culturally defined physical activities with considerable variation in the level and nature of organization and competition. What is important to stress is that the meaning of sport has changed quite dramatically in the last fifty years. While at mass participatory level, the 'fun' element remains as a central characteristic of sport, the evolution of many sporting forms, particularly in professional sport in 'developed' societies has seen a shift in general perceptions of the key characteristics of sport. This is partly associated with the changing political and economic environments within which sports organizations operate.

Given the international development context of the publication and inter-disciplinary profile of its contributors, this investigation adopts a broadly defined interpretation of what constitutes sport. For instance, while competitive sport does feature in the development process, many sport-in-development programmes use sport in a recreational or non-competitive manner. Examples from the sportandev.org website include dance and recreational cycling. This debate highlights that sport can be considered as a 'floating signifier'; defined by any commentator as they see fit, for a variety of purposes.

Linked to this discussion are writers from a range of academic disciplines, such as social history and sociology, who have reflected on the extent to which sports as social and cultural constructions in this increasingly globalized era, either continue to replicate the characteristics of the societies from which they are situated (Heinemann, 1993; Dunning, 1999; Dunning and Malcolm, 2003) or succumb to more homogenized traits because of the processes of colonialization, post-colonialism and globalization (Maguire, 1999). This in turn connects with wider debate concerning the extent to which sport has the capacity to act as an agent for change, as opposed to reflecting wider social and cultural change. Such debate has implications for how we subsequently interpret the impact of sport-in-development interventions.

It should be remembered that interpretation of what constitutes sport is much more than an academic exercise. Within the UK for instance, those activities classified as competitive sports have been able to access a variety of funding streams denied to other physical activities. Such classification may also form the terms of reference for policy change relating to investment in sport provision and the sport development process. This was recently articulated in the 28th November 2007 policy speech by James Purnell, (Secretary of State for Culture, Media and Sport, June 2007–January 2008) where, through a re-evaluation of what constituted 'sport' and the value of 'sport for sports sake', he set out the basis for policy shifts relating to the resourcing of sport development within the UK (Purnell, 2007).

1.3   International development defined

Debate as to the meanings attributed to the term 'development' has kept sociologists, economists, political theorists and anthropologists busy for many years. Until relatively recently, the dominant view of social and economic development, was for instance, associated with the idea of modernization through the processes linked to industrialization and corresponding economic growth. Such ideas fostered the concept of a linear path for development, which was quantifiable and which could be replicated given the correct pre-conditions. Sutton's 1955 (cited in Huntington, 1971: 283–322) summary of modern and traditional societies articulated this clearly.

This 'scientific' approach to the investigation of development fitted the Positivist perspective concerning the study of social phenomena and provided common ground for thinkers as diverse as Gunder Frank (who strongly criticized modernization approaches) and Rostow (1960).

Table 1.1   Characteristics of modern and traditional societies

Agricultural society	Modern industrial society
1. Predominance of ascriptive, particularistic, diffuse patterns	1. Predominance of universalistic, specific and achievement norms
2. Stable local groups and limited spatial mobility	2. High degree of social mobility (in a general, not necessarily 'vertical' sense)
3. Relatively simple and stable occupational differentiation	3. Well-developed occupational system, insulated from other social structures
4. A deferential stratification system of diffuse impact	4. 'Egalitarian' class system based on generalized patterns of occupational achievement
	5. Prevalence of 'associations' i.e. functionally specific, non-ascriptive structures

Source: Huntington, 1971: 284.

Within these approaches there is a long-standing belief that development is essentially good and dominated by a view that progress through economic growth and industrialization is possible. For modernization, these processes are often stimulated by a Northern donor organization (governmental or non-governmental) who enter into a relationship with a recipient from the Global South (governmental or nongovernmental).[5]

In practical terms, 'national' development continues to be measured by organizations such as the World Bank, through economic indicators like GDP. Indeed the core principle of development assistance remains the alleviation of absolute poverty and its consequences largely through policies advocated by modernization.

International development covers what is termed by various actors in the field (according to viewpoint) as the 'Third World', lesser developed regions of the world or the 'Global South' – in other words, countries or regions in the latter two categories of the World Bank's classification of developed countries, particularly in the lowest (low-income) bracket. These areas, predominantly in South America, Africa, Asia and the Pacific, are characterized by the following:

- Generally poor (material) standards of living
- Limited infrastructure (including education)
- Poor nutritional standards and/or limited access to clean water
- Prevalence of disease/ poor health care system
- Often unstable/authoritarian political systems
- Significant levels of discrimination and exclusion
- Low levels of trade, investment and general economic welfare.

The highest income countries are often collectively described as 'Northern' or 'Western'. These terms are used interchangeably throughout this publication.

We recognize that, because of the range of competing perspectives in the school of international development, there is a lack of common consensus surrounding what (international) development actually means. For the purposes of this research however, international development is taken to mean the processes by which there is an attempt to improve life chances throughout the world but particularly in countries considered to be low income.[6]

Clearly this rather traditional and standard definition of international development is open to many challenges, particularly that it is a Eurocentric/ethnocentric understanding of the world and that the indicators for development exclude characteristics that might portray 'developed' Northern/Western countries in a less privileged light. Furthermore, many of the characteristics listed above are evident within pockets of the Northern world. Sections of this book do return to this debate, especially through the terminology used to describe low-income countries, but we have used the term 'Global South' as our starting point.

1.4 'Sport' and 'development'

Modern sporting forms have, since their inception, often been tied to broad development objectives of some sort. This has either been in terms of individual skill acquisition and performance enhancement in developing sport or, as examples throughout this book highlight, in its adoption for the purposes of social, educational and cultural development. A well-rehearsed theme in recent literature is the differentiation between development *of* sport; that is activity designed to enhance participation and performance in sport as an end in itself, and development *through* sport; that is activity designed to use sport as a vehicle to achieve a range of other social, economic and political objectives (see for example, Houlihan and White's (2002) assessment of the politics of sports development). This latter understanding can be through specific development assistance programmes/projects or on a broader level within vaguer commitments to regional and national development strategies or via benefits generated with the hosting of sports events.

Clearly there are significant differences between these aspects of 'sports' and 'development'. Nevertheless, they are not mutually exclusive. This is articulated for instance, in the joint British Council and Youth Sport Trust sport leadership initiative entitled Dreams + Teams where there is parity between its aim of 'developing young leaders and global citizens through sport' (British Council, 2007) and the transference of specialist coaching skills. The initiative provides unique insights into the challenges and opportunities present when relationships with developing states are fostered through capacity building in sport and recreation. Engagement in delivery of sports leadership skills with a focus on international cultural awareness and inclusion, is then of equal importance to the enhancement of the coaching base within the recipient community.

At the same time, as has been discussed by Saavedra in Chapter 6, it is acknowledged by a number of sport-in-development practitioners, that the efficacy of many initiatives is largely dependent upon the capacity to secure skilled sports coaches with an appreciation of the

technical elements of skill acquisition as well as the soc
development context within which they are working. 'Sport de.
ment' programmes *may* then add to the development of sporting exce
lence, while at the same time contributing to broader development
objectives through the sporting activity.

Notwithstanding the linkage between these contrasting aspects of
sport development, it is nevertheless important to recognize the different rationales for engagement with the sport-in-development process
by a range of organizations and agencies. Coalter, in Chapter 3, introduces particularly useful terms to reflect this differential. On the one
hand he refers to those initiatives which are 'sport plus' – primarily
focused on the development of sport-oriented and those which are
'plus sport' – the focus principally on social and occasionally economic
development and how sport can assist this. It should be noted that the
'sport plus' category has very broad parameters where the articulation
of social and economic developmental spin-offs varies considerably.[7]
For example, as Akindes and Kirwin chart in Chapter 10, FIFA introduces two contrasting initiatives. The Football for Hope programme
has clearly outlined social development objectives that stipulate the
use of football for a youth target audience. FIFA's Goal programme
operates primarily to strengthen the football infrastructure in all of its
member states. However, a few social developmental side effects are
evident from this.

In these senses and for the purposes of this book, the term, 'sport-
in-development' is adopted, as representative of the perception that
the use of sport *may* assist the international development process. We
privilege this term above sport for development or sport through development (which are used elsewhere) because these latter terms imply that
the use of sport in the development process is an overwhelmingly positive one and tends to preclude the argument that sport might be detri-
mental to societies in the Global South.

As the preface to the publication and the opening paragraph highlight, there has been a noticeable increase in sport-in-development
initiatives. At the time of writing, 255 projects are listed on the
sportanddev.org website and considerably more undoubtedly exist. A
review of these schemes shows their recent intensification; 93% were
formed from 2000 onwards (28% from 2006 alone). The schemes can
be grouped into six major clusters:[8]

- Conflict resolution and intercultural understanding
- Building physical, social, sport and community infrastructure

- Raising awareness, particularly through education
- Empowerment
- Direct impact on physical and psychological health as well as general welfare
- Economic development/poverty alleviation

Some of these clusters are significant actors within the development sphere that they operate in. For example, the MYSA, is believed to be the largest grassroots organization in Kenya (Willis, 2000; Hognestad and Tollisen, 2004). However, most of these programmes are run on a micro-scale, reflected in initiatives that assist one or more of the themes highlighted above. Unsurprisingly, given the low levels of development that mainstream indicators give the region, most of the schemes – totalling 52% of all programmes – are located in sub-Saharan Africa. 18% (46 schemes) run in East Africa; 14% function in West Africa and 20% operate in Southern Africa. The target audience is over-whelmingly youth focused with 51% of schemes dedicated to children and young people. Sport is credited as having qualities that are particularly appealing to this section of community, where other traditional development initiatives might be perceived to be more staid or lacking interest/impact.

Furthermore, as many of the schemes are sport plus oriented, it is not surprising that 15% of the schemes are directed towards sport instructors. Other significant target groups are the disabled (9%), girls and women (10%) and refugees (10%).

Continuing with the 'Functionalist' perspective of sport and society, it is frequently claimed that sport may also contribute in less tangible ways to the development of a country (as true in Northern societies as it is within the Global South). For instance, there are those who argue that the Democratic Republic of Congo and Cote d'Ivoire attribute sport (mainly football) as one of the few successful vehicles at driving some form of integrative unity; something that is most noticeable when a national team performs well in an international tournament, whilst also projecting a positive image on a world stage. Success in sporting competitions has helped portray countries from the Global South in a more positive light (Levermore, 2004). These arguments were also used in the context of sport in the colonial and immediate post-colonial (independence) eras. For example, President Kwame Nkrumah was one of the first African statesmen to adopt the position that success at sporting events could assist the presentation of African countries in international society in the postcolonial era (Darby, 2005:

888). However, it could be argued that an equally negative portrayal, pandering to stereotypes and highlighting the backwardness of some countries, can also be articulated through such events (see chapter two for further discussion on this).

This chapter proceeds by considering the well-documented historical use of sport in development and nation-building processes within Global South countries. In so doing, it recognizes the call for a more critical approach to the study of sport in society. Moreover, a consideration of engagement of sport in the development process over the longer term provides a context within which the contemporary characteristics of the sport-in-development can be better understood. For example, Maguire and Young (2002: 1) refer to the 'threat of being tied too closely to the here and now and providing solutions to short term problems'. They point to the limited value of adopting an atheoretical and ahistorical approach to the investigation of sport in society. Similar concerns are echoed by contributors to this book. To that end, arguments have been embedded in a wider development theory with its concern with shifting power relations and the re-framing of the development agenda.

1.5   Historical perspectives on sport-in-development

Debate on the evolution of sport-in-development is generally character-ized by reference to its recent rapid expansion. Yet within the context of development assistance broadly defined, evidence points to a long history of development interventions involving sport. This has taken the form of support for institutional development and logistical and material assis-tance for athletes from colonies and former colonies as well as fostering engagement in sport as a mechanism for promulgating cultural values. As with mainstream development assistance, the form that sport-in-development has taken has historically been influenced by wider tensions in colonial and international relations. An appreciation of these historical experiences enhances understanding of challenges faced when engaging in contemporary development assistance programmes.

The link between colonialism (imperialism) and development is long established in literature. Townshend highlights the influence of socio-logist Herbert Spencer, on Hobson's classic work on imperialism that addressed the capacity of imperial intervention to contribute to the organic growth of international society (Hobson, 1988).[9] In the context of sport, such an idea of development assistance was articulated through attempts, as in the domestic sphere, to replace perceived 'barbaric' local customs with the 'civilizing' influence of particular sporting forms (Mangan, 2006).

This idea of sport having the capacity to 'civilize' was not limited to nineteenth century colonialism. Guttmann (1992) for instance, refers to attempts to export characteristics associated with ancient Hellenic culture through the early Olympic Games.[10] Nevertheless, it is in relation to the diffusion of modern sporting forms throughout empire, that the idea of its potential to contribute to the civilizing process becomes established.

The comprehensive body of literature relating to the international diffusion of modern sporting forms does then provide a valuable resource when investigating the challenges facing contemporary sport development assistance. The origins of contemporary initiatives seeking to use sport as a conduit for development remain within the frame of reference established during the period when these sports were going through the process of international transmission and translation. This is further underpinned by a separate but related body of sociological literature that investigates the place of sport in the 'civilizing process.' The belief that sport can have a civilizing influence on societies both in terms of the channelling of 'physical exertions' through the 'highly regulated form of sport [serving] as symbolic representations of non-violent competition between states' (Elias and Dunning, 1986: 23) and in terms of wider transference of cultural values, has provided the catalyst for a wide ranging debate, much of which is highly critical, on how sport relates to social development.

This perspective on the civilizing influence of modern sporting forms should be considered alongside the historically negative perception often shown by early commentators towards indigenous sport. Heinemann (1993: 144) for example, highlights the destructive impact of colonialism on traditional sport in the Global South, arguing that missionaries 'regarded popular sport, especially dancing, as immoral and felt it was too closely associated with the myths and cults of traditional society. They were also afraid that such pursuits could prevent people from attending church services'. The common strand running through this argument concerns power relations between the 'donor' and the 'recipient'. Sociologists such as Sugden and Tomlinson (2002: 8) have focused on the significance of sport as; 'one cultural form in which agency/power relations can be studied'. Their historical approach to social research can, when considered in the context of sport and development, facilitate a clearer appreciation of the influence of power dynamics on this process.

1.5.1 Development through new sporting forms: opportunities for imperial consolidation?

There has then been much scholarly debate concerning the contribution of modern sporting forms to ideas of development (MacAloon, 2006). Of particular note is reference to their contribution toward the development and consolidation of empire. Notwithstanding contemporary disagreement concerning the extent to which indigenous groups had agency in appropriation and translation of 'muscular Christian'[11] sport (Majumdar, 2006), the diffusion of modern sporting forms was it seemed, part of the cultural fabric associated with the expansion and consolidation of empire.

The relationship between the amateur sporting tradition and idealized notions of British imperialism has been explored in literature relating to both the history of sport and the history of empire. In both cases, it has been argued that the education process provided the environment within which sport was adopted as a means to communicate imperial responsibility. MacKenzie (1984), in his investigation of the perpetuation of empire, argued that sport was one aspect of a framework of curricular and extra-curricular activities through which attempts were made to imbue children at home, with a consciousness of imperial and military destiny.[12] The 'ideology of athleticism' had, it is commonly argued, become an integral part of public school culture, developing its own rituals and symbols and forming the basis of responsible, disciplined codes of behaviour. While there has been much scholarly debate about the nature of the 'donor–recipient' relationship in the context of imperial relations, attempts to transmit this value system to recipients through-out the empire, did clearly become a defining aspect of the colonial experience.

The claim that the diffusion of sport has contributed to the maintenance of empire, particularly in terms of disseminating 'British culture' and aiding the integration of indigenous elites, has then become a familiar theme of literature relating to the period (see for example MacKenzie, 1984). Mangan (1998) has made much of the adoption of the new sporting forms by indigenous elites in India. He refers to a number of Indian contemporaries of the late nineteenth century, as indicating their support for the use of the public school system in India and more specifically, the inculcation of codes of behaviour through engagement with English sports. The policy of promoting sport for the improvement of colonial populations had by the 1930s achieved tangible results in terms of internalizing the system of athletic education (Holt, 1989). Perkin (1989) went as far as, somewhat optimistically, suggesting that this diffusion had paradoxically also contributed to the emancipation of subject nations and so helped the British Empire to decolonize on a friendlier basis than was the experience with other imperial powers. Recent interpretations of this historical experience adopt a more critical approach to the process of diffusion and stress the translation of new sporting cultures within a variety of indigenous contexts (MacAloon, 2006; Majumdar, 2006). Notwithstanding lack of consensus among commentators regarding the extent to which sport contributed to cultural hegemony, attempts were certainly being made during this period to use assistance with the development of sport as a vehicle for managing imperial relations.

1.5.2   Interpreting contemporary developments

Understanding the colonial and post-colonial imperatives for such activity provides the context within which continued attempts to achieve development objectives through sport, can be explored. This is the case for instance, when investigating the role of sport leadership initiatives which, as part of international education programmes, are designed to inculcate a particular interpretation of roles and responsibilities in social development, as well as contributing to the enhancement of sporting infrastructure. Such activity is evident in a range of contemporary sport-in-development activities, most notably the joint British Council and Youth Sport Trust initiative Dreams + Teams (introduced above). Its aim of 'developing young leaders and global citizens through sport', provides unique insights into the challenges and opportunities present when relationships with developing states are fostered through capacity building in sport and recreation in developing states.

The existing framework of international contacts that the British Council has evolved over a number of years has provided an entry point for many of the Dreams + Teams projects. During Autumn 2004 and Spring 2005 a number of school links were developed in Hungary and the Czech Republic. The investigation identified that in the case of the Czech Republic, the enthusiasm of the Education Ministry led to a rapid expansion of the initiative. In addition it was argued that existing British Council programmes in South Africa have made a small contribution to the South African Government's strategy of training large numbers of young sports leaders in preparation for the football World Cup in South Africa in 2010.[13]

Finally it should be noted that the familiar themes of the social, physical and cultural value of sport continue to underpin calls for engagement with sport in a domestic development setting. This, despite limited tangible evidence concerning the true 'value' of sport (a theme explored later in the book). The heightened interest in development *through* sport domestically (in the UK) since the social unrest during the early 1980s,[14] continues with initiatives such as Positive Futures (explored in detail in chapter eight of this book). The re-interpretation of that message in the context of international development assistance forms the basis for themes throughout the book. Indeed, the experience in many donor countries, of using sport as a development tool in a domestic setting and the interest of a range of sports organizations and agencies in this process provides a basis upon which to expand activities into the wider development arena.

This expansion of sport-in-development initiatives from a domestic to an international setting, requires translation to align initiatives to new cultural contexts. Such translation, assessment and application need the engagement of policy makers and scholars across the North–South divide. By considering sport in the context of development theory and by engaging in a series of supporting case studies, this book contributes to that process.

1.6   Engaging sport-in-development discourse with mainstream development literature

Recognition of the role of sport as a potential engine of development is largely absent from the social sciences literature. Unsurprising, given its recent development, none of the seminal international development texts (such as Bhagwati, 1985; Amin, 1974; Frank, 1967; Rostow, 1960 and Balassa, 1978) or journals include even a cursory mention of sport. This trend has continued to present times – the last fifteen years of *International Development Abstracts*, found that from over 70,000 entries, only twelve mentioned sport. Contemporary texts on development (such as Hettne, 1995; Desai and Potter, 2002 and Kingsbury *et al.*, 2004), in which one might expect some discussion of the recent intensification of sport-in-development, fails to highlight or comment on the relationship. Only a poorly circulated and little known two page article in *International Development Review* (Anthony, 1969 – which argued that the benefits of sport-in-development had been neglected by practitioners and academics), Frey (1988) and a 2005 edition of *Third World Quarterly* discusses the role of sport (mega sporting events) in any detail from what might be termed loosely development academics. Other research emanates from sports studies, with Coalter (2005, 2007), Maguire (1999 and 2000), Armstrong (1997), Giulianotti (2004), Darby (2002), Arbena

(1993), Heinemann (1993) and Chappell (2004) amongst those who consider some of the relationships between sport and international development. However, and with notable exceptions (most of the authors above), sport-in-development is rarely the centre of their analysis and some are highly descriptive, noting simply that sport does play a role in promoting development around the world without embellishing further.

The 'disengagement' of sport and international development by the academic community is possibly due to the long-established and reasonably well documented unease with which sport has been viewed as being exclusive, male-dominated and somehow problematic because of its association with large-scale popular culture (despite the popularity of sport at the moment). Undoubtedly, exaggerated claims that sport is a panacea to 'cure all,' that some people make (particularly in the sport industry), is a further reason for a degree of alienation of sport by 'developmentalists' (Levermore, 2008b).

The central aim of this book is therefore to initiate a debate in academic international development circles on the use of sports based initiatives to establish and assist development. The critical appraisal will be concerned with identifying limitations as well as establishing contexts within which such initiatives can be considered beneficial. As catalysts for international development range from emergency and humanitarian aid, through to trade, investment, knowledge transfer and assistance with political transition, this book investigates the capacity of sport to act both as a conduit for traditional development assistance activities and as an agent for change in its own right. It argues that sport can, in certain contexts, contribute to the development process, particularly where traditional development approaches have difficulty in engaging with communities. It contends that understanding the opportunities and limitations for sport-in-development, contributes to an appreciation of the fundamental challenges currently facing the development community.

The book responds to a scholarly vacancy that, despite growing interest in the subject, exists in relation to sport-in-development. An assessment of the roles of sport based initiatives as a potential engine of development is largely absent from the social sciences literature. It is not just academic literature – as argued above – that largely neglects to highlight this growing trend. Notwithstanding some notable exceptions (see for example the UN statements on sport-in-development), many development agencies, such as the IMF and World Bank, or mainstream development NGOs, have failed to assess – and at times even recognize – the sport/development interaction. The UN tacitly admits this, noting in one policy document (2003: 2) that, 'Sport is seen as a by-product of development, not as an engine'.

1.7   The structure of the book

The book addresses a range of contemporary concerns emerging from the sport-in-development movement. It does this through a combination of analysis of conceptual debates and academic writing on the subject, investigation of the experience of key communities as 'recipients' of sport-in-development (identified above as young people, sports instructors, women and the disabled) and assessment of specific sport-in-development case studies. A central theme in the book is the call for more – and better – measurement of the impact that sport has on development. Coalter leads the way with a chapter devoted to this subject but all other chapters focus partly on this debate.

The structure of the book revolves around three broad areas; each comprising three chapters. The first of these highlights important general themes, issues and suggestions for analysis and measurement that are often echoed in more specific case studies or themed chapters that follow. The first of these chapters (Chapter 2), considers the contending views on sport and development from the perspective of development theories, by assessing the implications of different viewpoints in understanding donor-recipient relations in the context of sport development assistance. It suggests that the sport/development relationship highlights some benefits, especially in the dominant way of viewing development (modernization and neo-liberalism) whilst also posing a number of concerns from alternative theories that are not always confronted by practitioners who engage in sport-in-development. Criticisms range from sport perpetuating the 'core-periphery relationship' to the reinforcement of dominant perspectives of international development by conveying a message that Northern initiatives are best, often by portraying the Global South in a subordinate manner.

Chapter 3 addresses the call by many, especially donors, for more (and effective) evaluation of the impact of sport-in-development. It suggests that a key impediment to understanding the opportunities and limitations of sport as part of the development process is a misunderstanding of the nature of sport and how sport relates to wider society. It argues that an approach to monitoring and evaluation of such sport/development assistance initiatives based solely on impacts and outcomes, misunderstands the nature and potential of sport-in-development organizations. Considerations relating to sport as process, sport and the context of poverty and, most importantly, the relationship between sport-in-development organizations, social capital and weak civil societies require a 'process-led approach' to monitoring and evaluation. The chapter argues for an alternative approach by illustrating the value of theory-driven approaches which examine the assumptions about assumed program mechanisms and the extent to which they are legitimate and reflected in programme design and delivery.

Chapter 4 moves away from concentrating on sport-in-development projects by considering another dimension of the role of *sport in development* – the economic, social and political impacts of major sports events and the ramifications for development. A number of contending perspectives on this widely debated subject are explored. The chapter concludes with a discussion of the major developmental contours that sports events seem to have, and given the growing significance that the hosting of such events poses for policy, what factors should be taken into consideration for the promotion of sport-in-development at both the international and national levels.

The second area considers how different communities (the disabled, women and young people) relate to the sport-in-development movement. Chapter 5 addresses the issue of disability from the perspective of the sport-in-development movement. It considers a range of cross-cultural interpretations of what constitutes disability and considers the contrasting range of perspectives on disability rights across cultures. It argues that as inclusion and disability rights have moved up the domestic political agenda of Western Liberal Democracies, this has created a momentum toward responding to the needs of disabled people within the sport-in-development context. This trend is accentuated by the response of international organizations such as the UN, to rapidly increasing numbers of disabled people, resulting from a range of regional conflicts. These factors, combined with the organizational objectives of key international sports NGOs, have provided a new momentum for international assistance with the development of sport for disabled people. At the same time however, a number of recent initiatives have highlighted the difficulties that result from cultural tensions between donor organizations and recipients. They clearly illustrate the challenges faced by the wider development community when attempting to reconcile the objectives of donor organizations, with the perceived needs of recipients.

Chapter 6 addresses the tensions inherent in gender relations within the sport in development frame. It identifies efforts to empower – a central plank of the development agenda – as characteristic of effective sport-in-development programmes aimed at girls and young women. While this presents unique opportunities for development practitioners, it also presents dilemmas as established power relations are challenged. The chapter places gender, sport and development within wider historical context, with reference to nineteenth century attempts to achieve social and cultural development through sport, as well as highlighting the practical requirements for effective programme delivery. It argues that seeking to empower females through sport is somewhat paradoxical given that the world of sport can be a bastion for male privilege and power, an important arena for asserting a particular kind of male dominance over women (and some men), as well as furthering EuroAmerican hegemony *vis-à-vis* the Global South.

Chapter 7 is concerned chiefly with youth both as a major human resource for development and as key agents for social change. In light of the pivotal role of young people in the development process, Nicholls argues that sport-in-development 'is largely occurring on the backs of young people through peer education', as they carry the responsibility for achieving many of the sport-in-development objectives. The focus of her chapter is to better understand why policy and programming relating to sport-in-development appears to lack meaningful contributions from young people, while arguing for options to challenge and reshape this trend. It engages with the theoretical principles drawn principally from Michel Foucault's work. Feminist considerations, postcolonial analysis and empowerment theory will link aspects of Foucauldian power and knowledge to the field of sport-in-development and subsequent interaction with young people in order to offer a constructive critique of the barriers limiting the contribution of peer educators to strengthening the field.

The third area focuses on more specific case studies whilst also reflecting on the issues raised in preceding chapters. Chapters 8 and 9 build on the analysis conducted by Nicholls by concentrating on case studies that are targeted at young people. Crabbe links the engagement of sport and physical activity in a domestic (UK) social development setting, whilst highlighting how the scheme can – and is – being used in the Global South. It identifies the peculiar aspects of the Positive Futures initiative that was designed to avoid the limitations of previous 'command' programmes by adopting a locally negotiated approach to design and delivery, thus moving towards a horizontal decision-making structure identified by Nicholls to be important in the progress of sport-in-development programmes. It assesses evidence of the impact of the programme and identifies elements that may be appropriate in a wider development context. Through adopting a critical view of the development process the chapter assesses the limitations as well as the opportunities posed for development through such programmes, resulting from international power relations.

Chapter 9 interprets sport development from a Southern perspective. With a focus on youth (male) sport participation at community level, it assesses the capacity for development to take place on the basis of support from indigenous organizations and institutions. From there, it identifies how traditional donor states can both learn from the positives of such indigenous development and contribute most effectively to further capacity building.

Chapter 10 addresses with specific reference to the African subcontinent, the implications of dependency theories for understanding the development and movement of athletes across the north-south divide. It assesses recent developments in the context of the ongoing commodification and globalization of sport, especially football. Specifically, it looks critically at the motives and outcomes of sports as development programmes in Africa. While considerable potential exists for the use of sport as an instrument of development in Africa, the long term impact of these interventions remains open to question. Are they a net positive or do they exacerbate the exodus of talented people from Africa? Does the market for athletes have the exploitative aspects as do other market commodities such as natural resources? It argues that such wider political considerations must be taken into account in the evaluation process.

The concluding chapter joins the arguments and themes emerging throughout the book, identifying the opportunities and limitations for sport to contribute to the development process. Part of this is the level of inclusion and exclusion that is evident in the sport-in-development movement. Therefore, it considers the extent to which sport can – or should – be valued as a new engine for development. This helps us redefine the sport-in-development debates whilst charting new areas of research in this fast-evolving field.

Notes

1 These countries do so for a variety of domestic and geopolitical reasons. Many Western countries form part of the Development Assistance Committee of the OECD, which provides approximately 95% of development aid. However, it is important to note though that development concerns have not been confined to Western countries. During the Cold War, both the Soviet Union, China and 'non aligned countries' played an active role in promoting different forms of development around the world.

2 A UN initiative to encourage business to assist in contributing to the development process in a variety of manners through its ten core principles. For further details see: http://www.unglobalcompact.org/AboutTheGC/index.html

3 The sport-in-development 'movement' has been explicitly linked by advocates to eight MDGs that heads of state and multilateral international agencies adopted in 2000 to be achieved by 2015. Many would add a ninth goal, revolving around peace, reconciliation and post-conflict healing, to which, for some, sport seems ideally suited to contribute.

4 This refers to a process that usually begins with the codification of the sport and encapsulates the emergence of an organizational structure that governs its development.

5 Different interpretations exist concerning the relative roles of the donor and recipient in this relationship. Tisch and Wallace (1994, p. 4) adopt the more traditional state-centric approach through defining foreign development assistance simply as; 'resources provided by rich countries to help poor countries'. In contrast, the United Kingdom Government's Department for International Development (DFID) interpretation of the process highlights the pro-active role of the recipient as a partner in the development assistance process.

6 In this context, 'life chances' is taken to refer not just to living standards, but also related enhancement of personal welfare, and improved qualify of life for individuals and their dependents. To some, increased life chances relates to having access to the free market. The term has been used both in a domestic context, for instance *Life Chances and Social Mobility* (United Kingdom government, PM's Strategy Unit, 2004), and in the international context, for instance in the 2005 UNDP *Human Development Report.*

7 Some authors therefore further sub-divide this category. See Levermore (2008a) for more details.

8 This classification closely resembles recent attempts to categorize sport-in-development programmes. For example, The Sport for Development and Peace International Working Group (2006) demarcated schemes into individual development, health promotion and disease prevention, promotion of gender equity, social integration and the development of social capital, peace building and conflict prevention or resolution, post-disaster trauma relief and normalization of life, economic development, and communication and social mobilization. For a more detailed debate on the schemes that operate within these categories, please see Levermore (2008b).

9 The first edition was published in 1902. The third edition (1988) includes an introduction by Townsend. J. Hobson presents the idea of acceptable and unacceptable types of imperialism, with the form of imperial authority and the capacity to assimilate indigenous peoples, as central issues.

10 Guttmann does however, suggest that the process worked in reverse, when Roman ascendancy in the region, led to a more brutalized form of physical culture.

11 Muscular Christianity is a term used to encapsulate a system of ideals based on the combination of vigorous physical activity and Christian values that emerged, initially within the UK, during the Victorian period. It was articu-

lated through the so-called games ethic, the belief in the spiritual value of sports, which was central to the Victorian public school system. Mangan (1998) refers to English commentators and writers of the period, typically Kingsley, Almond and Hughes, as exhorting the young men of the time to train their minds and their bodies in service of the nation. An extensive body of historical literature has explored the meaning and implications of the muscular Christianity on the development of both sport and society.

12   MacKenzie identified this as taking place both through the school curriculum and through additional drill and exercise programmes. Outside school, youth organizations and the observance of Empire day rituals helped to further imbue children with the same world view.

13   For further information, see http://www.britishcouncil.org/sport-what-is-dreams-and-teams.htm.

14   See http://news.bbc.co.uk/1/hi/programmes/bbc_parliament/3631579.stm for reference to Lord Scarman's response to the Brixton Riots of April 1981. Also, see http://www.davidmiliband.info/sarchive/speech06_02.htm for reference to David Miliband's 'Scarman Lecture' entitled *Building a Community in a Diverse Society* (31st January 2006) which makes direct reference to use of sport in community development.

Bibliography

Amin, S. (1974) *Accumulation on a World Scale: A Critique of the Theory of Underdevelopment*. New York: Monthly Review.

Anthony, D. (1969) 'The Role of Sport in Development', *International Development Review*, **12** (December), 10–11.

Arbena, J.L. (1993) 'International Aspects of Sport in Latin America: Perceptions, Prospects, and Proposals', in Dunning, E., Maguire, J., and Pearton, R. (eds) *The Sports Process: A Comparative and Developmental Approach*. Champaign: Human Kinetics, pp. 151–167.

Armstrong, G. (1997) *Entering the Field: New Perspectives on World Football*. London: Berg Publishers Ltd.

Bairner, A. (2001) *Sport, Nationalism and Globalization: European and North American Perspectives*. New York: State University of New York Press.

Balassa, B. (1978) *Policy Reform in Developing Countries*. Oxford: Pergamon.

Beacom, A. and Levermore, R. (2008) 'International Policy and Sport-in-Development', in Girginov, V. (ed.) *The Management of Sports Development*. London: Elsevier, pp. 109–127.

Bhagwati, J.N. (1985) *Dependence and Interdependence*. Oxford: Blackwell.

Black, M. (2002) *No-Nonsense Guide to International Development*. London: New Internationalist.

Brailsford, D. (1992) *British Sport: A Social History*. Cambridge: Lutterworth Press.

British Council (2007) Welcome to Dreams + Teams. http://www.britishcouncil.org/sport-dreams-about.htm (accessed February 2007).

CAFOD (undated) 'Don't make war – play football', *Fairground*, Issue 16, p. 4, CAFOD, accessed on 27th March 2008 from, www.cafod.org.uk/content/download/5587/48063/version/1/file/sec.16.pdf.

Calderisi, R. (2007) *The Trouble with Africa: Why Foreign Aid Isn't Working*. London: Palgrave Macmillan.

Cashmore, E. (2005) *Making Sense of Sport*. London: Routledge.

Chappell, R. (2004) 'Sports Development in Botswana, Africa', *The Sports Journal*, 7(2), (internet journal, no page numbers provided).

Coalter, F. (2005) 'Measuring Success: evaluation methods and instruments', conference paper presented at the 2nd Magglingen Conference on Sport and Development, 4–6 December, 2005.

Coalter, F. (2007) *A Wider Social Role for Sport: Who's Keeping the Score?* London: Routledge.

Darby, P. (2002) *Africa, Football and FIFA: Politics, Colonialism and Resistance*. London: Frank Cass Publishers.

Darby, P. (2005) 'Africa and the "World" Cup: FIFA Politics, Eurocentrism and Resistance', *International Journal of Sport History*, 22(5), 883–905.

Desai, V. and Potter, R.B. (2002) *The Companion to Development Studies*. London: Arnold.

Dunning, E. (1999) *Sport Matters: Sociological Studies of Sport, Violence and Civilization*. London: Routledge.

Dunning, E. and Malcolm, D. (eds) (2003) *Sport: Critical Concepts in Sociology*. London: Routledge.

Easterly, W. (2007) *The White Man's Burden: Why the West's Efforts to Aid the Rest Have Done So Much Ill and So Little Good*. London: Penguin.

The Economist (7th–13th July 2007) Leader 'Are We There Yet?' 10–11 and 'Millennium Development Goals', 26–29.

Elias, N and Dunning, E. (1986) *Quest For Excitement: Sport and Leisure in the Civilizing Process*. Oxford: Blackwell.

Frank, A.G. (1967) *Capitalism and Underdevelopment in Latin America: Historical Studies of Chile and Brazil*. New York: Monthly Review.

Frey, J.H. (1988) 'The Internal and External Role of Sport in National Development', *Journal of National Development*, 1, 65–82.

Giulianotti, R. (2004) 'Human Rights, Globalization and Sentimental Education: The Case of Sport', *Sport in Society*, 7(3), 355–369.

Guttmann, A. (1978) *From Ritual to Record: The Nature of Modern Sports*. New York: Columbia University Press.

Guttmann, A. (1992) 'Chariot Races, Tournaments and the Civilizing Process', in Dunning, E. and Rojek, C. (eds) *Sport and Leisure in the Civilizing Process*. Basingstoke: Macmillan, pp. 137–160.

Guttmann, A. (1994) *Games and Empires*. New York: Columbia University Press.

Hargreaves, Jennifer (1994) *Critical Issues in the History and Sociology of Women's Sports*. London: Routledge.

Hargreaves, John (1986) *Sport, Power and Culture*. Cambridge: Polity Press.

Hargreaves, John (2002) 'Globalisation Theory, global sport, and nations and nationalism', in Sugden J. and Tomlinson A. (eds) (2002) *Power Games: A Critical Sociology of Sport*. London: Routledge, pp. 25–43.

Heinemann, K. (1993) 'Sport in Developing Countries', in *The Sports Process: A Comparative and Developmental Approach* (eds) Eric Dunning, Joseph Maguire and Robert Pearton, pp. 139–150.

Hettne, B. (1995) *Development Theory and the Three Worlds*. Harlow: Longman.

Hobson, J.A. (1988) *Imperialism: A Study* (3rd ed.). London: Unwin Hyman.

Hognestad, H. and Tollisen, A. (2004) 'Playing Against Deprivation: Football and Development in Nairobi, Kenya', *Football in Africa – Conflict, Conciliation and Community*. London: Palgrave Macmillan, pp. 210–226.

Holt, R. (1989) *Sport and the British*. Oxford: Clarendon Press.

Houlihan, B. and White, A. (2002) *The Politics of Sport Development*. London: Routledge.

Huizinga, J. (1955) *Homo Ludens: A Study of the Play Element in Culture*. Boston: Beacon Press.

Huntington, S. (1971) 'The Change to Change: Modernisation, development and politics', *Comparative Politics*, **1**, 283–322.

Jowell, T. (9th June 2005) Press release: *Sport as a tool for peace and reconciliation*, Next Step conference, Zambia.

Kingsbury, D., Remenyi, J., McKay, J. and Hunt, J. (eds) (2004) *Key Issues in Development*. Basingstoke: Palgrave.

Levermore, R. (2004) 'Sport's role in constructing the "inter-state" worldview', in *Sport and International Relations* (eds Levermore and Budd). London: Routledge, pp. 16–30.

Levermore, R. (2008a) 'Sport-in-International Development: Time to Treat it Seriously?', *Brown Journal of World Affairs*, **14**(2), 55–66.

Levermore, R. (2008b) 'Playing for Development: Outlining the Extent of the Use of Sport for Development', *Progress in Development*, **8**(2), 183–190.

Leys, C. (1996) *The Rise and Fall of Development Theory*. Bloomington: Indiana University Press.

MacAloon, J. (2006) 'Muscular Christianity after 150 Years', *The International Journal of the History of Sport*, **23**(5), 687–700.

MacKenzie, J. (1984) *Propaganda and Empire: The Manipulation of British Public Opinion 1880–1960*. Manchester: Manchester University Press.

Maguire, J. (1994) 'Sport, Identity Politics and Globalization', *Sociology of Sport Journal*, **11**, 398–427.

Maguire, J. (1999) *Global Sport: Identities, Societies, Civilizations*. Cambridge: Polity Press.

Maguire, J. (2000) 'Sport and Globalization', in *Handbook of Sports Studies* (eds, Jay Coakley and Eric Dunning). London: Sage, pp. 356–369.

Maguire, J. and Young, K. (eds) (2002) *Theory, Sport and Society*. Oxford: JAI/ Elsevier Press.

Majumdar, B. (2006) 'Tom Brown Goes Global: The "Brown" Ethic in Colonial and Post-Colonial India', *The International Journal of the History of Sport*, **23**(5), 805–820.

Mandell, R. (1984) *Sport; A Cultural History*. New York: Columbia University Press.

Mangan, J. (1998) *The Games Ethic and Imperialism: Aspects of the Diffusion of an Ideal*. London: Frank Cass.

Mangan, J. (2006) 'Christ and the Imperial Playing Fields: Thomas Hughe's Ideological Heirs in Empire', *The International Journal of the History of Sport*, **23**(5), 777–804.

Perkin, H. (1989) 'Teaching Nations how to Play: sport and society in the British Commonwealth', *International Journal of the History of Sport*, **6**(2), 145–155.

Purnell, J. (28th November 2007) *World Class Community Sport (Speech)*, Hansard.

Rostow, W. (1960) *The Stages of Economic Growth: A Non-Communist Manifesto.* Cambridge: Cambridge University Press.

Sachs, J. (2006) *The End of Poverty: Economic Possibilities for Our Time.* London: Penguin.

Sport for Development and Peace International Working Group (2006) *Sport for Development and Peace – From Practice to Policy*, Toronto, p. 173.

Sugden, J. and Tomlinson, A. (eds) (2002) *Power Games: A Critical Sociology of Sport.* London: Routledge.

Tisch, S. and Wallace, M. (1994) *Dilemmas of Development Assistance – The What, Why and Who of Foreign Aid.* Oxford: Westview Press.

United Kingdom Government, Department for International Development MDG Factsheet, November 2007, Millennium Development Goal 8: *To Develop Global Partnerships for Development.* http://www.dfid.gov.uk/pubs/files/mdgfactsheets/

United Nations Development Programme (2005) *Human Development Report.* New York: UNDP.

United Nations InterAgency Task Force for Development and Peace (2003) *Report: Sport for Development and Peace.* http://www.un.org/themes/sport/task.htm.

United Nations (2003) *Sport for Development and Peace: Towards Achieving the Millennium Development Goals.* New York: United Nations.

United Nations (2005) Common Ground: Sport as an innovative tool for Development and Peace: ECOSOC High Level Segment 2004 Ministerial Roundtable Breakfast, 30 June 2004, Summary document, prepared by UNICEF and UNFIP. New York: United Nations.

United Nations (2006) *International Year of Sport and Physical Education 2005 – Final Report.* New York: United Nations.

Willis, O. (2000) 'Sport and Development: The significance of Mathare Youth Sports Association', *Canadian Journal of Development Studies*, **XXI**(3), 825–849.

World Commission on Culture and Development (1995) *Our Creative Diversity: Report of the World Commission on Culture and Development.* Paris: UNESCO.

2
Sport-in-International Development: Theoretical Frameworks

Roger Levermore

2.1 Introduction[1]

The academic field of international development is characterized by often intense debates between competing perspectives which influence debate and therefore strategy and policy in the international development policy-making field (Hettne, 1995).[2] For example, Rostow (1960) was both a leading modernization theorist and senior administrator in post 1945 US administrations. Likewise, neo-liberal theorists and strategists significantly influence the work of major development agencies such as the World Bank and governments in some high income countries. This is an important point to note for those operating in, or assessing, sport-in-development because they occasionally need to engage with these debates in order to better understand how sport-in-development might be perceived, especially in highlighting its potential weaknesses and limitations.

This chapter therefore begins to address this scholarly vacancy, whilst also helping to contextualize debates and theories introduced in succeeding chapters. It starts with a section on the viewpoints (modernization and neo-liberalism) that have dominated Western forms of development thinking and policy for over sixty years and then moves on to the alternative perspectives; dependency, post-colonialism and critical feminist theories, that oppose much of these established theories' central tenets.

Analysis for this chapter stems from research undertaken for the author's initial investigation of sport and international relations (Levermore, 2004). A detailed contextual analysis of the literature provides a foundation upon which semi-structured interviews with over forty people engaged in sport-in-development were conducted. This includes representatives of traditional development, sport plus plus sport (these terms are explored in the introductory chapter) N(and programmes, sporting institutions (The English Football Association, UEFA and FIFA), the corporate sector and government. These interviews were conducted across the EU and South Africa from 2001 to date.

2.2 Dominant perspectives of development and sport-in-development

Concern with development, especially the material and moral improvement of people around the world can be traced back centuries, notably with ideas that emanated from the Western Enlightenment era in the eighteenth century. The legacy of this was that improved standard of living could be achieved particularly if industrialization occurred, there were increases in investment and free trade, expansion of infrastructure and society adopting established organized religious instruction rather than 'uncivilized' traditional practices. Many of these ideas were articulated in the approach to the governance of colonies in the nineteenth and early twentieth centuries and have been at the cornerstone of modernization and neo-liberal perspectives of development, which have dominated international development policy-making in the last sixty years (Rist, 2002).

A concise, if rather crude, definition of these perspectives would assert that this school of thought believes that the large cluster of less developed regions of the world (in many parts of Latin America, sub-Saharan Africa, Pacific Islands and Asia-Pacific) can follow virtually the same policies that appeared to have worked in high income, industrialized countries of the world (largely Western Europe and the US) in order to progress towards conventional (Northern) understandings of what being developed means. This binary understanding of the world was particularly associated with the work of Walt Whitman Rostow. He was a key member of US administrations in the post-war period and the work he was renowned for was published in 1960, entitled, *The process of economic growth*. Rostow argued that if the correct prescriptions were followed then any country or region could follow a series of stages of growth to become 'developed' via non revolutionary (in contrast to communism) means (Binns, 2002: 77–79).[3] The first stage was the least advanced – a traditional society that sees a barter system in place in a largely agrarian, subsistence economy with low levels of investment and technology. The most advanced stage is the mass-consumption society, experienced in high income countries of the world today, where tertiary industries dominate the economy as manufacturing reduces in importance.[4] The central ingredients to stimulate development from Rostow's perspective were:

(i)   *An increase in aid,* both financial and technical (expertise); many contemporary mainstream development institutions maintain that aid is still important. The UN for instance, advocates that the leading industrialized countries (mostly by OECD) devote 0.7% of their Gross Domestic Product to international development aid.

(ii)   *Stimulate free trade and foreign direct investment.* The Global South needs to be committed to the free market economy and open to technical assistance and advice, technology *etceteras* from industrialized, high-income countries and mainstream development agencies.

(iii) *Build a widespread infrastructure of communications.* This continues to be an important focus for development priorities. The 2006 *Human Development Report* notes that a lack of infrastructure remains a major hindrance to development (United Nations Development Programme, 2006).

Particularly important from Rostow's perspective, was the creation of a strong government which could intervene in society to provide the conditions for the growth in trade and investment and best utilization of aid and infrastructure as well as creating a stable political climate, develop a national media to disseminate key concepts of modernization and create an environment in which entrepreneurship thrives. All this was necessary in order to tackle the 'hindrance' of traditional forms of society with its reliance on subsistence agriculture and 'backward' social norms (large families, informal economic activity and 'immoral' beliefs). Some forms of modernization though, understood that selective features of traditional society could actually assist the modernization process. Despite these concerns with social obstacles, the principal stimulus for development for modernization was via economic growth (Willis, 2005).

Neo-liberalism shares many of the characteristics of modernization including the need for strong intervention from 'outside' agencies like the World Bank in the development of low-income countries and promoting further the importance of free trade and foreign direct investment. It points to the (perceived) success of countries in South East Asia, such as South Korea, who followed neo-liberal prescriptions to support their claims (Potter, 2002: 61). However, it differs from modernization in at least two ways; many of its adherents are concerned that aid distorts the performance of economies and are also wary of the role of the state, which has a tendency to hinder the development process through inefficiency and/or corrupt practices.

Many advocates of this perspective highlight corruption as one of the central impediments to development and that development aid and assistance should be reduced or curtailed in regions that show evidence of widespread corruption (*The Economist*, 2006). Its main adherents are major development institutions (such as the IMF and World Bank), governments from high-income countries (especially the US), businesses, some NGOs and development economists (Lal (1983), Balassa (1978 and 1981) and Friedman (1982)). Largely because of this, neo-liberalism is currently the most influential perspective shaping development policy (McKay, 2004: 61). Its supporters highlight further remedies that are needed to encourage development. First, the political and economic influence of (potentially corrupt) governments in low-income states can be reduced via strict regulations that effectively set policy, laid out by World Bank and IMF-inspired Structural Adjustment Plans (SAPs – now Poverty Reduction Strategies) in return for loans. Second, through encouraging other actors, particularly companies that operate globally, to have more responsibility in being engaged in the development process, either through core business competencies or via work in social responsibility.[5]

Many sport-in-development projects and the sport/development relationship in general, links in with the goals of neo-liberalism and modernization. As the introductory chapter (see section 1.5) notes, sport has long been seen as a tool that has the ability to *transform, or give the perception of transformation, of backward societies into more modern, civilized and unified ones* (Elias and Dunning, 1986). This has been more recently argued by Nelson Mandela in helping unify South Africa in the era after apartheid legislation had been repealed.[6] Arguably, Kenya and Ethiopia (through athletics) and Cameroon, Senegal and Brazil (through football) – and the media reporting of such success – have enhanced their international reputation as a result of success in international competitions. Moreover, some see sports as one arena with a level playing field where neo-liberalism appears to work (Milner and Elliott, 2002).

The remainder of this section reflects on three specific ways in which the sport-in-development movement might be viewed as linking in with the goals of modernization/neo-liberal development thinking. These are:

- Strengthening physical infrastructure.
- Creating a stronger social and economic environment, particularly through developing employment and other life skills and investment.
- Encouraging the escalation of business/private interest involvement in development.

2.2.1 Sport and infrastructure building

First, sport is particularly tied to strengthening the infrastructure of countries. This is seen partly in the work undertaken by sports federations, such as FIFA and the English Football Association, to develop a country's sports infrastructure, which primarily assists participation in sport but a secondary result is that a physical infrastructure (telecommunications, transportations systems *etceteras*) is also built. For instance, FIFA's Football for Hope and Goal programmes have resulted in developing sport and a wider infrastructure. Football for Hope, sees FIFA partner a number of NGOs around the world that focus on a range of development initiatives being aimed solely at children and young people, and uses football as an instrument to promote participation and dialogue (for education, inclusion and empowerment). It includes a scheme to generate US$10m (largely from FIFA's official partners – Adidas, Coca-Cola, Emirates, Hyundai, Sony and Visa) to fund 20 Football for Hope centres across Africa by the time the World Cup takes place in South Africa in 2010. The Goal programme, which started in 1999 with a three year budget of US$83.3 million (BBC, 2005) is a good example of a sport plus programme, aiming to reduce inequalities in the infrastructure of football in different countries, and allow for individual member associations to protect their autonomy from government interference (another link with neo-liberalism).

It has also been argued that the hosting of sports events in Global South countries can contribute to reinvigorating the physical (non-sport) infrastructure of a city or region through the building of roads and hotels, which also results in job creation and other forms of inward investment. The aura around bidding for sporting events is the veiled promise that it will be able to unlock significant levels of public and private investment, particularly directed at meeting infrastructural needs (Black and Westhuizen, 2004). A conference held by the South African embassy at Chelsea Football Club, London in May 2006, on creating foreign investment and business opportunities and strengthening

infrastructure around the 2010 Football World Cup (being
by South Africa) is a case in point. Indeed, reports from South .
highlight this belief. For instance the *Mail and Guardian* (2007) notes
that billions of rand have already been promised to improve infrastructure – from state, provincial government and private sector. It is
estimated that the South African government will contribute between
South African Rand (R) 17–20 billion (about US$2.27–2.67 billion at
the time of writing); of this R8.4 billion (US$1.12 billion) is designated
for stadium development and R6.7 billion (US$0.9 billion) to public
transport and surrounding infrastructure (*Business Day*, 2007a).
The Gauteng regional government has promised to spend R50 million
(about US$6.68m) to prepare the infrastructure for the World Cup
(Newmarch, 2007) in the greater Johannesburg area. This investment, along with private funding, resulted in new hotels and transportation systems having already been built or extended when research
was conducted by this author in late 2007. Other infrastructural projects are in the process of construction in order to accommodate
the anticipated influx of World Cup tourists. As a result, a *Business
Day* editorial argues that the 'World Cup's role as a catalyst for
investment in roads, buses, railways and communal facilities that
the cities need is arguably its most important role' (*Business Day*,
2007a). Moreover, the event is being labelled as one that will leave
a 'lasting legacy' for the African continent with the hope that infrastructure and tourism will be integrated in southern Africa (Pillay,
2007).

Similar hopes were expressed for the 2007 cricket World Cup held in
the Caribbean (*The Economist*, 2007a). Unfortunately, that tournament
resulted in a financial loss, leaving a legacy of debt and the bankruptcy
of businesses, especially in travel and tourism (*Barbados Free Press*,
2007; *The Economist* 2007b). Indeed, research conducted by Matheson
and Baade (2004) (and reiterated by Cornelissen in this publication)
suggests that there is little evidence to support the belief that events
result in a monetary boost especially from tourism as sports tourists
simply scare off (the 'crowding out' effect) tourists who would nor-
mally visit. It will be interesting to see the extent to which tangible
infrastructural and other economic benefits result from the Olympic
Games in Beijing.

2.2.2 Sport and socio-economic development

The second way in which sport might be considered to further the
objectives of neo-liberal development, is the argument that sport assists

social and economic development and poverty reduction. Advocates of sport-in-development regularly highlight the way that sport, sports events and specific sport related projects, increase capacity-building, strengthen empowerment, generate investment (as noted above) and establish a stable political environment for the economy and market to operate in.

There are two different methods that sport plays in helping strengthen such capacity-building. The first, and most quoted, is via sport-in-development schemes set up largely by sport plus and plus sport NGOs. Almost all of the 230 plus schemes identified on the sportanddev.org website highlight at least one capacity-building trait. Examples include:

(i) The much-vaunted and long-running MYSA engages in activities as diverse as cleaning slums of rubbish in this township in Nairobi to developing youth leadership skills for male and female youth. The role of creating peer leaders (discussed in length in the Nicholls and Crabbe chapters in this publication) is central to capacity building in this project (Willis, 2000).

(ii) Football for Peace uses football (through establishing a local football league) to teach children about building community involvement and leadership. Developing gender awareness and social cohesion is the main aim, especially in incorporating children back into their communities. This scheme was operated by BP, who partnered with UNICEF and local development NGOs in Medellin, Colombia.

(iii) SCORE is a community development organization, which trains volunteers to use sport to facilitate capacity building in rural communities across southern Africa. Specifically, SCORE explores how experience in managing sport at a community level through managing resources, writing business plans and managing organizational demands can effectively be transferred to enable similar good practice principles to be applied to more general business development.

(iv) The Catalonian football club, FC Barcelona, has a foundation that oversees domestic and international development activities. The club enthusiastically supports the UN's recommendation about the level of GDP that the highest income countries should be spending on international development by allocating at least 0.7% of its turnover to development activities each year. Specific programmes look at social integration initiatives, education, health and defense of human rights.

Aside from this, the second method sees some companies using their expertise to help organize, administer and run sports events to help train the local workforce. One example of this 'transferability' of skills is apparent in Deloitte in South Africa, who advertise that their experience with sports events helps them also develop enterprise and employment for underemployed black communities so that they can be a more skilled (and flexible) 'resource' in the national labour force. They estimate that 50,000 people will be trained and placed by the 2010 World Cup (*Business Day*, 2007b).

It is therefore contended that economic development builds on these skills, particularly through generating empowerment, employment skills and fostering organizational and administrative tools that would be useful to entrepreneurship. Furthermore, sport plays an enabling role in enabling a more secure economic environment. This is partly expressed through broad based 'macro' programmes run by the state and international financial institutions (such as the World Bank and IMF) sometimes with the help of sports federations. Examples include poverty reduction or national development strategies in Mozambique, Zambia and Belarus, where official documents point to the use of sport in governmental policy to stimulate education, highlight health awareness campaigns and encourage participation in sport (International Monetary Fund, 2007).

2.2.3   Sport and business

It is not surprising that companies (especially Multinational corporations – MNCs) are involved in many of the sport-in-development initiatives (especially as funding partners), given the popular appeal of sport (important for PR purposes), that modern sport 'is structured by a political economy in which multinationals play a decisive part' (Maguire, 1999: 35), and the understanding that business operates more effectively in a climate of peace and stability with a healthy and well-educated workforce. Therefore, many of the initiatives detailed in Table 2.1 are designed with peace, stability, health and education at the forefront of their plans. The table also intimates the growing range of businesses beginning to support sport-in-development initiatives including MNCs from the Global South (such as Arcelor Mittal).

The third aspect of neo-liberal oriented development associated with the sport/development relationship is the use of sport is in increasing

Table 2.1   Sample of corporate support for sport-in-development initiatives

Organization	Type of scheme (related to core business competencies and/or Corporate Social Responsibility initiatives?)	Further details
Nike: sports merchandising and leisure fashion company	CSR	Sponsor or directly contribute to a range of development programmes. Examples include 'Together For Girls' in refugee camps in East Africa, an initiative that promotes empowerment through boosting leadership skills for women
Standard Chartered, Unilever and Deloitte	'Magic Bus' project: CSR	Programme run by volunteers from these corporations, with partnerships with NGOs and local schools, to help children in slum areas of Indian cities to develop life skills. The programme creates an experiential timetable/curriculum that aims to develop skills that will enable these children to integrate into mainstream society. Enshrined in this is the child's right to play sport, promoting gender equality/equity, and bringing communities together through participation in sport
Deloitte	Consultancy/core business competency	Employment skills and transferability (details above)
BP	CSR	Football for Peace programme (details above)
British Airways	CSR	'Change for Good' Works with Charlton Athletic Football Club in Alexandra township on health, education and citizenship.
Adidas (notably the Adi Dassler Fund)	CSR	Funding support for four sport-in-development projects; Right to Play (see preface to this book), Diambars academy (see the chapter by Kirwin and Akindes in this publication), PeacePlayers International and Coaching For Hope.

Table 2.1   Sample of corporate support for sport-in-development
initiatives – *continued*

Organization	Type of scheme (related to core business competencies and/or Corporate Social Responsibility initiatives?)	Further details
Vodafone	CSR (voted best CSR report in 2008 at the CorporateRegister awards).	New Vodafone Group Foundation strategy launched in 2007 that uses sport and music to 'generate healthy and positive living in young people through education, health and welfare'. The Special Olympics has received specific support.
LaSalle Bank Sports Charitable Fund (subsidiary of ABN Ambro), US	CSR	Support healthy lifestyle initiatives for children and adults
BHP Billiton	CSR	The Kicking Goals sports education programme and focuses on improved educational performance, reduced truancy and increased youth volunteers.
CA Ron de Santa Teresa (CARST), Venezuala	CSR	Use of sport to deter youth crime (World Bank, 2007: 181)
UC Rusal	CSR	Since 2005 has helped build sports facilities for able bodied and disabled young people in Guinea and Eastern Europe. Some of these initiatives have been linked to health programmes.
Arcelor Mittal	CSR	Unspecified use of sport for social investment initiatives. Stated belief in local generation of ideas for initiatives

Sources: Sportanddev.org website, individual company annual reports and the Corporate
Register website.

business interaction in development in the Global South either as a 'top-down' process (Northern MNCs initiating or supporting sport-in-development) or from support generated by Southern MNCs and smaller businesses, for which there is growing activity. This can happen via:

(i)   Companies involved in supporting the delivery of sport and sports events, can intensify the level of business that takes place. This has partly been identified in the sections above, notably in generating Foreign Direct Investment.

(ii) More common is the use of sport in corporate social responsibility (CSR) initiatives that have a developmental focus. Some of these carry very explicit neo-liberal messages that clearly attempt to influence debate about the type of political and economic environment that is required for development to succeed. For example, The 'Partners of Americas' scheme that operates throughout South America uses soccer to 'help youth transfer sport skills into market driven vocational and employability skills' (International Platform on Sport and Development, 2006).

When considering the potential for altering the political and economic environment of countries to make them more receptive to neo-liberal notions of development, it is important to recognize the mutual compatibility that sport and business have to support, and sometimes supplant, the heavily-criticized (poorly governed) state as a deliverer of development. This is because sport has been credited as a useful non-political vehicle that strengthens the interaction of often hostile actors – business, NGOs and civil societies and encourages them to work together on many sport-in-development initiatives. Moreover, some initiatives promote principles of good governance. For example, the Supersports agreement with the University of Witwatersrand in Johannesburg allows for the utilization of the objectives of the Accelerated and Shared Growth Initiative for South Africa and Joint Initiative on Priority Skills Acquisition to improve skills and micro governance in South Africa. Seventy senior sports administrators across southern Africa were chosen to undertake good governance training under this initiative.[7]

To summarize, these characteristics of sport-in-development create an impression that the sport/development relationship is almost tailor-made to support the dominant mantra of development. This is an impression supported by both Heinemann (1993) and Frey (1988), who highlight how the revolution of modern sport can be so closely linked to modernization. Heinemann (1993: 147) notes how voluntary organizations (like sports NGOs) help facilitate conditions of modern society and gradually help in introducing new social structures, adding that, 'it is no coincidence that sports clubs in developing countries are very often directly government controlled and of political significance'.

Frey (1988: 69) says that sport assists in the transition from a traditional, agrarian society to an urbanized, modern/industrialized one through helping transmit messages that portray that change will occur soon, especially at sporting events where political figures are present. Messages about modern society, such as many of those discussed above as well as birth control and advanced agricultural policy have been disseminated through sport. Perhaps, unconvincingly to the perspectives this chapter is about to cover, Frey (1988: 70) adds that the 'acquisition of [educational, life and employment] skills, plus experience in operating sporting events... reduces the dependency on the developing country on larger and more powerful nations'.

However, few advocates of neo-liberal or modernization approaches to development appear to enthusiastically support the use of sport in development. There is also virtually no review by those academics attached to those viewpoints either. In terms of development practitioners, the World Bank comes closest to supporting the initiatives outlined in this publication, but only in a tacit manner, noting that far more evidence needs to be presented before it is treated as part of the mainstream development movement (World Bank, 2007:141). As the concluding chapter notes (see section 11.2) there is wariness from traditional development institutions about the claims made concerning the importance of sport in this area, especially when it comes to distracting communities and policy makers from pressing development realities which sometimes feeds into a distrust/dislike of sport. The following set of perspectives, which oppose many of the policies advocated by mainstream development thinking, largely share a mistrust of the one-way 'power of sport' from the Global North to Global South, particularly in its ability to further exacerbate the poverty divide between low and high income countries. A well-documented example of such sentiments comes from Frey (1988: 78) who argues that sport is a tool that diverts those who are marginalized by the global political economy (and dominant development practices) from protesting against more serious social and political problems. However, some theorists in these alternative schools of thought examine the potential that sport also has in offering, a platform for resistance to dominant practices and understandings of development. The following section reflects this polyseimic image of sport in the 'alternative' development reading of sport-in-development.

2.3　Critical theoretical reflections on sport-in-development

Having considered in some detail, how dominant (modernization/ neo-liberal) perspectives might view the sport/development relationship in a largely positive light, it is now time to consider alternative viewpoints. Hettne (1995), Potter (2002) and Willis (2005) are amongst many in development studies to have catalogued the broad diversity of perspectives that oppose these dominant development views. The three used here, dependency, post-colonialism and critical feminist stances, have well-documented criticisms of both the assumptions inherent in neo-liberalism/modernization approaches (that development can occur in a unilinear manner within distinct stages with little nuance provided for cultural differences), and their policies. They argue that these dominant approaches constitute a major reason for the widening of socio-economic conditions generally experienced between the wealthy North and largely poor Global South and that marginalization, discrimination and alienation of poor communities results. Indeed, 'Development can only take place when domination is reduced; development is not a matter of moving through stages as the modernists would suggest' (Frey, 1988: 80).

All these perspectives have also been utilized in a broad assessment of the impact of sport on society. Maguire (1999: 30–32) charts how Klein (1991), Arbena (1993) and Mandle and Mandle (1988) consider the politics of dependency through assessing the level of cultural imperialism of Northern sports in Latin America. Maguire also discusses Guttmann's (1994) assessment that Northern sport should be more realistically labelled a tool of cultural hegemony and Sage's (1995) evocation of Wallerstein's 'world system theory' in analysing how Nike's operations in the early 1990s was a stark example of a Northern corporation plundering the resources of Global South countries. Similarly, Darby (2002: 173–174) considers how dependent the CAF is on FIFA. Likewise, postcolonialism highlights the historical and contemporary dominance of sporting practices from colonial and postcolonial (i.e. Northern) powers noting in particular the exploitation of migrating athletes within this process (Bale, 2004; Bale and Cronin, 2003; Bale and Maguire, 1994). Critical feminist perspectives have focused on how sport has marginalized women, especially in their stereotyping (Hargreaves, 1994 and 1997; Harris and Humberstone, 2004; Stevenson, 2002).

It should be noted that, as with modernization and neo-liberalism, these 'alternative' schools of thought are marked by considerable disagreement and each description of these theoretical perspectives addresses what many regard to be their core characteristics. However, common agreement is seen over their opposition to the overly-optimistic and one-dimensional pronouncements made on sport-in-development and the failure to highlight how sport carries particularly divisive and dysfunctional traits that can extenuate unequal power relations. Sport should therefore be considered in the wider political and social environments in which it operates. Each school of thought will be briefly outlined before theorizing how each see the sport/ development relationship.

A) Dependency

Dependency is a school of thought that emerged from Latin America in the 1950s and is arguably close in orientation to Marxist analyses of society. Prebisch (and the 'Prebisch thesis' of 1957) (see Booth, 1975), Frank (1967) and Wallerstein (1979) are three of its best known theorists. It continues to have a strong base in Latin America but also resonates in Africa (Amin, 1974), Asia, the Caribbean and many other regions of the world. Dependency perspectives chronicle:

(i) How broad structural processes like global capitalism and colonialism have created conditions that peripheralize regions that are not at the core of the global political economy. Inevitably, the core regions are some of the most industrialized, powerful and high income nations or cities and the periphery is comprised of large areas of Africa, Asia, Latin America, and islands in the Pacific.

(ii) The inherent weaknesses in the belief that the process of 'trickle down' associated with modernization (and neo-liberalism) will somehow result in a more even distribution of wealth around the world.

(iii) The policies of neo-liberalism and modernization have resulted in a process of continuing *underdevelopment* in many regions, rather than improved development. Specifically, the periphery (or semi-periphery depending on the nuances of this perspective) serve the core regions by providing cheap primary resources (for example, minerals and labour) who add value to them in the manufacturing stage.

(iv) The periphery tends to specialize in only a few products; when their value is high then some of the population benefit materially – when it fails, the country/region suffers extensive underdevelopment.

(v) Many of the core countries became powerful because they did not follow the rules they prescribe for those countries in the periphery. This includes protecting domestic industries from outside competition and not reducing barriers to trade.

What is needed to combat underdevelopment is better regional collaboration by like-minded governments and partnerships, whilst still intensifying trade and developing an industrial society.

B) Post-colonialism

Post-colonialism touches on one of the central issues within development – the concept of power and how it shapes development thinking and policy (McKay, 2004). Similar to dependency, a common argument is that within the core-periphery relationship, peripheralized nations are vital to providing the raw materials necessary for the wealth of the most industrialized nations, who remain in a dominant position because of their military or economic weight (Escobar, 1995). Furthermore, colonial legacies still exert considerable influence over many countries and regions in the Global South (Crush, 1995) because old colonial powers are predominantly the main trading partners of their previous colonies. Moreover, development initiatives are, and have always been, dominated by powerful countries (including the colonizing influences of the Soviet Union in the Cold War years).

Post-colonialism characterizes dominant development institutions and policies as being overwhelmingly simplistic and Eurocentric. McKay (2004: 64–65) argues that, 'The West with its blind faith in technology and the effectiveness of planning has treated the Third World as a child in great need of guidance'. Of particular concern to post-colonialism is the way that the Global South is portrayed in a negative, derogatory and stereotypical manner within the development process (McEwan, 2002: 127; Said, 1978). A particularly crude example of this in the sporting sphere was given by the mayor of Toronto in 2003 who, when invited to Kenya to solicit support for the Toronto Olympic bid – said 'What the hell would I want to go to Mombassa for? I just see myself in a pot of boiling water with all those natives dancing around me' (Canadian Broadcasting Corporation, 2001).

To redress these concerns, what development thinking the Global South requires is the inclusion of more local, indigenous understandings/inputs in order to radically disrupt entrenched systems of (Northern) knowledge that create an air of immutability over development practices (and there representation). This again relates to wider debates in development circles, for example, who are best placed to stimulate development – external actors and 'experts' or an internal/local process (McKay, 2004: 50)?

C) Critical feminism

Similar to dependency and postcolonialism, 'gender perspectives' highlight the historical neglect of gender issues, such as the discrimination of women in many societies in the Global South in development (this is something discussed in further detail by Saavedra in this publication).

Hunt (2004b: 243) argues that large scale discrimination and marginalization of women is partly due to the unequal legal position of women in relation to men; 'there is not a single developing country in which women and men enjoy equal rights under law'. Hunt goes on to explain that at the turn of the millennium, women constitute 70% of world's poor and hold only 10% of parliamentary seats around the world, whilst earning around 73% of male wages. Women are prone to poverty because they often remain dependent on men and can cease to be a 'productive economic asset' in traditional development terms as a result of widowhood, separation or divorce. The future also looks unpromising as girls represent 60% of all primary school children not enrolled at school. 'Critical feminism', also termed 'gender and development', has been particularly concerned with the peripheralization of women in the neoliberal economic system, which some argue has resulted in the reduction of state welfare support and increased living costs. This leads to the disruption of traditional family life in many Global South communities as women have to find paid work, which is often very poorly paid (Willis, 2005: 130).

Although each of these alternative perspectives emphasize different concerns with mainstream development practices and policies, they combine in their deep anxieties over unequal power relations. This is demonstrated in the sport/development relationship with the dominance in the global political economy that higher income (core) countries and MNCs have over countries in the Global South, which has resulted in concern over; (i) the unequal power relations evident in the governance and political economy of the sports industry, (ii) the exclusion of communities by sport, and (iii), the negative portrayal that sport conveys on lower-income countries.

2.3.1   Unequal political power relations and governance

The governance of sport as well as sport-in-development schemes tend to be dominated by higher-income (Northern) countries. This is true of most international sports, especially football. Darby (2002: 168) views football's governing body, FIFA in such a way, noting that it 'is not uncommonly regarded as an instrument of neo-colonial domination by African and other non-European football associations and that ties between Africa and FIFA are often characterized by ambivalence and wariness on the part of Africans'. This is partly due to an allegedly long-standing ambivalence that FIFA and the European governing body – UEFA – have had towards regions such as Africa (Darby, 2005). Similarly, sport-in-development schemes are criticized for being administered or heavily influenced by Northern institutions and donors, which results in their aims, objectives and methods of accountability as well as the sports being chosen (largely football and basketball and not indigenous sports) dominating programmes. Indeed, the four most used sports in sport-in-development projects are football (listed in 27% of projects on the www.sportanddev.org website; 35% of programmes did not identify a specific sport), volleyball (7%), athletics (5%) and basketball (5%). Aside from two schemes that use traditional dance (and there are questions over whether this should be defined as a sport) the remainder of listed programmes could all be considered to use modern, northern-originated sports.

Sports sociologists, such as Maguire (1999), argue that these Northern (modern) sports carry with them dysfunctional aspects of the societies where they originated; namely a fixation with competition and winning, which has resulted in drug-taking (to enhance performance), violence, cheating and corruption and are infused with the worst traits of Northern corporate practices (some dependency theorists call this corporate, or Americanized sport – see Donnelly, 1996). Moreover, where some see sport and sport-in-development as an area where social integration and unity can be strengthened, more critical approaches consider that sport is a 'mechanism to reinforce the hegemony of the ruling elite' (Frey, 1988: 69) through helping control the population with the imposition of rules, order and norms of how to behave/ submit.

Added to that are the unethical practices and contradictory motives presented by Northern sports organizations and institutions. Corruption scandals surround some international sports federations and organizations. FIFA regularly attracts allegations about being implicated in the misuse (termed fungability in development terminology) of finance. One example was the use of Goal project funds to bribe officials in poorer countries to re-elect the FIFA president, Sepp Blatter (Turya, 2006). Moreover, much as World Bank infrastructural projects have been criticized for endangering the environment and forced displacement of communities, so too have sports events in the South'. For instance, considerable opposition has been raised the development of a sports village to be built along the Yamuna River for the 2010 Commonwealth Games in Delhi (Johnson, 2007) because it will lead to further deterioration of the ecology of the river.

However, sport has also been seen as a potential vehicle to allow for resistance against dominant political structures (Jarvie, 1991; Hargreaves, 1986). In colonial Africa, Wagg (1995: 34) highlights how football 'was wrested from European control and used by the African population to assert their new urban identity. The game became an expression of defiance towards the state and of independence from their colonial oppressors.' In the 1970s, FIFA was seen as a forum for resistance to dominant powers and it elected its President from Brazil and lobbied for African countries (and others from the Global South) to have more representation in world football. This is in contrast to how it is viewed today. More recently, Kuper (1994) in his research on football in Cameroon, illustrates how the hosting of a sports event can provide an arena for subtle and more explicit forms of resistance against the government (the population showing their displeasure with the President by boycotting the final of a football tournament). The protests surrounding the route of the Olympic torch (BBC, 2008) at the time of writing (March 2008) could signal regular focus for protests about the political status of Tibet in its relations with the Chinese government.

2.3.2 Unequal economic relations

These alternative perspectives can also point to how Northern private interest in sport, especially European professional football, perpetuates unequal economic relations by extracting far more from 'peripheral' regions in the Global South than is given back. The fact that the value of leading sport franchises can exceed the GDP of many developing countries arguably demonstrates this. For example, Nauright (2004) documents that leading sports franchises exceeds the GDP of countries like Paraguay, Honduras and Zambia. O'Connor (2005) details that £1.049 billion (US$2.04 billion) was spent on wages and transfers within English professional football (92 clubs and over 2000 footballers) for the 2003–4 season, which was more than the GDP for Lesotho (population in 2003 of 1.8 million).

This allure of wealth is a major reason for the dramatic growth in the migration of athletes from countries in the Global South to Northern countries. Black and Van der Westhuizen (2004) note that at the start of the century, 1000 footballers from Africa and 5000 from Brazil travelled to play in Europe. The few that become successful generate considerable income for their club, without much trickling back to where they originated. Those that are not successful can be trapped in poverty in the countries which they migrated to.[8]

Some commentators term this a new type of slave trade, where young athletes are enticed to richer sports leagues in the North, such as the football leagues of Western Europe and basketball and baseball in the US (Bale and Maguire, 1994; Bale and Cronin, 2003; Bale, 2004). This results in the weakening of the leagues of modern sports and more worryingly the 'obliteration' of more traditional sporting forms in these Global South countries as athletes turn to sports that promise a better life (Bale and Cronin, 2003). The issue of the parlous nature of traditional sport is discussed in more detail in the concluding chapter. Klein (1991) provides an example of the former problem in his analysis of US baseball interest in the Dominican Republic, which led to the gradual dismantlement of domestic Dominican baseball (this is an argument echoed by Kirwin and Akindes in this publication).

All these perspectives also see danger in the involvement of private interest (especially from Northern MNCs) in sport-in-development schemes, especially for health development schemes. Some of the corporations involved in these projects are fast food, soft drinks or tobacco companies. This inevitably resulted in concerns about the motives, and contending messages that supporting sport-in-development whilst simultaneously continuing to encourage its customers to consume unhealthy products sends out. For instance, tobacco companies continue to sponsor many sporting events around the world, especially in East Africa, where laxer rules on advertising and sponsorship exist. Professional football clubs and federations in particular have been condemned for being sponsored at various levels by companies such as McDonald's, Pepsi and Coca Cola, whilst also promoting healthy eating initiatives. The Food Commission (2003) notes a particularly embarrassing example where the English Football Association's 'Medical Education Centre' distributed health educations packs to parents and football academies. This carried an endorsement by Mars Snickers bars. Therefore, sport federations have faced criticism concerning their eagerness to attract sponsorship, without clearly considering some of the possible contradictions this might have in terms of their – or their partners' – social responsibility.

Such concerns build on fears that private and commercial interests from companies with their headquarters in the North hijack more altruistic developmental creeds. For example, just as there are questions over the precise motives for business involvement in general development initiatives, there are those who worry that the involvement of some private interest in sport-in-development projects. For instance, the Head of a prominent sport-in-development NGO during the interview process for this research raised his concern that many sport-in-development projects are supported by sports merchandising companies like Nike and Adidas. They (logically) provide these projects with equipment but this can be at the expense of indigenous (or NGO) suppliers, who are more likely to use local supplies and labour. This is an example replicated throughout development programmes, where Northern private interest can sometimes clash with local/Southern development priorities by usurping either domestic suppliers or non-profit organizations.

Very closely associated to this is the way in which some companies might be accused of using sport (and sport-in-development) as a vehicle by which to further their brand and purchasing power without delivering on promises (often made in corporate social responsibility reports), of delivering on the development objectives that they claim to. This is particularly the case for marketing to the largest target audience of sport-in-development programmes – children and youth (Hawkes, 1998). An example includes the tactic by some tobacco companies to organize or target sports events where free cigarettes have been distributed (Westhead, 2000). What compounds this is the well-chronicled criticism that many sports retail companies face in using labour forces that are poorly paid, exploit children or create environmental degradation (Oxfam, 2006). Therefore, partly because of such examples, some sport-in-development projects are often perceived to be driven more by the needs of the donor, rather than the needs of the community for which the development programme is tailored to. This contradiction is partially linked to what Hamann (2006) calls the 'greenwash strategy', where the difference between rhetoric and practice to ethical/development behaviour by private interest (particularly Northern MNCs) belies MNCs' commitment to good corporate citizenship.

2.3.3   Marginalizing communities

There is evidence that sport and sport-in-development does exclude certain communities and groups. This is a theme developed further in the conclusion (11.2.1). However, in relation to the alternative perspectives of development introduced in this chapter there are two examples to discuss. First, well-documented Feminist concerns have been articulated, especially by Hargreaves (1997) who argues that there has been significant and systematic gender inequality in promoting sport-in-development because of substantial funding differences being available for boys rugby, cricket and soccer development as opposed to girls sport (her research focused on South Africa in the 1990s). Furthermore, there are questions around how far women influence those schemes that are directed at girls and women. Often their presence is seen as a token gesture. This sentiment is echoed in the chapters by Beacom (disability sport-in-development) and Nicholls and Crabbe (young people) in this publication.

Second, a very large proportion (51 per cent) of projects listed on the sportanddev.org website highlight that, for whatever altruistic intentions, the sport-in-development initiatives are overwhelmingly addressed at youth audiences with other segments of the population (adult, elderly etceteras) largely ignored or excluded. For example, FIFA's Football for Hope programme specifically stipulates that funding can only go to youth development. In addition, Willis (2000) suggests that there is evidence that schemes sometimes accidentally exacerbate the marginalization process by raising expectations of participants on sport-in-development programmes to unrealistically high levels. When the participants become politically aware they realize that the social, political and economic structures continue to limit their life choices and standard of living is likely to remain low. The alternative perspectives featured in this section might well argue that what is required is the dismantlement of unequal power relations and not the maintenance of schemes that reduce resistance to dominant political and economic structures.

2.3.4 Negative stereotyping

International sport events, rather than articulating modernization, more often than not represent teams or athletes from Northern countries as being successful and modern, whilst parodying or highlighting the backwardness of the Global South. One interviewee (from a 'plus sport' NGO) in the research conducted for this chapter remarked in 2005 that sport perpetuates a form of apartheid as, 'Global sporting events regularly provide an embarrassing mirror of the widening wealth/poverty divide' and deepen negative stereotypes. This point is reinforced by Cornelissen (2004: 1293) who argues that, 'Postcolonial discourse draws attention to the fact that prevailing Western portrayals of the African continent tend to depict its environment, landscape and people in a certain way... Africa is consistently represented as wild, exotic, subordinate, barbaric, infantile and open for the simultaneous exploitation and civilising force of Westerners', particularly in sport events. This is evidenced through a series of email circulars from 2006 that question the validity of South Africa hosting the football World Cup in 2010, including power point slides with pictures 'highlighting' the backwardness of South Africa. Even events that appear to proceed well and attract positive sounding headlines, such as the African Nations Championship (football) held in Ghana in 2008, show negative stereotyping when reading the small print. *The Economist* (2008) highlighted in an article on the event, the 'ropey' administration, visitors' 'smirking' at the long grass, allegations of match-fixing, 'shoddy' hotels, and half empty stadiums under a headline 'A Happy taste for the future'.

It is also fairly commonplace to see evidence of the process of 'stacking' in different sports, where athletes are allotted positions (and excluded from others) within teams based on racial typologies. For Giulianotti (2004: 4), this, 'reproduces the racist structure of Western societies through sport'.

2.4 Conclusion: sport for development: a neo-liberal vision?

Many of the benefits listed within the sport/development relationship (increasing trade and investment, strengthening life and employment skills, providing better governance, and a more stable environment), appear close to modernization and neo-liberal understandings about the approved path of development. Therefore, a good 'fit' is apparent. However, as this chapter and the concluding chapter in this publication highlight, these perspectives in development still need convincing that sport is a reliable and long-lasting partner that can be used to progress such a vision of development. Indeed, the lack of enthusiasm (or interest) displayed by modernization/neo-liberalism comes close to matching the antipathy historically shown by critical theoretical perspectives, which underpin much of the three alternative perspectives discussed in the second part of this chapter. Giulianotti (2004: 4) shows how they are 'popularly associated with a cerebral contempt for mindlessness of popular cultural pastimes', quoting Adorno who thought that modern sport trained 'men all the more inexorably to serve the machine. Hence sports belong to the realm of unfreedom, no matter where they are organized'. Given the close association that sport, particularly at an elite level, has with the dominant political economic and development strategies and philosophy, it is no surprise that the critical perspectives outlined here would continue to be concerned with the increase in the sport/development relationship, either through the hosting of sports events (which clearly display consumerist messaging through sponsorship and other marketing narratives) or via sport-in-development programmes. This chapter speculates how both can exacerbate unequal political and economic relations, further marginalizing communities (especially women) and promoting damaging negative stereotyping in the process. Crabbe (Chapter 8) illustrates how sport-in-development can transmit dominant, consumerist messages, despite programmes being set up without such intentions. The opportunities that sport presents to enable forms of resistance to dominant development and political economic processes/ relationships appears to pale into insignificance against the weight of concerns raised above. That said, a number of projects have emerged in the last five years that encourages grassroots/indigenous input, or are led at a local level and appear to deliver a range of development goals. Examples of such programmes include EduSport and Sport in Action, which operates in Zambia. Clearly, as Nicholls argues adeptly in chapter seven, many more are needed. Furthermore, some sport-in-development programmes are focused on the empowerment of young women. More critical theoretical perspectives might criticize this as cultural imperialism or even false consciousness, but does at least redress some of the perceived injustices of other sport/ development aspects noted in section 2.3.

This chapter therefore, in common with many others in this publication, calls for a strengthened engagement within the academic development studies community to think about the measurement of the sport/development relationship. This could come from the perspectives that dominate debate and shape development policy, to examine the sport/development relationship more seriously. As noted in the introductory chapter, it is somewhat surprising that the increased utilization of sport-in-development has received such little critical attention. The chapter has partially addressed this gap by suggesting how contrasting perspectives from the international development field might regard the growing escalation of sport-in-development.

Notes

1   This discussion recognizes that it takes place within the context of similar contending debates within sports studies on the impact of sport on society. This issue is one that is debated in the concluding chapter here.

2   For a detailed discussion on the range of debates that take place in development studies see Willis (2005) and McKay (2004).

3 More nuanced forms of modernization emerged – see McKay, 2004 (52–3) for a more detailed discussion of them.
4 Rostow's five stage growth theory starts with a traditional society. This is defined as subsistence economy based mainly on farming with very limited technology or capital to process raw materials or develop services and industries. *Preconditions for take-off*, the second stage, are said to take place when the levels of technology within a country develop and the development of a transport system encourages trade. During the next stage, *take-off*, manufacturing industries grow rapidly, airports, roads, and railways are built, and growth poles emerge as investment increases. Stage four is termed the *drive to maturity* during which growth should be self-sustaining, having spread to all parts of the country, and leading to an increase in the number and types of industry. During this stage more complex transport systems and manufacturing expand as transport develops, rapid urbanization occurs, and traditional industries may decline. In Rostow's final stage, the *age of mass consumption*, rapid expansion of tertiary industries occurs alongside a decline in manufacturing.
5 Further details on modernization and neo-liberalism can be found in Preston (1996), Simon and Närman (1999) and Simon (2002: 86–92).
6 Furthermore, Mandela is often quoted as saying, 'Sport has the power to change the world. It has the power to inspire in a way that little else does. It speaks to youth in a language they understand. Sport can create hope, where once there was despair. It is more powerful than governments in breaking down barriers. It laughs in the face of discrimination' (*The Guardian*, 2004).
7 Supersport – an amalgamation of sports teams and organizations – funded this programme with R6 million (US$0.767 million).
8 McDougall (2008) highlights the growing trade in football-related trafficking of children from West Africa to Europe.

Bibliography

Amin, S. (1974) *Accumulation on a World Scale: A Critique of the Theory of Underdevelopment.* New York: Monthly Review.
Arbena, J.L. (1993) 'International Aspects of Sport in Latin America: Perceptions, Prospects, and Proposals', in Dunning, E., Maguire, J., and Pearton, R. (eds) *The Sports Process: A Comparative and Developmental Approach.* Champaign: Human Kinetics, pp. 151–167.
Armstrong, G. (1997) *Entering the Field: New Perspectives on World Football.* London: Berg Publishers Ltd.
Baker, W.J. (1987) 'Political Games: The Meaning of International Sport for Independent Africa', in Baker, W.J. and Mangan, J.A. (eds) *Sport in Africa: Essays in Social History.* New York: Africana, pp. 272–294.
Balassa, B. (1981) *The Newly Industrializing Countries in the World Economy.* Oxford: Pergamon.
Balassa, B. (1978) *Policy Reform in Developing Countries.* Oxford: Pergamon.
Bale, J. (2004) 'Three Geographies of African Footballer Migration: Patterns, Problems and Postcoloniality', in *Football in Africa: Conflict, Conciliation and Community* (eds) Gary Armstrong and Richard Giulianotti. Basingstoke and New York: Palgrave Macmillan, pp. 229–246.

Bale, J. and Cronin, M. (2003) *Sport and Postcolonialism*. London: Frank Cass.
Bale, J. and Maguire, J. (1994) *The Global Sports Arena: Athletic Talent Migration in an Interdependent World*. London: Frank Cass.
Barbados Free Press (2007) 'The Legacy of Cricket World Cup: Debt, Debt and More Debt', 6th July.
BBC (2005) 'Blatter wraps up African tour', posted 15 April, accessed 21st December 2007, http://news.bbc.co.uk/sport1/hi/football/africa/4447955.stm.
BBC (2008) 'Olympic torch lit despite protest', posted 24th March 2008, accessed 25th March 2008, http://news.bbc.co.uk/1/hi/world/europe/7310654.stm.
Binns, T. (2002) 'Dualistic and unilinear concepts of development', in *The Companion to Development Studies* (eds) Desai and Potter, pp. 75–79.
Black, D. and Van Der Westhuizen, J. (2004) 'The allure of global games for 'semi-peripheral' polities and space: a research agenda', *Third World Quarterly*, 25(7), 1195–1214.
Blowfield, M. (2005) 'Corporate Social Responsibility: reinventing the meaning of development?', *International Affairs*, **81**(3), 515–524.
Booth, D. (1975) 'Andre Gunder Frank: an introduction and appreciation', in I. Oxaal, T. Barnett and D. Booth (eds) *Beyond Dependency*. London: Routledge & Kegan Paul, pp. 50–85.
Business Day (2007a) (26th November) 'Footing the bill (editorial)', p. 10.
Business Day (2007b) (27th November) 'Deloitte: Getting ready for 2010', pp. 6–7.
Canadian Broadcasting Corporation (2001) 'Toronto mayor hurts Olympic bid with comments', 22nd June, 2001, accessed 23rd March 2008, from http://www.cbc.ca/canada/story/2001/06/21/lastman010621.html
Chappell, R. (2004) 'Kenyan Sport in the Aftermath of the Commonwealth Games, Manchester 2002', *Sport in Society*, 7(2), 175–191.
Cornelissen, S. (2004) "It's Africa's turn!' The narratives and legitimations surrounding the Moroccan and South African bids for the 2006 and 2010 FIFA finals', *Third World Quarterly*, 25(7), 1293–1309.
Crush, J. (ed.) (1995) *Power of Development*. London: Routledge.
Darby, P. (2002) *Africa, Football and FIFA: Politics, Colonialism and Resistance*. London: Frank Cass Publishers.
Darby, P. (2005) 'Africa and the "World" Cup: FIFA Politics, Eurocentrism and Resistance', *International Journal of Sport History*, 22(5), 883–905.
Desai, V. and Potter, R.B. (2002) *The Companion to Development Studies*. London: Arnold.
Dimeo, P. and Kay, J. (2004) 'Major sports events, image projection and the problems of 'semi-periphery' a case study of the 1996 South Asia Cricket World Cup', *Third World Quarterly*, 25(7), 1263–1276.
Donnelly, P. (1996) 'The local and the global: globalization in the sociology of sport', *Journal of Sport and Social Issues*, 20(3), 239–257.
Dunning, E., Maguire, J. and Pearton, R. (1993) *The Sports Process: A Comparative and Developmental Approach*. London: Human Kinetics.
The Economist (2006) 'The World Bank and Corruption', 2nd March.
The Economist (2007a) 'Beyond a boundary', February 24th, p. 54.
The Economist (2007b) 'Stumped', May 3rd, accessed from http://www.economist.com/world/la/displaystory.cfm?story_id=9116953, 21st October 2007.
The Economist (2008) 'A Happy taste for the future', 14th February.

Edelman, Kennedy School of Government and International Business Leaders Forum (2005) *Business and International Development: Opportunities, Responsibilities and Expectations*, p. 26.

Elias, N. and Dunning, E. (1986) *Quest for Excitement: Sport and Leisure in the Civilizing Process*. Oxford: Basil Blackwell.

Escobar, A. (1995) *Encountering Development: The Making and Unmaking of the Third World*. Princeton: Princeton University Press.

FIFA (2005) *FIFA World Report on Football Development*. Zurich: FIFA.

The Food Commission (2003) (27th January) 'Football sells out to junk food brands', *Food Magazine*.

Frank, A.G. (1967) *Capitalism and underdevelopment in Latin America: historical studies of Chile and Brazil*. New York: Monthly Review.

Frey, J.H. (1988) 'The Internal and External Role of Sport in National Development', *Journal of National Development*, 1, 65–82.

Friedman, M. (1982) *Capitalism and Freedom*. Chicago: University of Chicago Press.

Frynas, J. (2005) 'The false developmental promise of Corporate Social Responsibility: evidence from multinational oil companies', *International Affairs*, **81**(3), 581–598.

Giulianotti, R. (ed.) (2004) *Sport and Modern Social Theorists*. Basingstoke and New York: Palgrave Macmillan.

The Guardian (2004) 'The penny's dropped', 21st August.

Guttmann, A. (1994) *Games and Empires: Modern Sports and Cultural Imperialism*. New York: Columbia University Press.

Hamann, H. (2006) 'Can business make decisive contributions to development? Toward a research agenda on corporate citizenship and beyond', *Development Southern Africa*, **23**(2), 175–195.

Hargreaves, Janet (1994) *Sporting Females*. London: Routledge.

Hargreaves, Janet (1997) 'Women's Sport, Development and Cultural Diversity: The South African Experience', *Women's Studies International Forum*, **20**(2), 191–206.

Hargreaves, John (1986) *Sport, Power & Culture*. Cambridge: Polity Press.

Harris, J., and Humberstone, B. (2004) 'Sport, gender and international relations', in *Sport and International Relations* (eds) Roger Levermore and Adrian Budd, pp. 48–61.

Hawkes, T. (1998) 'Scoring an Own Goal? Ethical issues in the UK professional soccer business', *Business Ethics: A European Review*, **7**(1), 37–47.

Heinemann, K. (1993) 'Sport in Developing Countries', in *The Sports Process: A Comparative and Developmental Approach* (eds) Eric Dunning, Joseph Maguire and Robert Pearton, pp. 139–150.

Hettne, B. (1995) *Development Theory and the Three Worlds*. Harlow: Longman.

Hunt, J. (2004a) 'Aid and Development', in *Key Issues in Development* (eds) Kingsbury *et al.* Basingstoke, UK: Palgrave Macmillan, pp. 67–90.

Hunt, J. (2004b) 'Gender and Development', in *Key Issues in Development* (eds) Kingsbury *et al.* Basingstoke, UK: Palgrave Macmillan, pp. 243–265.

International Monetary Fund (2007) Zambia: Poverty Reduction Strategy Paper, accessed from http://www.imf.org/external/pubs/ft/scr/2007/cr07276.pdf, 11 December 2007.

International Platform on Sport and Development (2006) 'Project detail: A Ganar', accessed from http://www.sportanddev.org/en/projects/americas/a-ganar-vencer-in-brazil.htm, accessed 6th January 2008.

Jarvie, G. (1991) 'Sport, Popular struggle and South African culture', in *Sport, Racism & Ethnicity* (ed.) Grant Jarvie. London: Falmer Press, pp. 175–189.

Jennings, A. (2007) *Foul!: The Secret World of FIFA: Bribes, Vote Rigging and Ticket Scandals*. London: HarperCollinsWillow.

Johnson, J. (2007) 'Sports village for Delhi river opposed', *Financial Times*, 15th/16th June, p. 9.

King, G. (2006) 'Tackling the Tigers: the Wanderers on Tour', *The Guardian* (2nd September).

Kingsbury, D., Remenyi, J., McKay, J. and Hunt, J. (eds) (2004) *Key Issues in Development*. Basingstoke: Palgrave.

Klein, A.M. (1991) *Sugarball: The American Game, the Dominican Dream*. New Haven, Conn: Yale University Press.

Kuper, S. (1994) *Football Against the Enemy*. London: Orion.

Lal, D. (1983) *The Poverty of Development Economics*. London: Institute of Economic Affairs.

Larrison, T. (1998) 'Ethics and International Development', *European Review*, 7(1), 63–67.

Levermore, R. (2008) 'Playing for Development: Outlining the extent of the use of sport for development', *Progress in Development*, 8(2), 183–190.

Levermore, R. (2004) 'Sport's role in constructing the 'inter-state' worldview', in *Sport and International Relations* (eds) Levermore and Adrian Budd, pp. 16–30.

Levermore, R. and Budd, A. (2004) *Sport and International Relations: An Emerging Relationship*. London and New York: Routledge.

Maguire, J. (1999) *Global Sport – Identities, Societies, Civilizations*. Cambridge: Polity.

Maguire, J. (2000) 'Sport and Globalization', in *Handbook of Sports Studies* (eds) Jay Coakley and Eric Dunning. London: Sage, pp. 356–369.

Maguire, J. (2005) *Power and Global Sport*. London: Routledge.

Mail and Guardian (August 10–16, 2007) 'Bad for business', p. 46.

Mandle, J. and Mandle, J. (1988) *Grass Roots Commitment: Basketball and Society in Trinidad and Tobago*. Parkesburg, Ia: Caribbean Books.

Matheson, V.A. and Baade, R.A. (2004) 'Mega Sporting events in developing nations: Playing the way to prosperity?', *South African Journal of Economies*, 72(5), 1084–1095.

May, G. and Phelan, J. (2005) *Shared Goals: Sport and Business in Partnerships for Development*. London: IBLF.

McDougall, D. (2008) 'The investigation: This is Baba', *The Observer Sports Monthly*, January, pp. 50–55.

McEwan, C. (2002) 'Postcolonialism', in *The Companion to Development Studies* (eds) Desai & Potter, pp. 127–131.

McKay, J. (2004) 'Reassessing Development Theory: 'Modernisation' and Beyond', in *Key Issues in Development* (eds) Kingsbury *et al.* Basingstoke, UK: Palgrave Macmillan, pp. 45–66.

Milner, M. and Elliott, L. (2002) 'This is a level playing field', *The Guardian*, 28th May, p. 22.

Nauright, J. (2004) 'Global games: culture, political economy and sport in the globalised world of the 21st century', *Third World Quarterly*, 25(7), 1325–1336.

Newmarch, J. (2007) 'Billion rand ball', *Mail & Guardian*, 10–16th August.

O'Connor, A. (2005) 'The billion-pound revolution', *The Times*, 8th June, p. 80.

Oxfam (2006) *Offside – Labour rights and sportswear production in Asia*. Oxford: Oxfam.

Peet, R. (1991) *Global Capitalism: Theories of Societal Development*. London and New York: Routledge.

Pillay, U. (2007) (14th August) 'Africa's lost opportunity', *Business Day*, p. 9.

Potter, R.B. (2002) 'Theories, strategies and ideologies of development', in *The Companion to Development Studies* (eds) Desai and Potter, pp. 61–64.

Preston, P.W. (1996) *Development Theory: An Introduction*. Oxford: Blackwell.

Rist, G. (2002) *The History of Development – From Western Origins to Global Faith*. London and New York: Zed Books.

Rostow, W.W. (1960) *The Process of Economic Growth*. Oxford: Clarendon Press.

Sage, G. (1995) 'Deindustrialization and the American sporting goods industry', in Wilcox, R.C. (ed.) *Sport in the Global Village*. Morgantown, W.Va: Fitness Information Technology, Inc, pp. 39–51.

Said, E. (1978) *Orientalism*. London: Routledge and Kegan Paul.

Sayer, J. (2005) 'Guest editor's introduction: Do more good, do less harm: development and the private sector', *Development in Practice*, 15(3&4), 251–268.

Simon, D. (2002) 'Neo-liberalism, structural adjustment and poverty reduction strategies', in *The Companion to Development Studies*, eds Desai and Potter, pp. 86–91.

Simon, D. and Närman, A. (1999) *Development as Theory and Practice*. Harlow: Longman.

Sport for Development and Peace International Working Group (2006) *Sport for Development and Peace – From Practice to Policy*, Toronto.

Sports Sans Frontiers (2005) *Our Vocation, Our Actions*.

Stevenson, D. (2002) 'Women, Sport and Globalization; Competing Discourses of Sexuality and Nation', *Journal of Sport and Social Issues*, 26(2), 209–225.

Stuart, O. (1995) 'The Lions Stir; Football in African Society', *Giving the Game Away: Football, Politics and Culture on Five Continents*, (editor Stephen Wagg). London/New York: Leicester University Press, pp. 24–51.

Turya, M. (2006) 'FIFA – Failing International Football Advancement', *bulb*, Issue 10, 14–15.

United Nations Development Programme (2006) *Human Development Report 2006: Beyond Scarcity: Power, Poverty and the Global Water Crisis*. New York: United Nations.

Wagg, S. (1995) *Giving the Game Away – Football, Politics & Culture on Five Continents*. London and New York: Leicester University Press.

Wallerstein, E. (1979) *The Capitalist World Economy*. Cambridge, UK: Cambridge University Press.

Westhead, J. (2000) 'UK tobacco firm targets African youth', *BBC News*, accessed from http://news.bbc.co.uk/1/hi/uk/933430.stm, accessed 9th November 2006.

Willis, K. (2005) *Theories and Practices of Development*. London and New York: Routledge.

Willis, O. (2000) 'Sport and Development: The significance of Mathare Youth Sports Association', *Canadian Journal of Development Studies*, **XXI** (3), 825–849.

World Bank (2007) *World Development Report, 2007: Development and the Next Generation*. Washington: World Bank.

Young, Y. (2002) 'WID, GAD and WAD', in *The Companion to Development Studies* (eds) Desai and Potter, pp. 321–325.

3
Sport-in-Development: Accountability or Development?

Fred Coalter

3.1 Introduction

This chapter is based on extensive fieldwork in Africa and India to develop a user-friendly monitoring and evaluation manual for UK Sport and UNICEF (Coalter, 2006).[1] The chapter explores issues relating to the intersection of two recent policy developments. Firstly, the dramatically increased growth in interest in the role of sport in international development (see section 1.2) and the often rhetorical and grandiose claims made for sport's contribution – ranging from individual self-esteem via the strengthening of communities to creating the conditions for conflict resolution and peace. For example, at the World Sport's Forum in March 2000 Louise Fréchette, the UN Deputy Secretary General, stated that:

> The power of sports is far more than symbolic. You are engines of economic growth. You are a force for gender equality. You can bring youth and others in from the margins, strengthening the social fabric. You can promote communication and help heal the divisions between peoples, communities and entire nations. You can set an example of fair play. Last but not least, you can advocate a strong and effective United Nations (United Nations, 2000: 4).

In such policy rhetoric, sport seems to be presented as an all-purpose social vaccine, frequently based more on the almost mythic nature of 'sport' (rarely defined) and supported by *ad hominem* illustrations and anecdote, rather than any substantive research evidence (Coalter, 2007).

However, paralleling such rhetoric, Pollard and Court (2005) refer to a second policy development which has led to growing pressure on NGOs to improve the standard of their monitoring procedures, to become more accountable, justify their roles, and work more effectively in order to retain their legitimacy. Although their analysis relates more to the content and nature of NGOs' advocacy and mediation work, it also refers to service provision. For example, the UN Business Plan for the International Year of Sport (UN, 2005a: 11) refers to the need for 'monitoring and evaluation of sport and development programs and ... the selection of impact indicators that would show the benefits of sport and development programs in the field.' A UNICEF publication on monitoring and evaluation of such programmes (UNICEF, 2006: 4) states that 'there is a need to assemble proof, to go beyond what is mostly anecdotal evidence to monitor and evaluate the impact of sport in development programmes.'

Not surprisingly, there is little systematic evidence about the impacts of such sport-in-development programmes. Many are relatively new, they have limited access to technical and financial resources and the environment is frequently not conducive to undertaking robust research. Further, the limited available research on the impact of such programmes in the area of HIV/AIDS education is not wholly encouraging (Kruse, 2006; Botcheva and Huffman, 2004). The major methodological difficulties relating to measuring *any* outcomes of sports programmes, even in much more favourable circumstances, are well documented (Collins *et al.*, 1999; Coalter *et al.*, 2000; Coalter, 2007). However, many of the wide-ranging and ambitious claims being made in the policy rhetoric of sport-in-development pose even more substantial issues of definition and measurement. To quote Pawson's (2005) comment about many social policy interventions, much of the policy rhetoric in sport-in-development can be viewed as proposing 'ill-defined interventions with hard to follow outcomes'.

In addition to posing major methodological difficulties, the nature of sport-in-development organizations also raises fundamental issues about the purpose of, and approach to, monitoring and evaluation. For reasons which will be outlined in this chapter, there is a need for a theoretically informed, process-led approach, which is concerned as much with *organizational development* as with various types of (ill-defined) outcomes. While not arguing that we should not attempt to measure outcomes, it is proposed that there are inherent methodological difficulties (and policy limitations) with such an approach and that these are compounded by the environments within which sport-in-development organizations operate. It is argued that sport-in-development organizations are important *qua* organizations and this is illustrated via a brief case study of the Kenyan MYSA. This is used to outline the argument that a theory-driven, participatory, process-led approach to monitoring and evaluation can provide the basis for capacity-building, greater ownership, understanding and integration and greatly improved programme delivery. Further, it is an essential first step to formulating more precise and realistic outcome measures.

3.2 Development, civil society and the new importance of sport

As outlined in introductory chapter, via a series of resolutions and the designation of 2005 as the International Year of Sport and Physical Education, the UN acknowledged sport as an important sector of civil society (United Nations, 2005b) and turned to 'the world of sport for help in the work for peace and the effort to achieve the Millennium Goals' (United Nations, 2005a: v). Areas of engagement included universal primary education, promoting gender equality and empowering women, combating HIV/AIDS and addressing issues of environmental sustainability.

Such initiatives serve to promote and legitimize a range of sports-based initiatives, under the collective term of 'sport-in-development'. Of course, many bottom-up sport-in-development initiatives had existed prior to the recent UN interest. For example, the MYSA was established in Nairobi in 1987 and the community-development oriented SCORE was established in South Africa in 1991. In fact, the high profile achievements (and lobbying) of such organizations played a major role in the UN's embracing of sport as a contributor to development. Further, government organizations such as the Norwegian Agency for Development Cooperation (NORAD) and the Norwegian Olympic Committee and Confederation of Sports (NIF) have a long history of investing in sports programmes to strengthen civil society.[2]

3.2.1 Sport plus and plus sport

Because of the wide variety of very ambitious desired outcomes, it is not surprising that there is a variety of 'sport-in-development' programmes with a diversity of aims and objectives. Although traditional sports development objectives of increased participation and the development of sporting skills are part of these programmes, they are rarely the sole rationale and very rarely the basis for external investment and subsequent evaluation. Almost without exception, the presumed instrumental role of sport is emphasised (with outcomes often constructed with an eye to aid agencies' (non-sporting) objectives rather than a realistic assessment of what is possible).

As the introductory chapter notes, within this context it is possible to divide sport-in-development projects into two broad approaches. First, sport plus programmes, give primacy to the development of sustainable sports organizations, programmes and development pathways. However, even within such organizations sport is also used to address a number of broader social issues (e.g. gender equity; HIV/AIDS education). These outcomes are pursued via varying mixtures of organizational values, ethics and practices, symbolic games and more formal didactic approaches. Second, plus sport programmes give primacy to social and health programmes where sport is used, especially its ability to bring together a large number of young people, to achieve some of their objectives. Short-term outcomes (e.g. HIV/AIDS education and, much more ambitiously, behaviour change) are more important than the longer-term sustainable development of sport. Of course, there is a continuum of such programmes and differences are not always clearcut. Nevertheless, the broad division has implications for the definition of outcomes and 'success' and appropriate timescales for evaluation.

3.3   Need for evaluation?

However, as noted earlier, the increased emphasis on the developmental role of sport has been accompanied by an emphasis on evidence of the results of such programmes, with the UN Business Plan for the International Year of Sport (United Nations, 2005a: 11) referring to the need for monitoring and evaluation and the selection of relevant impact indicators (see also UNICEF, 2006). Within this context the *Sport in Development: A Monitoring and Evaluation Manual* (Coalter, 2006) was produced, based on the basis of four in-depth case studies (three in Africa and one in India) and the rest of this chapter outlines and explores the political, organizational and methodological issues encountered in the development of this manual. In order to illustrate these issues we begin with an outline of one of the organizations visited in the process of producing the manual.

The MYSA has been chosen for a number of reasons. Firstly, it is among the longest standing sport-in-development organizations in Africa (established in 1987). Secondly, it clearly is a sports development organization, with a development pathway leading to two semi-professional soccer teams (Mathare United) and has produced several Kenyan international soccer players. Thirdly, it has sought to identify the development needs of the young people of Mathare and to adapt soccer and the organization to these needs. While MYSA is certainly not typical of sports plus projects, it provides a clear illustration of the potential of such programmes, has acted as a template for more recently emerging sport-in-development organizations and provides a clear antidote to simplistic assertions about 'sport', by embedding soccer in a much broader programme of activities based on a coherent developmental philosophy. Finally, MYSA illustrates many of the complexities facing attempts to monitor and evaluate the contribution of 'sport' to development.

3.3.1 Mathare Youth Sport Association (MYSA)

Mathare, in north east Nairobi, is one of the largest and poorest slums in Africa, with a population of about 500,000 people living in an area of 2 kilometres by 300 metres (1.2 miles by .2 miles). It is a maze of low, rusted iron-sheeting roofs with mud walls. Housing is wholly inadequate, with most houses measuring around 8 by 6 feet and holding up to 10 people. Few houses have running water, open gutters of sewage run throughout, the road infrastructure is extremely poor, refuse and litter dominate the area and the local authority provides few services (Brady and Kahn, 2002; Willis, 2000).

MYSA, was started by Bob Munro (a Canadian UN development officer) in 1987 as a small self-help project to organize sport (mostly soccer) and slum cleanup and environmental improvements. It is now the largest youth sports organization in Africa, with more than 1,000 teams and 17,000 members. MYSA's teams range from under 10 to 18 years of age, organized in 16 zones – the biggest league in Africa. MYSA also has two male semi-professional teams, Mathare United A and B (Atkins, nd). These teams were established for two reasons. Firstly, to provide the top of the sports- development pyramid and provide motivation and role models for the junior players – in 2004 MYSA supplied eight players for Kenya's African Nation's Cup squad. Secondly, it was hoped to benefit from transfer fees which could be used to provide economic security for the broader MYSA programme. However, reflecting wider aspects of corruption in Kenyan society and sport, football agents in association with the Kenyan Football Federation (KFF) undermined this strategy, by depriving MYSA of its legitimate share of two transfer fees and leading to an intervention by FIFA and a threat of sanctions on the KFF (for a systematic and detailed analysis of the corruption of the KFF see Munro (2004)).

3.3.2 Producing citizens

MYSA initially attracted young males who played on waste ground in the slums with footballs made of recycled plastic bags and twine. The attraction of MYSA was three-fold. Firstly, access to real footballs (not to be under-estimated in conditions of such poverty). Secondly, organized and structured games, which simulated the professional game. Thirdly, MYSA provided an ordered and protective environment, which was especially important for the many street children. However, it soon developed into a more complex and ambitious project, whose ultimate ambition is 'to help produce the leaders needed for building the new Kenya' (Munro, 2005) – a complex theme which is both explicit and implicit throughout all aspects of the organization and its programmes.

In effect, MYSA compensates for major failures of the local and national states' welfare provision and, in many ways, could be viewed as a 'state within a state' – facilitated and given coherence by soccer and soccer-related programmes. Part of the key to MYSA's success is to be found in the broader social relationships, inter-dependence and trust which it develops, especially in reducing the social isolation of young women. The organization seems to have generated a form of *social capital* (Coalter, 2008; Portes and Landolt, 2000; Putnam, 2000), with many members referring to MYSA as a 'family'. This is reinforced by the fact that its sixty full and part-time employees are recruited from MYSA members, born in Mathare. Most of these administrators, peer leaders and coaches appear to possess a deep sense of responsibility to act as positive role models. The sense of involvement, responsibility and values of active citizenship are reinforced by member-involvement in decision-making at all levels, with a strong emphasis on mutual self-help – succinctly expressed by Munro (2005: 2) as 'you do something, MYSA does something, you do nothing, MYSA does nothing'.

3.3.3 Empowering young women

Football for young women started in 1992 and required MYSA staff to address issues of restrictive domestic labour and parental opposition, which is an ongoing struggle (Brady and Kahn, 2002). The concentration on soccer can be explained by a desire to use a presumed male preserve to challenge gender stereotypes. With boys expressing scepticism about girls' ability to play the game, the provision of 'girls' sports' would risk simply re-enforcing deep rooted gender stereotypes. The subordinate economic and social position of young women present obstacles to recruitment and is reflected in programming which is flexible enough to permit both the completion of domestic tasks and to address parental fear about safety after dark. For example, 'out-of-school girls work eight times as many hours in unpaid domestic work as out-of-school boys' (Brady and Kahn, 2002: 5). A major goal for MYSA has been to use sport to reduce young women's social isolation by providing them with public spaces and opportunities to develop. As Brady and Kahn (2002: 1–2) state:

> Typically, the kinds of public spaces that are seen as legitimate venues for females – markets, health clinics, and so forth – are those that enable women to fulfil their domestic roles as homemakers and mothers......'public space' de facto becomes men's space....

Although there is little robust empirical data about the effectiveness of this approach at either a personal or community level (e.g. the link between poverty and sexual exploitation remains widespread), Brady and Kahn (2002: 1–2) state:

> We posit that participation in non-elite sports programs appropriate for girls of average physical ability and skills can meet the simultaneous needs of offering girls new venues in which to gather and breaking down restrictive gender norms .... Girls' participation can begin to change community norms about their roles and capacities. In this way, sports may be a catalyst for the transformation of social norms.

3.3.4 Sporting talent and social responsibility

More generally, the ethical and philosophical issues of respect for self and others, responsibility and citizenship are embedded in all activities. For example, during soccer games a yellow card is awarded to anyone other than the captain who speaks to a referee (a substitute player is permitted). The player then has to referee six junior matches to put him or herself in the place of a referee before being permitted to play again. In addition, a green card is awarded to the most sporting player and is a highly valued award as it is accompanied by educational scholarship points.

As part of its commitment to help young leaders to stay in school, MYSA has about 400 annual Leadership Awards (it also provides small libraries and study rooms to compensate for the lack of study space in over-crowded dwelling). Although schooling is free up to the age of 14, many schools require pupils to wear uniforms (prohibitive for many living in poverty) and in the post-14 schools fees are required. The awards are paid to the school of the winners' choice and are used to pay for tuition, books and uniforms. Points towards these scholarships are also linked to volunteer and peer-leadership work undertaken within MYSA.

Community service is compulsory for all members of MYSA, including Mathare United. The work is aimed at increasing environmental awareness and mostly entails a 'clean up' in which teams from the various zones clear drains, cut grass, remove litter and so on. Although this work makes little impact on the overwhelming environmental problems of Mathare, the core value being emphasized here is that 'if you get something from the community you must put something back into the community' (Munro, 2005: 2). Of course, such work also raises MYSA's profile and assists in the building of trust (especially among parents). The extent of programme integration and re-enforcement of citizenship values is emphasized by the fact that each completed cleanup project earns a soccer team 6 points towards its league standings – success being a combination of sporting talent and social and collective responsibility.

3.4   From outcomes to process

It is clear from this case study that sport-in-development organizations have complex and multi-stage processes and outcomes which raise substantial questions about traditional, outcome-oriented, approaches to monitoring and evaluation – nearly all sport-in-development organizations are sport *plus*. Further, such processes raise significant questions about easy generalizations about 'sport' and the generalizability of the findings from any single study. For these reasons it is argued that monitoring and evaluation needs to move beyond simple definitions of 'outcomes' and accountability and from summative to formative approaches. Such an approach can assist in the shift from funder/client relationships based simply on accountability to *partnerships* concerned with organizational development and sustainability. To explore these issues we need to distinguish three levels of analysis:

(i)   Developing people, creating citizens
(ii)   Sport and poverty
(iii) Sport as process

3.4.1   Developing people, creating citizens

In most traditional sport-in-development programmes leaders and coaches are regarded simply as *inputs* – qualified sports development officers who use their professional expertise to develop programmes for local communities. However, the increasing emphasis on *developing communities through sport* has led to a greater emphasis on a 'bottom-up' approach (Deane, 1998; Witt and Crompton, 1996; Coalter *et al.*, 2000), with local leadership being regarded as a vital factor in the success of many programmes. Such strategies are based on recognition that the involvement of local people increases the sense of ownership and credibility of sports programmes (Witt and Crompton, 1996; Utting, 1996; Deane, 1998) and also a desire to ensure longer-term sustainability.

Most sport-in-development programmes are based on the development of *youth peer leaders* (see also specific chapters on youth leaders by Nicholls (Chapter 7) and Crabbe (Chapter 8) in this publication) and they train young people to coach and lead their peers in sport and life skill programmes. Many involve young people (especially young women) at various levels of planning, implementation and decision-making, providing important experience of control, empowerment and a sense of collective responsibility (via the much emphasized status of 'role models'). In other words, *people* (or 'responsible citizens') are a major outcome of such organizations, one that underpins their sustainability and precedes the more general sports programmes whose inevitably more varied impacts are often the subject of evaluation. In fact it is these aspects of sport-in-development organizations which best illustrate the UN's (2005b: 2) reference to sport as 'an important sector in civil society'.

Munro (2005: 4) illustrates the importance placed on role models by asking rhetorically, 'role models for youth: is anything more important in development?'. He argues that in many African countries the poor are the majority and youth constitute the majority of that poor majority and that 'among the many debilitating aspects of poverty is that the poor, and especially the youth, lack confidence and belief in themselves'. Consequently, 'after food, water, shelter, health and education, nothing is more important for future development than providing good role models for our youth' (Munro, 2005: 4). Although there is much talk of the importance of role models in sport, much of this relates to the assertion that elite sports people can have a positive impact on young people's commitment to, and participation in, sport. However, a review of evidence by Payne *et al.* (2003) illustrates that, to be effective, role models must be 'embedded', based on the development of supportive, longer term relationships, with attention paid to the selection and training of mentors. Further, self-efficacy theory (Bandura, 1977), suggests that a major factor underpinning the effectiveness of role models is their *perceived similarity to the learner*. Learning is more likely to occur when the learner perceives that they are capable of carrying out the behaviour (self-efficacy expectancy), think that there is a high probability that the behaviour will result in a particular outcome (outcome expectancy) and if the outcome is desirable. Many, if not all, sport-in-development programmes are based on such, often unarticulated, understandings (see Nicholls in this publication).

3.4.2 Sport and poverty

Sport-in-development organizations often compensate for wider failures of national and local states, weak civic structures, disintegrating families, poorly developed labour markets, failing educational institutions, deeply rooted gender inequalities and poverty of an order, scale and depth unknown in developed economies. For example, Burnett (2001: 49), in discussing the issues involved in assessing the impact of sport-in-development projects, refers to the pervasive influence of poverty. Poverty is however not simply a quantitative or economic phenomenon, but indicates a particular location and experience of being human. Kotze (1993: 3) refers to the all-embracing nature of poverty 'in the sense that it encompasses material, social, physical and intellectual insecurity'.

Such circumstances raise significant conceptual, methodological and cultural issues about the definition of outcomes, the nature of baseline data and the setting of realistic performance targets. Drawing on her work in South African townships Burnett (2001: 43) emphasizes the need for 'a unique and context-sensitive research instrument' and the need 'to establish the 'value-added' dimension of the impact on the community (represented by social networks, institutions and groups) and on the individual'. In other words, there is a need for a consideration of realistic definition is of locally relevant outcomes, grounded in material circumstances (again raising significant issues about generalizability, especially in the absence of information about context and process).

3.4.3 Sport as process: why do we assume that our programmes will work?

Although summative, outcome-based evaluations may provide some indication as to some (limited) aspects of the effectiveness of the programme

– for example, the extent to which self-efficacy has been improved, HIV/AIDS knowledge has been increased; values and attitudes have been modified – such an approach has two major limitations. Firstly, it is difficult to over-estimate the difficulties in undertaking such evaluations in the circumstances in which many sport-in-development programmes work. Limitations on financial and human resources (barely enough for programme delivery), lack of research expertise, the absence of robust base-line data, issues of language, literacy and meaning, the relatively chaotic lives and irregular attendance of many participants all combine to raise significant questions about the logistics of meaningful outcome measurement and evaluation (leaving aside the generic methodological issues associated with intervening and confounding variables – e.g. the role of school/ church/media in disseminating HIV/AIDS information).

Secondly, as Pawson (2006) argues, such evaluations can rarely answer the question as to *why* programmes have been either successful or unsuccessful (however defined). The simple measurement of outcomes fails to address Patriksson's (1995) questions about what sports and sports' *processes* produce, what outcomes for which sections of the population and in what circumstances. Policy makers and funders seek to establish the easy empirical generalization that 'sport can....' in order to underpin a process of 'heterogeneous replication' (Pawson, 2006). However, such approaches frequently ignore the conditionality of findings, the varying cultural contexts, issues of validity (are we measuring and comparing the same things when cultural contexts and language vary so much?) and, most importantly, ignore process – the nature of the interactions and exchanges which produce outcomes. Whereas outcome-oriented approaches are satisfied with *necessary conditions* (i.e. participation in sport), Pawson (2006) insists that we need to explore *sufficient conditions* and to do this we need to adopt a 'generative approach' to causation and the analysis of programmes. *Sport* does not have causal powers. It is the *process of participation* – how sport is provided and experienced – which begins to explain success and failure (Pawson, 2006; Coalter *et al.*, 2000; Patriksson, 1995). Such an analysis leads to a process-led, formative, approach to monitoring and evaluation as it enables (in fact requires) *theory-driven evaluations,* rather than the more traditional quantitative approach to output and outcome measurement. This requires a clear, articulated understanding and evaluation of the conceptualization, design and delivery of a programme, rather than the traditional concentration on (assumed or desired) outcomes – *why* do you think that your programme will produce the outcomes that you (and your funders) desire?

Such an approach requires those seeking to use sport for development purposes – both funders and sport-in-development organizations – to articulate clearly and precisely the nature of their assumptions about the mechanisms underpinning their specific sports programmes and how participation is presumed to lead to specific *intermediate impacts* (changes in individuals' self-perceptions and attitudes) and then to broader intermediate *outcomes* (changes in individuals' behaviour). The answers to such *process* questions are central to the development of organizational understanding and capacity, increasing the effectiveness of programmes and, more generally, to the further growth and development of emerging sport-in-development programmes.

A clear understanding and articulation of desired outcomes and the nature of the processes of participation – the sufficient conditions – through which these may be achieved should inform provision (and applications for funding) and enable an approach based on *managing for outcomes* – i.e. understanding how to maximize the possibility of the achievement of the assumed outcomes. This requires the adoption of general theories of change (Granger, 1998), which relate to such (often unexamined) questions as:

- Why do we assume that participation in sport (or a particular type of sport) can have certain impacts on certain types of participants and communities?
- What are the properties of sports participation that lead to such outcomes? For example, Biddle (2006), among others, emphasizes that the widely desired outcomes of increased self-efficacy and self-esteem are most likely to be achieved via programmes based on a mastery climate (rather than performance) and one which matches participants' skills to the challenges posed by the programme.
- Can we define clearly the theory of the relationship between participation in sport and a range of *intermediate outcomes* (e.g. changed attitudes to HIV/AIDS, increased self-efficacy)? For example, whereas some sport-in-development programmes use integrated and symbolic games (Mwaanga, nd) to address issues of HIV/AIDS, others use traditional didactic, information-giving approaches to large groups of young people on sports programmes; others rely on a 'social learning' approach, based on role models and emulation. Which of these approaches is proposed and why?

3.5 Developing a programme theory for sport and HIV/AIDS

Such issues can be illustrated via an example of a logic model which seeks to make theoretical sense of the claims that participation in sport can contribute to the reduction of the incidence of HIV/AIDS. The rather crude and one-dimensional version of these claims seems to be that sport (especially soccer), via its ability to attract large numbers of young people, provides an ideal opportunity to provide information (and often dire warnings) about HIV/AIDS. Consequently, it is sometimes assumed that the 'success' of these programmes can be assessed via an outcome measurement defined as sports participants' level of knowledge of HIV/AIDS (frequently ignoring the relative importance of other sources of information – school, church, community, widespread posters and, sadly, personal experience of the HIV/AIDS-related deaths of family and friends). For example, one small indicative research study of two Zambian sports organizations (members of the Kicking Aids Out Network), based on 40 participants and 40 non-participants (Kruse, 2006: 33) reported that 'there are only insignificant differences in level of knowledge about HIV/AIDS and in attitudes to stigma and discrimination' between the participants and the control group. However, Kruse (2006: 34) also hints at the potential complexity of undertaking evaluations of the effectiveness of such organizations by suggesting that sports participants had greater aggregate 'life skills' than the control group, defined as 'the ability to make independent decisions and say no in matters of sex and also the level of self-confidence'. Kruse (2006: 34) argues that,

> The wide difference between the exposed who acquired the skill to make their own decisions and their unexposed counterparts could be attributed to the emphasis laid by the KAO programme on decision-making as a fundamental skill in the fight against HIV/AIDS.

Although this conclusion seems to be based on the answer to a single question about learning rather than behaviour – 'Have you learned that you can make your own decision to say no?' – it does point to the need to move beyond one-dimensional outcome measurement and to address issues of process (and programme evaluation based on theory). Such an approach is supported by Kerrigan's (1999) work on the role of peer educators in HIV/AIDS programmes, which concludes that the key to successful peer education lies in the fact that it makes possible a

Develop sporting skills

⇩

Develop sporting/ethical attitudes

⇩

Develop self-efficacy/confidence

⇩

HIV/AIDS information

⇩

Gender equity attitudes/behaviour

⇩

Self-esteem *[more likely to be peer leaders?]*

⇩

Reduced risk-taking sexual behaviour

Self-efficacy + information + attitudes ⇨ changed sexual behaviour

...maybe

Figure 3.1   A model of sports-based HIV/AIDS: education and sexual behaviour change

dialogue between equals and collective planning the adoption of practices which are contextually and culturally relevant. Within this context it is possible to develop a basic *programme theory* (Weiss, 1997) – a sequence of causes and presumed effects – which provides the basis for a process-led approach to monitoring and evaluation (Figure 3.1).

The logic outlined in Figure 3.1 (each stage of which can be monitored and evaluated) is that the process of developing practical sporting skills (via effort and practice) leads to the increase in a sense of self-efficacy and self-confidence (the ability to set and work towards certain goals; the ability to overcome certain obstacles). Of course, as suggested above (Biddle, 2006), consideration needs to be given to the optimal and most inclusive approach to this – a mastery climate or one based on competition. In addition, by operating within an ethical framework, it is assumed that participants will develop a certain degree of moral reasoning via an emphasis on sporting and ethical attitudes (e.g. respecting opponents; the need for fair play and obeying rules; collective responsibility). Within this context of the developing individual, information about HIV/AIDS is provided and the approach adopted – didactic versus a more symbolic and integrated approach – is a possibly significant factor. This information is communicated within the context of an emphasis on gender equity and respect – changing young men's attitudes to young women and providing young women with 'empowering' experiences (e.g. via a peer leadership role). The issue of gender-relations, power and respect are regarded by many as central to addressing the issues of HIV/AIDS, especially communicated via the role model approach of peer leadership (Kruse, 2006). These various *intermediate impacts* may also lead to an increase in self-esteem and self-worth, although this is a much misused and misunderstood concept (see Fox, 1992; Emler, 2001; Coalter, 2007), which needs care in both measurement and interpretation. It is also probable that any meaningful increase in self-esteem is most likely to occur among the heavily involved peer leaders rather than general participants, as the former are more likely to experience enhanced status and changes in self-definition.

Consequently, the programme-theory outlined in Figure 3.1 (others may wish to emphasize different elements, processes and contexts) suggests that it is a *combination* of increased self-efficacy, the understanding of relevant information, changed gender attitudes and improved self-worth which *may* lead to a reduction in risky sexual behaviour. Of course, there are obvious limitations to the outcome measurement of sexual behaviour, with survey questions about such matters having obvious limitations. Nevertheless, if the programme theory is regarded as plausible and the programme is delivered consistently as theoretically intended (not an easy task in the circumstances in which many such organizations operate), then it provides a plausible basis for assuming that it has *maximized the possibility* of achieving the desired outcomes of safer sexual behaviour (even if this cannot be measured directly). Consequently, the programme theory, with its broadly sequential steps of cause and effect, provides the basis for a systematic process-led monitoring and evaluation of the relative effectiveness of the programme. However, within the context of the 'maybe' in Figure 3.1, it is worth noting Mwaanga's (2003) somewhat pessimistic interpretation of the outcome of such processes in the absence of a change in women's economic circumstances.

Such an approach provides the basis for theoretically-informed process monitoring and evaluation, rather than simple (and frequently crude) outcome measurement. Further, as process monitoring is inherently participatory it can develop a greater ownership and understanding of the philosophical and theoretical basis of the programme by those delivering it (see Nicholls in this volume).

- It provides the basis for identifying *sufficient conditions* and *managing for outcomes*. Understanding how and why programmes are supposed to work will improve peer leader training, programme design and implementation and increase the ability to manage for outcomes.

- It is essential in the many circumstances where there are difficulties in measuring certain impacts and outcomes. Where organizations can systematically illustrate the theoretical basis of their programme design and implementation and, via process monitoring can ensure that programmes are delivered as theoretically intended, they can more confidently claim that, all other things being equal, their programme maximizes the probability of achieving the desired outcomes. Where outcome measurement is possible, such an approach provides robust explanations for both success and failure. Too frequently the lessons that can be gained from failures are ignored, or more likely suppressed because of fear of losing funding. In this approach a theoretical understanding of the reasons for failure provides the basis for programme improvement.

3.6   Evaluating sport-in-development programmes: accountability or development?

It is not unusual for organizations to be resistant to monitoring and evaluation – especially when it is disruptive of programme delivery in resource-poor organizations. This reaction is often based on a belief that monitoring and evaluation relate solely to *accountability*, providing largely quantitative evidence that programmes have been provided, have attracted the target type and number of participants and have achieved the outcomes desired by sponsors and partners (e.g. effective HIV/AIDS education programmes). In such circumstances it is not unusual for those who collect the data to not be involved in its analysis, or in subsequent decision-making processes (Shah *et al.*, 2004; Nicholls in this publication).

It is not suggested that accountability and measures of performance are *not* important – they are. Transparency and accountability are important not only to funders, but also to the sport-in-development organizations – especially in societies where transparency might not be the norm (see Munro, 2004, 2005). However, the argument proposed here is that monitoring and evaluation can play a much wider developmental role (Coalter, 2006, 2007). For example, Shah *et al.* (2004) argue that monitoring and evaluation should provide the basis for a dialogue, both between organizations and funders and *within* organizations.

Although it could be argued that such an approach to monitoring and evaluation is generic (Weiss, 1997; Pawson, 2006) – it should apply in all contexts – it has a particular relevance to sport-in-development organizations, because they are important *as organizations*. The importance of such organizations *qua* organizations (as well as their programmes) means that it is essential that monitoring and evaluation are *formative*. Summative evaluations tend to be conducted for the benefit of funders and be concerned with determining the effectiveness of programmes. Although the definition of 'effectiveness' will vary, it tends to be confined to quantifiable and measurable aspects – outputs such as programmes delivered, teams developed, participants attracted and certain outcomes such as the extent of HIV/AIDS knowledge or the development of self-efficacy. However, formative evaluations are concerned with examining ways of improving and enhancing the implementation and management of interventions. This approach is accepted by the UK Government's Department for International Development (DfID, 2005: 12), which states that:

> The over-arching goal for evaluation in international development is to foster a transparent, inquisitive and self-critical organizational culture…so we can learn to do better.

Such a philosophy necessarily leads to a participatory approach to monitoring and evaluation, which contributes to personal and organizational development in a number of ways. This is because, when organizations involve their members in process-led monitoring and evaluation this is likely to lead to:

- Capacity-building. To achieve sustainability, to achieve their many aims and to improve their programmes, organizations need to develop internal capacity (Sports Coaches' Outreach, 2005).
- Greater ownership, understanding and integration. A broad agreement about and understanding of the relationship between aims and objectives can provide the basis for an integrated and coherent organizational culture and associated programmes.
- An ability to reflect on and analyse attitudes, beliefs and behaviour (Shah *et al.*, 2004). The involvement of staff in the monitoring and evaluation of all aspects of organization and programme delivery contributes to the development of a self-critical and self-improving organizational culture (DFID, 2005).

3.7   Conclusions

The increased emphasis being placed on sport as a vehicle for delivering a wide variety of development objectives has been accompanied by a concern, often from understandably sceptical funders with little understanding of 'sport', about the effectiveness of sport-in-development programmes. These issues are often exacerbated because many resource-poor sport-in-development organizations feel under pressure to construct funding applications with an eye to aid agencies' (non-sporting) objectives, rather than a realistic assessment of what is possible.

Approaches to the effectiveness of such programmes based solely on the traditional outcome-based approach (perhaps understandably encouraged by some funders) fail to acknowledge the *generic* methodological and *specific* environmental difficulties involved in such measurement. The adoption of a programme theory approach to process monitoring and evaluation would move some way to de-constructing the almost mythic nature of sport in policy rhetoric, which is frequently based on ill-defined interventions with hard-to-follow and unrealistically ambitious outcomes. We need to be as clear about the limitations of 'sport' as its strengths and to recognize that sport needs to be embedded in much broader policies and practices to contribute to development.

Such an approach is also based on a recognition of the importance of sport-in-development organizations *qua* organizations and their often complex role in civil society (as illustrated via the MYSA case study) – producing 'citizens', offering models of ethical practice, providing experience of decision-making, addressing gender issues in an organizational context and generating forms of social capital (Coalter, 2008). Within this context there is a need to acknowledge the potentially significant contribution that participatory, theoretically-informed, process-led monitoring and evaluation can make to the development and sustainability of such organizations and the eventual effectiveness of their programmes. In societies with weak civic structures, funders should recognize the importance of organizational development and the production of peer leaders, as much as narrowly defined sports-related outcomes. Weiss (1997) argues that the attraction of this approach is that it necessarily entails a 'conversation' between researchers, policy makers and practitioners. Such a conversation is overdue.

Notes

1 The four case studies undertaken for the development of the monitoring and evaluation manual were the Mathare Youth Sport Association, Nairobi, Kenya; Go Sisters, part of EduSport, Lusaka, Zambia; Youth Education through Sport (YES), Zimbabwe; Magic Bus, Mumbai, India.
2 For further details please refer to www.norad.no.

Bibliography

Atkins, H. (n.d.) *Mathare United: A Model CECAFA Club*, accessed from www.toolkitsportdevelopment.org.

Bandura, A. (1977) 'Self-efficacy: toward a unifying theory of behavioural change', *Psychological Review*, **84**(2), 191–215.

Biddle, S. (2006) 'Defining and Measuring indicators of psycho-social well-being in youth sport and physical activity', in Vanden Auweele, Y., Malcom, C. and Meulders, B. (eds) *Sports and Development*. Leuven, Lnoocampus, pp. 163–184.

Botcheva, L. and Huffman, M.D. (2004) *Grassroot Soccer Foundation HIV/AIDS Education Program: An Intervention in Zimbabwe*. White River Junction, VT: Grassroot Soccer Foundation.

Brady, M. and Kahn, A.B. (2002) *Letting Girls Play: The Mathare Youth Sports Association's Football Program for Girls*. New York: The Population Council.

Burnett, C. (2001) 'Social Impact Assessment and Sport Development: Social Spin-Offs of the Australia-South Africa Junior Sport Programme', *International Review for the Sociology of Sport*, **36**(1), 41–57.

Coalter, F. (2008) 'Sport-in-development: development for and through sport?', in Nicholson, M. and Hoye, R. (eds) *Sport and Social Capital*. London: Elsevier; Butterworth-Heinemann, pp. 149–161.

Coalter, F. (2006) *Sport-in-Development: A Monitoring and Evaluation Manual*. UK Sport, London.

Coalter, F. (2007) *A Wider Social Role for Sport: Who's Keeping the Score?* London: Routledge.

Coalter, F., Allison, M. and Taylor, J. (2000) *The Role of Sport in Regenerating Deprived Urban Areas*. Edinburgh: Scottish Executive Central Research Unit.

Collins, M., et al. (1999) *Sport and Social Inclusion: A Report to the Department of Culture, Media and Sport, Institute of Sport and Leisure Policy*. Loughborough: Loughborough University.

Deane, J. (1998) 'Community Sports Initiatives – An Evaluation of UK Policy Attempts to Involve the Young Unemployed – The 1980's Action Sport Scheme', in *Sport in the City: Conference Proceedings Volume 1*, Sheffield, 2–4 July 1998, Loughborough University/Sheffield Hallam University/The University of Sheffield, pp. 140–159.

Department for International Development (2005) *Guidance on Evaluation and Review for DFID Staff*, Evaluation Department, Department for International Development, London.

Emler, N. (2001) *Self-Esteem: The Costs and Causes of Low Self-Worth*. York: Joseph Rowntree Foundation.

Fox, K.R. (1992) 'Physical education and the development of self-esteem in children', in N. Armstrong (ed.) *New Direction in Physical Education, vol 2 Towards a National curriculum*. Leeds: Human Kinetics, pp. 33–54.

Granger, Robert C. (1998) 'Establishing causality in evaluations of comprehensive community initiatives', in *New approaches to evaluating community initiatives. Vol 2: Theory, measurement, and analysis* (eds) Karen Fulbright-Anderson, Anne C. Kubisch and James P. Connell. Washington, DC: Aspen Institute, accessed from, www.aspenroundtable.org/vol2/granger. htm

Grootaert, C., Narayan, D., Jones, V.N. and Woolcock, M. (2004) *Measuring Social Capital: An Integrated Questionnaire*, World Bank Working Paper No. 18, Washington, World Bank.

Hognestad, H. (2005) *Norwegian Strategies on Culture – and Sports Development with Southern Countries*, A presentation to the Sports Research Forum, Australian Sports Commission, Canberra, 13–15 April 2005.

Kerrigan, D. (1999) *Peer Education and HIV/AIDS: Concepts, Uses and Challenges*. Washington, DC: Horizons/Population Council.

Kotze, J.C. (1993) *In their Shoes*. Kenwyn, Johannesburg, Juta.

Kruse, S.-E. (2006) 'Review of Kicking AIDS Out: Is Sport an Effective Tool in the Fight against HIV/AIDS?', draft report to NORAD (The Norwegian Agency for Development Cooperation), unpublished.

Munro, B. (2004) 'Greed vs Good Governance: The fight for corruption-free football in Kenya', paper presented at *Play the Game 2005 – Governance in Sport: The Good, The Bad and The Ugly* Copenhagen, accessed from http://www.playthegame.org.

Munro, B. (2005) *Role Models: Is anything more important for future development?*, Role Models Retreat, Laureus Sport for Good Foundation, South Africa, November 23–24, 2005, in Pretoria, South Africa.

Mwaanga, O. (2003) *HIV/AIDS: At-risk adolescent girls' empowerment through participation in top level football and Edusport in Zambia*, MSc thesis submitted to the Institute of Social Science at the Norwegian University of Sport and PE, Oslo.

Mwaanga, O. (nd) 'Kicking Aids Out Through Movement Games and Sports Activities', http://www.norad.no/items/1028/38/3357469240/Kicking_AIDS_out.pdf

Patriksson, G. (1995) 'Scientific Review Part 2', in *The Significance of Sport for Society – Health, Socialisation, Economy: A Scientific Review*, report prepared for the 8th Conference of European Ministers responsible for Sport, Lisbon, 17–18 May 1995, Council of Europe Press.

Pawson, R. (2005) 'Evaluating Ill-Defined Interventions with Hard-to-Follow Outcomes', paper presented to ESRC seminar Understanding and evaluating the impact of sport and culture on society. Leeds Metropolitan University, January 20th.

Pawson, R. (2006) *Evidence-based Policy: A Realist Perspective*. London: Sage Publications Ltd.

Payne, W., Reynolds, M., Brown, S. and Fleming, A. (2003) *Sports Role Models and their Impact on Participation in Physical Activity: A Literature Review*. Victoria: VicHealth.

Pollard, A. and Court, J. (2005) *How Civil Society Organisations Use Evidence to Influence Policy Processes: A Literature Review*, Working Paper 249. London: Overseas Development Institute.

Portes, A. and Landolt, P. (2000) 'Social Capital: Promise and Pitfalls of its Role in Development', *Journal of Latin American Studies*, 32: 529–547.

Putnam, R.D. (2000) *Bowling Alone: The Collapse and Revival of American Community*. New York: Simon and Schuster.

Renard, R. (2006) *The Cracks in the New Aid Paradigm*, Discussion Paper, Antwerpen, Belgium, Institute of Development Policy and Management.

Shah, M.K., Kambou, S., Goparaju, L., Adams, M.K. and Matarazzo, J.M. (eds) (2004) *Participatory Monitoring and Evaluation of Community- and Faith-based Programs: A step-by-step guide for people who want to make HIV and AIDS services and activities more effective in their community*, Core Initiative, accessed from www.coreinitiative.org/Resources/Publications/PME_2nd/index.php.

Sport Coaches' Outreach (SCORE) (2005) *Partnership in Practice: Assessing Our Capacity to Deliver Sustainable Sport and Development: Workshop Report*.

United Nations (2000) Press Release DSG/SM/88, 17 March 2000.

United Nations (2005a) *Business Plan International Year of Sport and Physical Education*. New York, NY: United Nations.

United Nations (2005b) *Sport for Development and Peace: Towards Achieving the Millennium Development Goals*. New York, NY: United Nations.

UNICEF (2006) *Monitoring and Evaluation for Sport-Based Programming for Development: Sport Recreation and Play*, Workshop Report. New York, NY: UNICEF.

Utting, D. (1996) *Reducing Criminality among Young People: A Sample of Relevant Programmes in the United Kingdom*. London: Home Office Research and Statistics Directorate.

Van Rooy, A. (ed.) (2004) *Global Legitimacy Game: Civil Society, Globalisation and Protest*. London: Palgrave Macmillan.

Weiss, C. (1997) 'How can theory-based evaluation make greater headway?', *Evaluation Review*, 21(4), 501–524.

Willis, O. (2000) 'Sport and Development: The Significance of Mathare Youth Sports Association', *Canadian Journal of Development Studies*, 21(3), 825–849.

Witt, P.A. and Crompton, J.L. (eds) (1996) *Recreation Programs that Work for At-Risk Youth*. Pennsylvania: Venture Publishing Inc.

World Bank (n.d.) *Social Capital and Civil Society*, accessed from, http://web.worldbank.org/wbsite/external/topics/extsocialdevlopment.

4
A Delicate Balance: Major Sport Events and Development

Scarlett Cornelissen

4.1 Introduction

Major or hallmark sport events – those which are organized on a competitive and international basis, involve a very large number of participants and spectators, and are held according to a regular and agreed upon schedule – have become prominent and significant in recent years (Roche, 2000). Their importance stems partly from the greater degree of commercialization, and as a result, the volume of private capital which has come to be associated with such events. Their significance also relates in the extent to which their hosting has become part of public policy objectives. Today, major sport events are prominent in the planning and development itineraries of many urban and national governments across the world. They tend to be viewed by such decision makers as possible stimulants for short term and more permanent economic growth. They are commonly noted for their potential to provoke greater levels of domestic and foreign investments, to encourage the development of infrastructure that could support long-term advance, and to accelerate the growth of key sectors such as tourism (e.g. Bale and Moen, 1995; Hall, 1992; Baade and Matheson, 2002). Increasingly too, such events have political features – in the manner in which they may be used by political or sport elites toward the attainment of certain targets, or by which policy objectives may be set (see for instance Black and Van der Westhuizen, 2004; Hiller, 1998; Hall, 2006) – which may have repercussions on host societies long after the event has come to an end. As such, discourse about the impacts of sport events – long celebratory about their potential gains – has progressively become influenced by a more critical body of scholarship which emphasizes some of their unanticipated negative externalities (e.g. Hiller, 2000; Crompton, 1995; Tribe, 2005).

On the whole, however, the nature of the discourse on sport event impacts is a complex one. Marked by intense and often acrimonious exchanges between proponents and opponents, the debate centres on the extent to which a major event can have catalytic effects on hosts and on the durability of such effects. Most accounts focus on the economic dimensions of events. While in recent years aspects such as the socio-cultural dimensions of events have received a greater deal of scholarly attention (e.g. Owen, 2002; Hall and Hodges, 1996; Valera and Guardia, 2002), this is something which for the most part has been absent in the planning schedules or official discourses of authorities or the event practitioners and consultants they employ (Waitt, 2001). Significantly therefore, the debate on the impacts of major events lacks a cogent discussion of how these impacts articulate with broader processes of development in host cities or countries (Smith, 2007). Indeed, the very concept of development – defined for the purposes of this chapter as tangible and sustainable improvement in the life situation of a given population[1] – may be said to be largely uncultivated in a body of scholarship which has grown both in vibrancy and empirical depth over the years (Horne and Manzenreiter, 2006).

This differentiates studies on major sport events from other distinctive scholarly currents where (as for instance in the sport-in-development movement) the developmental dimensions of sport has been more saliently explored. As highlighted in the introductory chapter, 'development' is in no way uniformly understood in the scholarship on sport-in-development, with many different attributions pervading this area of study. Yet this scholarship reflects an important conceptual progression, in the way development has been approached closely following trends in wider development discourse over the years. This has not been the case with literature on major events.

There have been a few notable shifts in events literature in recent years. An influential discourse on the longer-term and multiple legacies of events has arisen by which scholars attempt to assess the impacts of events. Also, within the framework of the Olympic Movement there have been more directed attempts at improving the sustainability standards of the Olympic Games, expressed in triple bottom line components (i.e. economic, environmental and social impacts). In 1999 the IOC adopted a resolution by which its members should seek to promote sustainable development through sport. While encouraging, all of these emergent trends have not fostered a commonly accepted definition of development as it may take shape through the hosting of a major sport event, nor is there consensus on how the varied impacts from a sport event could contribute to broader based development (Jones, 2001). This has not thwarted a vigorous, if largely unsubstantiated promotion of the developmental potential of major events by many public authorities in contemporary times (Hall, 2006). Indeed, while the purported benefits of events have largely been proclaimed in industrialized environments in the Global North (and usually as supportive to urban regeneration programmes), it is increasingly the case that urban and national authorities in the Global South seek to host major events (e.g. Hiller, 2000; Swart and Bob, 2004; Du Plessis and Maening, 2007). Although often deployed to signify different intentions and meanings in the Global North and South, the developmental virtues of sport events seem to be a shared leitmotif (Black, 2008). Northern and Southern public authorities are commonly animated by the prospects of attracting the international capital which has increasingly become linked to major events. For intended hosts in the Global South, however, events are often also seen as opportunities to project or 'showcase' achieved levels of modernity to the outside world (e.g. Van der Westhuizen, 2007; Cornelissen, 2008).

The manifold values and meanings surrounding the developmental aspects of major sport events in some ways complicate cross-national comparisons of the longer-term effects of these events. This chapter explores the developmental dimensions of events at two levels; first by sketching the debates on the impacts of major sport events and investigating the manner in which 'development' has figured or has been absent in these debates; and second, by drawing out the major themes and contrasts characteristic to the role that events that have come to play in Northern and Southern contexts.

Four arguments are presented. First, whilst the promotion of development has been an overriding rationale for the growing number of public authorities who have aimed to host major events, this has usually been based on a vague understanding of how an event's impact translates into development. Second, the current-day significance of events – and the growing international competitiveness around them – should be understood in relation to the more intense commercial character of international sport, which in turn has raised events' allure for public authorities. An increasing number of such authorities have come to view events as alternative avenues for development. Stemming from this, the third argument is that the way in which major events are ascribed value in the contemporary era, raises a number of challenges for the widely accepted precepts of development theory, central of which is the extent to which developmental processes are similar in settings as different as the Global North and South.

Fourth, major sport events encourage a particular interaction between developed and developing countries. Both assign worth to events' potential capacity to generate revenue, to spur on growth or even to demonstrate attained levels of economic advance. As such, events constitute an arena for contest. Literature on the role of sport in international development lays emphasis on the collaborative relationships that can be fostered between developed and developing countries, often in a donor-recipient relationship and mediated through non-governmental actors (e.g. Vanden Auweele, Malcolm and Meulders, 2006). In contrast, major sport events found on an international political economy by which limited incentive exists for the establishment of initiatives which explicitly address international developmental exchange through sport.

The first part of the chapter reviews the processes which have caused major sport events to gain the prominence they have today, recounts their main characteristics, and considers some of the factors as a result of which much contestation surrounds the presumed impacts of such events. The second part discusses the manifold impacts and legacies – positive and negative – of events in greater detail. As a body of scholarship, analyses of the impacts of major sport events has had little direct contact with cognate studies related to sport's role in international development. Some conclusions on the developmental contours of major events, and their implications for an understanding of the role of sport in broader development processes, are provided in the third part.

Hall (1992) delineates hallmark events by whether they are of a first-order (or -mega) nature (such as the Olympic Games and football's World Cup) or of lower rank (such as the Commonwealth Games or continental competitions), in terms of the level of spectatorship, participation and commercial turnover they command. His delineation is adopted here to present a general portrait of the dimensions and impacts of major sport events. However, because of the extent to which they dominate the landscape of hallmark events through their sheer size, the focus falls to a greater degree on the developmental contours of events of first-order scale.

4.2   Multiple dimensions: sport mega-events in the contemporary era

In a letter of correspondence to the IOC more than a quarter-century ago, Abram Ordia, president of the Supreme Council for Sports in

Africa, the continental sport body tasked, *inter alia* with organising the All Africa Games, lamented the manifold obstacles to preparing for, or hosting, the regional Games. While by their own statute the All Africa Games was meant to be held on a rotational, four-yearly basis, chronic under-funding and poor organization prevented the Supreme Council for Sport in Africa from attaining this. Instead, after the inaugural Games in the central African city of Brazzaville in 1965, the event was held very erratically, and often by capricious hosts – the next Games, scheduled to be held in Mali in 1969 had to be cancelled due to the occurrence of a coup d'état, and the lack of adequate financing saw the postponement or cancelling of many other later Games. In describing the state of affairs, Ordia (1980) also wrote to the IOC:

> It had been my secret policy to award the staging of the Games to a city with no sports facilities at all or those of (low) international standards. By so doing the government would be committed to constructing modern facilities which will remain for the youths of the country long after the Games. In this way more and more sports facilities would emerge throughout Africa. Under the situation which I now find myself, I shall depart from that policy temporarily.

Much ahead of his time, and rather incongruous with socio-economic conditions in sub-Saharan Africa which by then had seen numerous years of decline, Ordia was here expressing a view on the catalytic effects which the hosting of a sport event of some magnitude could have on national economies.

The rise to prominence of major sport events can be seen as the result of four interrelated processes which have unfolded over the past thirty years. The first is the growing significance of sport as an international economic sector. It is estimated that sport today contributes close to three percent to the world economy (World Tourism Organization, 2006). Shifts in the wider international political economy have provided the context against which this occurred. Prompted by factors such as continual and predictable rises in disposable incomes in some of the world's largest economies, concomitant changes in lifestyle and the greater value that became accorded to leisure activities, the economic importance of sport has increased over the past three decades. Underpinning this has been a second process, by which sustained efforts by large corporations to restructure sport sectors toward the goal of profit generation have fed sport's steady commercialization. The incr commodification of sport is visible in the extent to which sport memorabilia are popularized and sold, sport brands have become firmly established and sport celebrities are created and marketed to world audiences (Slack, 2004). Fomenting this has been the emergence of global and powerful media corporations, their creation of omnipresent and standardized sport broadcast channels and the advent of global sport coverage. In brief, sport's value today stems from both its intensified production and consumption.

The growth in the economic significance of sport over the past three decades paralleled a third process, which was the rising eminence of the world's largest sport federations and organizations, such as the IOC and the FIFA. Such organizations sought to enlarge their influence, in part by enhancing the prominence of their world competitions (e.g. Tomlinson and Young, 2006). For the IOC this came through the hosting of the 1984 Los Angeles Games, which following on the political fiascos (Munich 1972 and Moscow 1980) or over-expenses (Montreal 1976) of the three prior tournaments, was marked by the extent to which the Los Angeles authorities succeeded in drawing a profit from the Games (Gruneau, 1984). The FIFA World Cups have also grown in magnitude and importance, bolstered by the increasing international popularity of football, and the growing prominence of some of the world's main football leagues (predominantly located in Western Europe). Indeed, sport's commercialization has been particularly pronounced in world football, with the sale of merchandising, television coverage and the creation of revenue out of football being proportionately large (Goldblatt, 2006). This has provided much incentive to an international federation which has sought to encourage the further growth of the sport not only through the promotion of its flagship World Cup, but also through a more diverse range of international competitions (Sugden and Tomlinson, 1998).

Many of the world's other sport federations have followed suit so that youth, regional and women's tournaments are more numerous today. As such, the crowded contemporary annual events calendars should perhaps be seen in a more cynical light, as testimony to the strong mercantilist thrust which has come to underlie major sport events, rather than these events being noted for their display of sporting prowess or to foster good sporting relations. This is underscored by the fact that, while the Olympic Games and FIFA World Cups are archetypal for their magnitude, levels of participation and volumes of resources they involve, they also tend to exemplify much of what is regarded as reprehensible in the planning for and consequences of sport events (e.g. Jennings, 2006; Sugden and Tomlinson, 2002).

The fourth process which occurred and served to solidify the contemporary importance of sport mega-events in particular, is political in nature. It involves the search for and increasing utilization of 'alternative' development activities by political authorities, and how progressively, national and urban governments have come to view the development of sport economies and the pursuit of event-driven growth as viable policy options. This process has been protracted and variable, having differential features for governments of greater or lesser means, but arose in a context where the assumption that 'traditional' industries such as manufacturing are declining and can no longer provide a sufficient economic foundation, has increasingly shaped policy making. Instead, priority is given to enlarging the consumer sector, to enhance activities based on consumption and to lure the capital – assumed to be global and mobile – which is tied to these industries (e.g. Zukin, 1995). The growing battle among governments to attract footloose international capital, described by Cerny (1990) as the emergence of the 'competition state,' has focused on sectors such as tourism and the so-termed creative industries, but sport and sport events have increasingly come to be part of governments' development prioritization (Euchner, 1999; Hall, 2006).

In urban settings this can be explained by the degree to which sport and events provide useful anchors around which authorities can design place-based promotion activities: sport's easy appeal and values that are universally applied to it such as amiability, goodwill and also competitiveness, allow for the creation of destination imaging which can readily be disseminated. At a wider level however, national governments are also increasingly utilising major sport events to defined political aims. This could be inwardly directed, to support unpopular domestic programmes, enhance the legitimacy of the government, or to foster nationalism; or it could be intended to serve distinct foreign policy goals. A growing body of scholarship (e.g. Black, 2008; Van der Westhuizen, 2007) suggests that, under a specific set of circumstances, major sport events can be deployed as political instruments by governments to which activities of signalling, legitimization or constituency-building could be aligned.

To add to this, there has been a growing complexity across the range of hallmark sport events over the years. With this, the ability of potential hosts to provide requisite infrastructure becomes all the more central for world sport governing bodies in deciding who would host flagship events. For this reason, despite a discourse of the ubiquity of events and a narrative underlying this of the expansive reach and increased 'democratization' of events – by which it is tacitly understood that a host of any size or geographical location has the opportunity to be selected in bidding competitions – there is a growing rift between the industrialized and developing worlds. There are indeed few examples of cities or countries in the developing world which have hosted the events of today's size and requirements. These factors often make it prohibitive for many developing states to consider bidding for them. Notwithstanding, there are an increasing number of states from what may be termed the semi-periphery who are engaging in the more intense international contests to host events (see e.g. Black and Van der Westhuizen, 2004). Significantly too, what seems to define these contests is an unyielding faith in the intrinsic developmental worth of events. Yet, as the next section explores to greater depth, in spite of a vibrant debate which has arisen in time about the developmental effects of mega-events, this is part of what may be characterized as events' great 'known unknowns' (Horne, 2007), with there being little clarity on how potential event impacts could be converted into a more solid process of development (Kirkup and Major, 2007).

4.3   The varied impacts and legacies of major sport events

Two major reasons for the intricacy of major sport events are the manifold attributions that are made with respect to their impacts and the lack of consensus on what shape or longer term implications these impacts may have (Jones, 2001). Nor do events play out uniformly in different settings. The debate about the impacts of events is composed of competing sets of narratives by proponents and opponents, who are often equally vocal and vehement in their claims. Champions of mega-events draw attention to short and long-term potentials and the broad spread of gains to be made. Detractors tend to challenge precisely those, for instance contending that particular effects (such as tourism visitation) can only be assessed in an extended period of aftermath; that there is a time lag for impacts to be visible, and that the way in which events are planned and managed is really instrumental in determining their benefits and costs. In the event, yay-sayers and nay-sayers are probably equally guilty of what Crompton (1995) described as the 'science of (mis-)estimation' of major sport events.

A useful delineation of what is a complicated and often acrimonious discussion of the impacts of major sport events, is with respect to their economic, socio-cultural and political impacts on the one hand, and by whether impacts are direct, indirect or induced on the other. Further, events unfold over a lengthy period, from the time when bids are prepared, planning takes shape, events are hosted, and the immediate aftermath. Each phase is affected by different types of actors, and involves a linear and cumulative progression by which learning takes place and policy becomes made and adjusted (e.g. Weed and Bull, 2004). In terms of assessing events' developmental effect, it is important to consider a given event's impact in terms of the entire time spectrum in which it has played out (Jones, 2001).

The economic impacts of sport mega-events are mostly cited as their most important aspects and generally constitute the prime motivation for states or urban authorities to show a willingness to commit fiscal resources and undertake what could amount to risky political wagers to present bids to sport federations. Economic effects could relate, directly, to the generation of revenue (sourced from both domestic and foreign investors) in the development of event infrastructure; the accrual of new income derived from spectators and participants to the event; the creation of short-term employment through the development of stadia and other event facilities; and indirectly, in the increase in the tax base of governments, and the longer-term maintaining of new employment positions after the event. Sport events can also induce growth in ancillary sectors, in particular leisure consumption, tourism and construction. This aspect, and the fact that events could provide extended publicity to hosts, lead proponents to celebrate their possible longer-term consequences.

In truth, however, the economic dimensions and potential impacts of events are varied and could have differential effects on different sectors within a given economy. They could also encourage host cities or regions to disproportionately draw resources from neighbouring regions, impacting negatively on the latter. For example, while the Sydney Olympics of 2000 are generally held as one of the economically more successful Games in recent times, the host state, New South Wales had to extract some revenue for the planning and hosting of the Games from other states (NSW Treasury, 1997). Often also, the expansion and growth benefits that can be prompted by a construction boom during the preparation phases for an event are absorbed by a small number of larger or dominant corporations (Horne and Manzenreiter, 2006).

In addition, it is common for the pre-event assessments used during bid campaigns to (unknowingly or deliberately) over-inflate the potential economic consequences of a given event, so as to heighten the appeal of the campaigns to major domestic constituencies. Frequent errors stem from the incorrect application of indicators such as economic multipliers, confounding gross economic output with the impacts flowing from an event, and the imprecise demarcation of the geographical region by which an event's impacts are measured (e.g. Crompton, 1995). In addition, most *ex-ante* impact studies either underplay or miscalculate the costs associated with the hosting of an event, commonly neglecting to include aspects such as expenses incurred from the start of bid processes (Gibson, 1998). Many other hidden costs frequently surface during an event itself, or in its immediate aftermath, causing there to seldom be a match between cheery ex-ante studies and more sober, if less widely publicized ex-post analyses (Kirkup and Major, 2007).

In recent years acknowledgement of the potentially negative effects of sport mega-events has contributed to a discussion about how to ensure constructive legacies from these events. Much of this discussion focuses on the infrastructural developments, facilities and sport sites which remain after a tournament has come to an end. Perhaps much influenced by the sight of underutilized Olympic stadiums and sport venues, the IOC recently indicated that in the interest of post-event relevance and durability, it would require of future hosts to reduce costs and to prevent redundant construction of sites (IOC, 2001). In addition, the 1999 Session of the IOC adopted a resolution by which its members commit themselves to the promotion of sustainable development through sport.

Yet, as noted by Frey, Iraldo and Melis (2007), the IOC has been a latecomer to the international debate on sustainability, and as an event of often excess dimensions, the Olympic Games has not been subjected to extensive sustainability testing, in terms of its economic, social and ecological consequences. The IOC has moved somewhat closer toward this with the introduction of the Olympic Games Global Impact Project (OGGI), an attempt to assess the impacts of an Olympiad from its inception (with the launch of a bid campaign) to shortly after its closure – in total an eleven year period. With the OGGI, the IOC aims to gauge the effects of the Olympic Games in its totality, to draw lessons from previous host cities and to apply experience gained to future hosts (IOC, 2006). Since analysis of impact commences with an intentional host's bid campaign and carries through to two years after a Games has ended, it is thought that as an instrument, the OGGI could provide an appraisal of a full Olympiad cycle, as well as assist in measuring as far as possible all revenue and costs accrued by a host during this cycle. While not fully covering the mandatory eleven-year period of assessment, the 2008 Beijing Olympic Games will be the first Olympiad for which an OGGI study will be carried out. Brownell (2006:53) notes that although much can be learnt from this OGGI report, the study will not focus on the impacts of the Games on:

> cultural heritage – such as the preservation of culture to enrich the Olympic cultural programme versus the destruction of historical sites for new construction, the growth of traditional sports versus their replacement by Olympic sports, or the effects of the Olympic Games on traditional cultural beliefs.

While potentially a useful tool therefore, and far-reaching in its scope, the emphasis of the Olympic Games Global Impact Project remains on the 'hard' infrastructural legacies of the mega-event. This is important, but discourse on event legacies has in recent years shifted to place more accent on facets such as the environmental and social consequences of events (e.g. Owen, 2002; Waitt, 2001). On these counts, experience from the two prime mega-events, the Olympic Games and the FIFA World Cup, has been mixed. Aspects concerning the environment have started to receive more serious attention within the Olympic Movement from about fifteen years ago, when the organizers of the Lillehammer Winter Olympics of 1994 proclaimed it an 'ecological Games' (Furrer, 2002). Since then a tradition of placing emphasis on environmental protection through the hosting of the Games has become fairly entrenched, marked by the bid campaigns and plans of numerous successive hosts.[2]

The FIFA World Cups have yielded even fewer best practice lessons for positive environmental and social impacts. Indeed, football's world regulators have not shown much interest in the development of instruments such as OGGI, although some belated activities aimed at improving research and knowledge about the effects of football's World Cup have been undertaken by FIFA. These include the establishment of a research division at FIFA's headquarters in 2004 and the start of collaborative research projects with a number of academic institutions around the world.

4.3.1   Appraising events' legacies

On the whole most mainstream debates on the impacts of large-scale events have been slow to incorporate discussions on their social consequences. A growing and largely critical number of studies in recent years have illustrated some of the negative social outcomes of events. More than inconveniences or disturbances to host societies' regular patterns of life, some of the social impacts have involved serious transgressions of civic rights. These have included lax interpretation or even outright disregard of housing or tenure rights by event authorities where tenants were residing in areas earmarked for event development, and instances where evictions, voluntary or forced and justified as part of 'event regeneration' schemes occurred.[3] The 1992 Barcelona Games, while otherwise heralded as exemplary for its long-term positive infrastructural legacies, witnessed the eviction of small-scale businesses from underdeveloped areas during the city's preparations for the event (Raco, 2004). Stricter social surveillance within cities, and efforts by authorities to portray cities in more appealing ways to outside audiences, have also tended to impact more adversely on the poor and more marginalized stratum within urban areas (Waitt, 2003), although the hosting of sport events has also been known to restrict, rather than enlarge many communities' access to facilities (e.g. Nash and Johnstone, 2001).

Generally caustic in tone, the increasing volume of scholarly literature on the social impacts of events, and a wider sensitization among ordinary citizens of the potentials and hazards of events in the context of their growing prominence probably account for the greater demand for accountability that the organizers of events have to succumb to – even if only tacitly so. Increasingly too, intentional hosts are required to provide details not only of how they will comply with the technical specifications laid down by the sport governing bodies in whose name the rights to host an event are awarded, but they also have to indicate the longer-term legacies or regenerative potential of their bids. As such, although not very systematic in approach, more large-scale events in recent times have contained social programmes or social emphases of some or other form. These could include the launch of cultural awareness or activity programmes by host cities or regions before or during an event, the implementation of community regeneration programmes to dovetail with broader urban regeneration initiatives, or the use of events to bolster urban skills development (see Smith and Fox, 2007 for a review). Underpinning many of these programmes is a widespread if unchallenged belief that sport poses many potential advantages for social development, such as raising self-esteem, improving community integration, stimulating latent entrepreneurial spirits within communities, providing positive incentives and reducing crime and vandalism. Although positive associations have for long been made with respect to the social prospects of sport, as noted by Long and Sanderson (2001) evidence for this has been rather sparse. Demonstrating positive social impacts from major sport events has been even more tricky (Owen, 2002; Waitt, 2003).

4.4   Events as developmental impetuses

The above discussion highlights the dense and disparate nature of the debate on the impacts of major sport events. In brief, most standard contemporary accounts seek to incorporate the multidimensional character of these events and therefore the compound ways in which impact can be reflected. In practice, however, the economic dimensions of events have received by far the greater attention (Roberts, 2004), while others such as the socio-cultural, environmental and political aspects have largely been underplayed. In more recent years, the emergence of a discourse on maximising positive legacies from the hosting of events has encouraged a more integrative approach, by which some attempt is made to round up all the facets of events in assessments of their impacts. Somewhat still inchoate, however, this discourse has also tended to privilege the advancement of 'hard' (i.e. the development of infrastructure) over 'soft' (social) legacies.

What is most striking is that after several decades in which international sport events have grown in size and stature, and amid robust scholarly deliberation and the incremental accumulation of practice-generated knowledge, there is as yet no clear understanding nor a cogent hypothesis of how event impacts translate into development. A cohort of scholars has provided empirical substantiation that events can provide piecemeal injections to specific sectors in host environments; there is however little hard evidence on how those impacts provide momentum on a general basis over an extended period of time. Even more significantly, there is not a common approach among the world's large sport federations and organizations – the proprietors of major sport events – to what development could mean in relation to these events.

In part this is due to the wider context within which major sport events have evolved, where progressively defined by commercial and corporate interest, questions of development have been matters of lesser concern in the expansion of what today have become well established industries of sport, events and media-entertainment complexes (Nauright and Schimmel, 2005). Growing popular pressure on the world's major sport federations to show greater levels of accountability has been an important impetus for these organizations to take the issue of the broader developmental significance of their events more seriously, even if in a disjointed fashion. The IOC only recently developed a mechanism by which the promotion of long-term, positive impacts through the Olympic Games could be monitored and transferred from one host to another. Its recent adoption of the notion of sustainable development through sport, however, has not fed through in a systematic fashion to the Games. Indeed, as perceptively commented by Frey *et al.* (2007: 2):

> (A)ctually, the high concentration implied by the Games in terms of *time* (a two-week event), *space* (one host city only, or even specific areas within the city) and *investment* (the operating and infrastructure costs of the Games are in billions) seems to conflict with the concept of sustainable development, that calls for the distribution and sharing of environmental, social and economic impacts across time and space for spreading benefits and minimising negative effects on the whole society.

As it is, the international political economy of major sport events – disproportionately shaped today by corporate interest – has tended to provide little incentive for a systematic discourse on development through events to take shape. This has been further encouraged by the manner in which public authorities, predominantly in the North, but increasingly in the South, have been inclined to utilize major sport events toward a particular objective, in which an attained level of development has been presumed. Differential accreditation is given by public authorities in the North and South to the developmental dimensions of events. In the urban settings of the Global North, doused within a much utilized, although also weakly defined discourse of 'regeneration,' it would seem as if development is equated with the presumed manner in which a sport event could revive cities where economic performance has been sluggish, or where social conditions have declined. As used by the national governments of the North, the language may differ slightly and may be adapted to the wider political intentions behind hosting campaigns, but contains the same implicit understanding of the intrinsic regenerative effects – and hence developmental potential – of large-scale events. In the context of the Global South, much more usually tends to be ascribed to large scale events, and more direct associations tend to be made between 'development,' poverty alleviation, the ending of deprivation and even political advance.[4] The assumption however

– keenly sustained through the application of rigorous host applicant criteria and which lends a sense of elitism to international bidding competitions – is that major sport events can only be presented by hosts who have already attained a particular level of development and can therefore provide the requisite hard infrastructure (cf Hiller, 1998). Major events therefore are often used to showcase development; 'development' as such is not problematized.

These aspects set scholarship on major sport events apart from scholarship on sport's role in international development in two important ways. First, events pose some key tests to the standard precepts of conventional development theory, and those upon which the sport-in-development debate has evolved. Large in scale, sectorally focused and concentrated in duration, major sport events jar with what are today widely accepted notions of inclusive and broad-based development. The temporal and spatial distinctions of these events fundamentally shape the type of short-term and long-term effects these events can generate. Also, concepts and processes which have long been discarded by development practitioners – such as trickle-down effects – have regained salience among political classes keen to profess the benefits of events to their populations. By contrast, principles, which have with shifts in the wider development discourse found firm footing in the documentation and policy rhetoric of national governments and international development bodies, such as the importance of emphasising social distribution, have not been put into much practice with events. What is perhaps most worrisome, however, is the extent to which sport development tends to receive short shrift from event practitioners, with the accent falling more squarely on sport's *commercial* development.

Second, whereas praxis related to sport-in-development lays emphasis on the importance of North-South engagement and the provision of developmental assistance through or for sport, the current political economy of major sport events has not spawned structures for international developmental exchange to the same extent. Some initiatives have recently been introduced by large sport federations which are in a similar mould to the sport-in-development programmes, loosely built on donor-recipient patterning. Examples of these include developments around South Africa's hosting of the 19th FIFA World Cup™ and attempts to utilize the event to encourage regional growth. The 2010 finals have been framed 'the African World Cup', signifying both the political significance of the inaugural African hosting of the world tournament, and the attempt by the South African government to use the 2010 tournament to achieve long-set foreign policy objectives around the revival of the African continent and African unity (cf Cornelissen, 2004). As part of this, the African Union declared 2007 as the 'International Year of African Football,' aiming to support attempts by the CAF, the continental football governing body, to use sport 'as an instrument for the promotion of solidarity, peace and reconciliation, and (CAF's) preventive campaigns against scourges, such as HIV/AIDS, (which) affect the youth of the Continent' (African Union Commission, 2007). In the same year FIFA introduced its 'Win in Africa, With Africa' project, which seeks to 'establish long-term development and solidarity programmes as a means of perpetuating and reinforcing the legacy of the 2010 FIFA World Cup™ in Africa' (FIFA, 2007). One of the principal initiatives under the FIFA project is the installation of synthetic football pitches in all of the remaining 52 CAF members. Additionally, courses on coaching, refereeing and club management, and the provision of training equipment and information technology to African football clubs, is envisaged. Finally, FIFA has signed agreements with two South African and one Senegalese university according to which FIFA-accredited courses on sport organization, marketing, finance and event management are offered.

Importantly, although the 2010 finals is the principal framework under which these initiatives have been set up, they are not specifically linked to this event, nor are they aimed at providing assistance in South Africa's, or other African countries' preparations toward the tournament. On the whole, pledges by the South African government, the 2010 Local Organizing Committee and CAF officials to support efforts to promote regional development through the tournament, have seen limited implementation thus far. Many of the countries neighbouring South Africa, motivated by the prospects to host teams before and after the tournament, have undertaken to upgrade or construct stadia, often at great expense. For example, Mozambique has undertaken to build three new stadia and upgrade existing infrastructure, an expenditure that will draw US$42 million from the national budget (*City Press*, 23 October 2005). The extent to which involvement of other African countries outside of South Africa will be possible or allowed within the rules of compliance by FIFA and its corporate sponsors, is however not clear. As such investments undertaken by neighbouring countries may be made on tenuously premised returns which, if they do not materialize, could jeopardize the longer term economic prospects of many Southern African states.

The 2010 FIFA World Cup in many regards constitutes a test case for the degree to which a large-scale event could mobilize and assemble efforts by sport organizations, NGOs and governments from the South and North to promote development in African countries. As yet, however, the initiatives which had been launched have been unsystematic, have not specifically been directed at the event itself, nor have they had the required scale of financial backing. Few lessons may yet come from the event that could contribute to greater comprehension of the linkage between major sport events and international development.

4.5   Conclusion

While the varied *impacts* of major sport events have received a great deal of scholarly attention and there by now exists a voluminous scholarship on how the manifold socio-economic, political and ecological consequences of these events can be anticipated and even managed, an understanding of how these multiple effects could be channelled into a coherent process of *development* is lacking. This does not mean that major sport events are necessarily the antithesis of development. Nor, however, should these events be regarded as a panacea for the social and political ills of bidding states or cities. Rather, it suggests that a much greater degree of thought should go into event campaigns, that consideration is given to how resources could be directed at sectors and activities that in the context of the host economy, fulfil a strategic function, and that in the targeting of resources attempts are made to address social and other imbalances. Evidence is also mounting that the adoption of an incremental approach to the development of sport economies, with the hosting of such events being a pinnacle in an extended and gradually cumulative event hosting programme, yields greater benefits over the long term (Higham, 2005). In this, the focus for intentional hosts should be on developing the ability to offer a standardized and more diversified range of sporting competitions, with greater priority given to lower-order events and amateur sport development.

The scholarship on major sport events has accreted as a discrete body, not having integrated very well with cognate scholarships on sport and (international) development. The latter has seen some advance toward more refined understandings of the role of sport in development. For instance, the initially over-optimistic view of the development potential of sport is steadily being replaced by a more qualified approach, by which it is understood that sport development, and the initiatives implemented by donor agencies can also carry negative consequences for the communities they are intended to assist. More balanced assessments of both the positive and negative aspects of sport-in-development have served to deepen this scholarship.

As far as the developmental effects of major events are concerned, there is no overriding prescription for how sport events can contribute to development, although gaining a sense of the institutional, cultural and socio-political context in which events are hosted, could enhance understanding of the developmental role events can play. With respect to the broader debate on sport's role in development, a few comments are in order. First, the prevalence, commercial size and political importance of large scale sport events today do evoke a number of normative questions about the place of sport's main governing bodies in the international political economy of sport, and the duties they carry to assist in not only the overall development of sport, but the fairer distribution of the commercial gains of their flagship events. They also have a role to play in the development and implementation of a roster of impact and sustainability indicators. Second, in tandem with this, such events could encourage collaboration among states of the North and the South to a greater extent than currently is the case. This could come through the sharing of knowledge or experiences, or joint efforts to encourage the democratization of international sport and the practices by which events gain significance. Third, an emergent politics of major events in divergent settings suggests that these events increasingly affect national process of policy making and decisions. This implies on the one hand, the need to gain a better understanding of how internal processes around such events overlap or deviate from main political shifts and development in a given environment. On the other hand, it also provides the opportunity for assessing how as a sector, sport can contribute to social and political development, for instance by constituting the forum by which greater demand for accountability, as in the instance of event bidding campaigns, is provoked. Finally, the uneasy fit between emergent conventions around the impacts of major sport events and established development discourse provides occasion to fine-tune some of the contradictions in this discourse.

Notes

1 Needless to say, development is a complex phenomenon and a highly contested concept. After several decades of scholarly dispute and revision, the most accepted approach to development today is one which emphasizes the improvement of the social, cultural and economic quality of an individual's

life (or human development). This approach is considered to better reflect the complexity of development than do 'traditional' GDP-based measures of economic growth (e.g. UNDP, 1990). Although the notion of human development is itself contested (e.g. Sagar and Najam, 1998), and scholarship on sport's relation to development has itself undergone many changes over the years, this scholarship roughly reflects the precepts upon which the concept of human development is founded.

2 For example, Cape Town's failed bid for the 2004 Olympics was strongly developmentalist in nature, emphasising the maintenance of environmental integrity (Swart and Bob, 2004), while the organizers of all of the Sydney 2000, Torino 2006 and Beijing 2008 Games claimed those events as 'green' (see Sydney Olympics Bid, 1993; Toroc, 2002).

3 This was the case for the 1996 Atlanta Games (Owen, 2002), the 1988 Winter Olympics held in Calgary, and during Vancouver's hosting of the 1986 Expo (Olds, 1998).

4 Illustrative of the gravity with which such events can be regarded by political authorities in the South, is the following statement by South Africa's minister of sport, who suggested, '(T)he awarding of the 2010 World Cup host to South Africa by FIFA is a legacy on its own. For South Africa and the rest of Africa, the memory of that tournament will be a lasting legacy. But we cannot end there... (We) believe that preparations for the 2010 World Cup must leverage the fast-tracking of some elements of our transformation agenda... (We) must use this opportunity to level the proverbial playing grounds, both in respect of infrastructure and otherwise' (M. Stofile, address at the International Year of African Football and 2010 World Cup workshop, Johannesburg, 7 March 2007). Similarly, after an intense bid campaign by the authorities in New Delhi, the city was awarded the rights to host the 2010 Commonwealth Games. An argument that was made by the New Delhi campaigners was that the Games would enhance 'democracy, progress, knowledge and peace' in India (Black, 2008).

Bibliography

African Union Commission (2007) 'Concept paper: Launch of 2007 as the international year of African football, 8th Ordinary Session of the Assembly, 29–30 January 2007'. Accessed at www.africaunion.org.

Baade, R.A. and Matheson, V.A. (2002) 'Bidding for the Olympics: Fools' gold?' in C. Barros, M. Ibrahim and S. Szymanski (eds) *Transatlantic Sport: The Comparative Economics of North American and European Sport*. London: Edward Elgar Publishing, pp. 127–151.

Bale, J. and Moen, O. (eds) (1995) *The Stadium and the City*. Keele: Keele University Press.

Black, D. (2008) 'Dreaming big: the pursuit of second order games as a strategic response to globalisation', *Sport in Society*, 11(4), 467–480.

Black, D. and Van der Westhuizen, J. (2004) 'The allure of global games for the "semi-peripheral" polities and spaces: a research agenda', *Third World Quarterly*, 25(7), 1195–1214.

Brownell, S. (2006) 'The Beijing Effect', *Olympic Review*, June–September: 52–55.

Cashman, R. (2006) *The Bitter-Sweet Awakening – The Legacy of the Sydney 2000 Olympic Games*. Petersham: Walla Walla Press.

Cerny, P. (1990) *The Changing Architecture of Politics: Structure, Agency and the Future of the State*. London: Sage Publications.

City Press (2005) 'LOC Sells World Cup 2010', 23 October.

Cornelissen, S. (2008) 'Scripting the nation: sport, mega-events and foreign policy in post-apartheid South Africa', *Sport in Society*, 11(4), 481–493.

Cornelissen, S. (2004) "It's Africa's Turn!' The narratives and legitimations of the Moroccan and South African bids for the 2006 and 2010 FIFA finals', *Third World Quarterly*, 25(7), 1293–1309.

Crompton, J. (2006) 'Economic impact studies: instruments for political shenanigans', *Journal of Travel Research*, 45(1), 67–82.

Crompton, J. (2001) 'Public subsidies to professional team sport facilities in the USA', in C. Gratton and P. Henry, P. (eds) *Sport in the City: The Role of Sport in Economic and Social Regeneration*. London: Routledge, pp. 15–34.

Crompton, J. (1995) 'Economic impact analysis of sports facilities and events: eleven sources of misapplication', *Journal of Sport Management*, 9(1), 14–35.

Du Plessis, S. and Maennig, W. (2007) 'World Cup 2010: South African economic perspectives and policy challenges informed by the experience of Germany 2006', *Contemporary Economic Policy*, 25(4), 578–590.

Euchner, C.C. (1999) 'Tourism and sports: The serious competition for play', in D.R. Judd and S.S. Fainstein (eds) *The Tourist City*. London: Yale University Press, pp. 215–232.

FIFA (2007) 'CIES concludes partnerships with South African universities', press release, 5 June 2007, accessed at www.fifa.com.

Frey, M., Iraldo, F. and Melis, M. (2007) 'The impact of wide-scale sport events on local development: an assessment of the XXth Torino Olympics through the Sustainability Report', Conference Paper, *RSA Region in Focus? International Conference*, Lisbon, 2–5 April 2007, 21pp.

Furrer, P. (2002). 'Sustainable Olympic Games, a dream or a reality?', *Bollettino della Società Geografica Italiana*, 32(8), 4.

Gibson, H.J. (1998) 'Sport tourism: a critical analysis of research', *Sport Management Review*, 1(1), 45–76.

Goldblatt, D. (2006) *The Ball is Round: A Global History of Football*. London: Penguin.

Gruneau, R. (1984) 'Commercialism and the modern Olympics', in A. Tomlinson and G. Whannel (eds) *Five Ring Circus: Money, Power and Politics at the Olympic Games*. London: Pluto, pp. 1–15.

Hall, C.M. (2006) 'Urban entrepreneurship, corporate interests and sports mega-events: the thin policies of competitiveness within the hard outcomes of neoliberalism', in J. Horne and W. Manzenreiter (eds) *Sports Mega-Events: Social Scientific Analyses of a Global Phenomenon*. Oxford: Blackwell, pp. 59–70.

Hall, C.M. (1992) *Hallmark Tourist Events*. London: Belhaven Press.

Hall, C.M. and Hodges, J. (1996) 'The party's great, but what about the hangover? The housing and social impacts of mega-events with special reference to the 2000 Sydney Olympics', *Festival Management and Event Tourism*, 4(1), 13–20.

Higham, J. (2005) Sport tourism destinations: issues, opportunities and analysis, in J. Higham (ed.) *Sport Tourism Destinations: Issues, Opportunities and Analysis*. Oxford: Elsevier Butterworth Heinemann, pp. 1–14.

Hiller, H. (2000) 'Mega-events, urban boosterism and growth strategies: an analysis of the objectives and legitimations of the Cape Town 2004 Olympic Bid', *International Journal of Urban and Regional Research*, 24(2), 439–458.

Hiller, H. (1998) 'Assessing the impact of mega-events: a linkage model', *Current Issues in Tourism*, 1(1), 47–57.

Horne, J. (2007) 'The four "knowns" of sports mega-events', *Leisure Studies*, 26(1), 81–96.

Horne, J. and Manzenreiter, W. (2006) 'An introduction to the sociology of sports mega-events', in J. Horne and W. Manzenreiter (eds) *Sports Mega-Events: Social Scientific Analyses of a Global Phenomenon*. Oxford: Blackwell Publishing, pp. 1–24.

International Olympic Committee (2006) *Olympic Games Global Impact*. Olympic Review, June–September.

International Olympic Committee (2001) *Olympic Charter*. Lausanne: International Olympic Committee.

Jennings, A. (2006) *Foul! The Secret World of Fifa Bribes, Vote Rigging and Ticket Scandals*. London: Harper Collins.

Jones, C. (2001) 'Mega events and host region impacts: determining the true worth of the 1999 Rugby World Cup', *International Journal of Tourism Research*, 3, 117–133.

Kirkup, N. and Major, B. (2007) Doctoral foundation paper: the reliability of economic impact studies of the Olympic Games: A post-Games study of Sydney 2000 and considerations for London 2012, *Journal of Sport and Tourism*, 11(3–4), 275–296.

Long, J. and Sanderson, I. (2001) 'The social benefits of sport: where's the proof?', in C. Gratton and I. Henry (eds) *Sport in the City: The Role of Sport in Economic and Social Regeneration*. London: Routledge, pp. 187–203.

Nash, R. and Johnstone, S. (2001) 'The case of Euro 96: where did the party go?', in C. Gratton and P. Henry, P. (eds) *Sport in the City: The Role of Sport in Economic and Social Regeneration*. London: Routledge, pp. 109–124.

Nauright, J. and Schimmel, K. (eds) (2005) *The Political Economy of Sport*. Houndmills, Basingstoke: Palgrave.

New South Wales Treasury (1997) *The Economic Impact of the Sydney Olympic Games*. [Online] Available at http://www.treasury.nsw.gov.au/pubs/trp97_10.

Olds, K. (1998) 'Urban mega-events, evictions and housing rights: the Canadian case', *Current Issues in Tourism*, 1(1), 2–46.

Ordia, A. (1980) Correspondence to Monique Berlioux, secretary-general of International Olympic Committee. Lausanne: IOC Archives.

Owen, K. (2002) 'The Sydney 2000 Olympics and urban entrepreneurialism: local variations in urban governance', *Australian Geographical Studies*, 40(3), 563–600.

Raco, M. (2004) 'Whose Gold Rush? The Social Legacy of a London Olympics', in A. Vigor, M. Mean and C. Tims (eds) *After the Gold Rush: A Sustainable Olympics for London*. London: IPPR/DEMOS, pp. 31–50.

Roche, M. (2000) *Mega-events and Modernity: Olympics and Expos in the Growth of Global Culture*. London: Routledge.

Roberts, K. (2004) *The Leisure Industries*. London: Palgrave.

Sagar, A.D. and Najam, A. (1998) 'The human development index: a critical review', *Ecological Economics*, 25(3), 249–264.

Schimmel, K.S. (2006) 'Deep play: sports mega-events and urban social conditions in the USA', in J. Horne and W. Manzenreiter (eds) *Sports Mega-Events: Social Scientific Analyses of a Global Phenomenon*. Oxford: Blackwell, pp. 160–174.

Slack, T. (ed.) (2004) *The Commercialisation of Sport*. London: Routledge.

Smith, A. and Fox, T. (2007) 'From "event-led" to "event-themed" regeneration: the 2002 Commonwealth Games Legacy Programme', *Urban Studies*, 44(5–6), 1125–1143.

Stofile, M. (2007) 'Opening address by Sport and Recreation Minister M. Stofile at the International Year of African Football and 2010 World Cup workshop, Pretoria, 7 March 2007'. Pretoria: Government Communication and Information System.

Swart, K. and U. Bob (2004) 'The Seductive Discourse of Development: The Cape Town 2004 Olympic Bid', *Third World Quarterly*, 25(7), 1311–1324.

Sugden, J. and Tomlinson, A. (2002) 'International power struggles in the governance of world football: the 2002 and 2006 World Cup bidding wars', in J. Horne and W. Manzenreiter (eds) *Japan, South Korea and the 2002 World Cup*. London: Routledge, pp. 56–70.

Sugden, J. and Tomlinson, A. (1998) *Fifa and the Contest for World Soccer: Who Rules the People's Game?*. Cambridge: Polity Press.

Sydney Olympics 2000 Bid Ltd. (1993) *Environmental Guidelines for the Summer Olympic Games Sydney*: SOBL.

Tomlinson, A. and Young, C. (2006) 'Culture, politics and spectacle in the global sports event – an introduction', in A. Tomlinson and C. Young (eds) *National Identity and Global Sports Events: Culture, Politics and Spectacle in the Olympics and the Football World Cup*. Albany: State University of New York Press, pp. 1–14.

Torino Organising Committee for the XXth Olympic Winter Games (Toroc) (2002) *Strategic Plan 'Environment'*, working document, Turin.

Tribe, J. (2005) *The Economics of Recreation*. (3rd Edition). Oxford: Elsevier Butterworth Heinemann.

United Nations Development Programme (UNDP) (1990) *Human Development Report 1990*. New York: Oxford University Press.

Valera, S. and Guardia, J. (2002) Urban social identity and sustainability: Barcelona's Olympic Village. *Environment and Behavior*, 34(1), 54–66.

Vanden Auweele, Y., Malcolm, C. and Meulders, B. (eds) (2006) *Sport and Development*. Leuven: Lannoo Campus.

Van der Westhuizen, J. (2007) 'Glitz, glamour and the Gautrain: Mega-projects as political symbols', *Politikon: South African Journal of Political Studies*, 34(3), 335–352.

Waitt, G. (2003) 'The social impacts of the Sydney Olympics', *Annals of Tourism Research*, 30(1): 194–215.

Waitt, G. (2001) 'The Olympic spirit and civic boosterism: The Sydney 2000 Olympics', *Tourism Geographies*, 3(3), 249–278.

Weed, M. and Bull, C. (2004) *Sports Tourism: Participants, Policy and Providers*. Oxford: Elsevier/Butterworth.

World Tourism Organisation (2006) *Tourism Highlights 2006 – First Edition*. Madrid: WTO.

Wright, R.K. (2007) 'Planning for the Great Unknown: The challenge of promoting spectator-driven sports event tourism', *International Journal of Tourism Research*, 9, 345–359.

Zukin, S. (1995) *The Cultures of Cities*. Cambridge, MA: Blackwell.

5
Disability Sport and the Politics of Development

Aaron Beacom

5.1 Introduction

While recognizing the increasingly pluralist nature of the development process, states through public policy, continue to provide the frame of reference through which development activity takes place. In that sense international development assistance programmes are generally informed and directed by domestic and foreign policy concerns of donor states (e.g. Noel and Therien, 1995; Humanitarian Policy Group, 2001). In the context of disability, as inclusion and disability rights have moved up the domestic political agenda of Western Liberal Democracies, a moral imperative for responding to the needs of people with disabilities internationally, through development assistance has been created. Contributing to this is the response of international organizations such as the UN to the rapidly increasing numbers of people who are disabled as a result of a range of regional conflicts such as Cambodia, the Balkans, Sri Lanka, North Africa and the Middle East. These factors, combined with the organizational objectives of key international disability sports federations that have recognized the challenges such a phenomena presents, have provided a new momentum for providing assistance with the development of sport for people with disabilities. At the same time, a number of recent disability sport-in-development initiatives have highlighted the difficulties that result from cultural tensions between donor organizations and recipients. They clearly illustrate the challenges faced by the wider sport-in-development community when attempting to reconcile the objectives of donor organizations, with the perceived needs of recipients. Experiences with the delivery of disability sport-in-development initiatives suggest opportunities for alleviating these tensions through shared recognition by donors and recipients, of fundamental human rights.

While, as discussed in the introductory chapter, there is evidence of a long history of attempts to facilitate the development process through sport – contrasting with the perception that it is a new phenomena – the emergence of organized sporting forms for disabled participants is indeed, a relatively recent dimension to the evolution of sport. An articulate international disability rights lobby, medical and prosthetic developments and enhanced rehabilitation programmes, have combined with growth in the number of people disabled as a result of regional conflicts to create an environment conducive to the use of 'disability sport' as an aspect of development assistance programmes. In the light of these changes, this chapter is concerned with investigating focal points in the expansion of disability sport as it relates to the development process and identifying linkages with wider policy change at domestic and international level.

The chapter begins by assessing disability in development from the perspective of wider political debate. It pays particular attention to the relationship between the domestic (UK) and international political agenda and the locus of organizations representing disability rights in international relations. It then contextualizes these arguments through an assessment of provision for the needs of the disabled within the changing development agenda. The contribution of the rapidly evolving network of disability sports initiatives within international development assistance can then be considered. This leads to a re-evaluation of the traditional distinction between development through and development of sport. For example, an assessment of the role of development assistance in support of competitive disability sport highlights the significance of social and personal development throughout the range of development initiatives. In this context, particular attention is given to the wider social and developmental objectives of the Paralympic movement articulated through its engagement with the development process. The chapter concludes by identifying key challenges to engagement of disability sport as an aspect of development assistance, given wider debate relating to the politics of development.

Since the aim of the chapter is to encourage cross-disciplinary debate relating to the challenges of responding to the needs of disabled groups within the development process, research was necessarily linked to a wider body of development studies and international studies literature. Regarding the investigation of recent and current initiatives, this was carried out through a combination of archive and documentary research as well as, where appropriate, interviews with representatives of specific development organizations.

5.2   Perspectives on disability and development

Representations of disability have shifted significantly over the past 30 years and a large body of material has emerged over that time, contrasting the so-called 'medical' and 'social' models of disability (Tregaskis, 2004; De Pauw and Gavron, 2005). Essentially this represents an underlying shift away from a focus on medically defined categories of physical or intellectual disability, towards a concern, not with the impairment itself, but with the 'disabling' impact that society, in terms of physical accommodation and social relations, places on people with impairments. This is articulated in the UN Convention on the Rights of Persons with a Disability (2006), which noted that:

> Disability is an evolving concept and results from the interaction between a person's impairment and obstacles such as physical barriers and prevailing attitudes that prevent their participation in society. *The more obstacles there are, the more disabled a person becomes.* Persons with disabilities have long-term physical, mental, intellectual, or sensory impairments such as blindness, deafness, impaired mobility and developmental impairments. Some people may have more than one form of disability and many, if not most people, will acquire a disability at some time in their life due to physical injury, disease or aging (*italics added*).

In this context, disability emerges as a relative term, influenced by wider social and political considerations. Development assistance relating to any aspect of disability predictably becomes enmeshed in such considerations.

5.2.1   Disability and development – a political context

The debate concerning disability and society is dominated by the continuing struggle for social and political change aimed at addressing what is still considered to be systemic discrimination against persons with a disability. This is reflected for instance, in ongoing debate concerning progress in the implementation of the 1995 and 2005 Disability Discrimination Acts, (UK) and the 1992 Disability Discrimination Act (Australia). Domestic policy is then considered primarily in the context of enactment of such relatively enlightened 'inclusive' legislative developments. Increasingly however, concern is shifting toward the need to address the issue at international level. In part, this reflects the wider globalization debate and concerns over the universality of human rights as well as what appears to be the limited capacity of some states to affect change without external pressure and assistance.

Long established 'pluralist' perspectives (which suggest that international society is becoming less dependent on or influenced by the state) on the re-distribution of political and economic influence in international society, share in common, a belief in the move away from the position where power relations were dominated by states and state sponsored agencies.[1] Amongst the myriad non-state actors that are purported to have gradually acquired the capacity to influence international politics, recent growth in NGOs advocating social change, is noteworthy. A decade ago Keck and Sikkink (1998, preface) noted that approximately half of all non-governmental organizations working for social change, operate in one of the three areas of; human rights generally, women's rights specifically and the environment. They further argued that; 'voices that are suppressed in their own societies, may find that advocacy networks can project and amplify their concerns into an international arena, which in turn can echo back into their own countries'. A significant number of organizations engaged in the mobilization of support for disability rights, now feature within the wider category of human rights advocacy groups. The recent, rapid increase in international Disabled Peoples Organizations (DPOs) reflects the relationship between rights of the disabled and the wider human rights movement, as well as the increasing expectations of disabled people, concerning their capacity to influence the policy process at national and international level.

5.2.2   Disability and the development agenda

The relationship between poverty, political instability and numbers of disabled people, has been recognized by commentators for some time. The WHO estimate that approximately 650 million people live with disabilities of some kind.[2] It identified approximately 80% of these as living in the Global South, with a significant proportion struggling to survive. It highlighted the continuing increase in the number of disabled people, identifying a range of reasons, in particular, war injuries, antipersonnel landmines, HIV/AIDS, malnutrition, environmental damage and chronic diseases. On that basis, the development and disability agendas have converged. A number of significant issues however, have influenced the manner of that convergence.

The separation of national and international politics is becoming increasingly difficult in the emerging global political environment. The concept of disability rights and inclusion and its establishment as part of the domestic political agenda of Western liberal democratic states has set the frame of reference for policy relating to disability in the context of international development assistance. In the case of the UK, developments in the so-called 'inclusion agenda' prior to and during the New Labour administration of 1997, has seen an increase in activity at organizational and legislative level. The implementation of the 1995 and 2005 Disability Discrimination Acts is a case in point. The current merging of organizations representing minority interests, particularly the Commission for Racial Equality, women's rights and disability rights organizations into one body known as the Commission for Equality and Human Rights is intended to enhance their capacity to influence the policy process. While that organizational change is proving to be highly controversial,[3] it does nevertheless demonstrate the level of priority attributed to this area of policy.

Having set standards for the inclusion of disabled groups in the domestic context, it is argued here that this development in public policy in the UK on disability rights, creates a moral imperative that informs and directs both negotiation on international conventions relating to disability rights and decisions regarding provision for the needs of the disabled within international development programmes. While there clearly continue to be many obstacles (cultural and resource based) to equitable provision for the needs of disabled people internationally, nevertheless the principle (if not the practice) of 'universality' is applied to the determination of rights of such minority groups.[4]

5.2.3 The internationalization of disability rights

International institutions engaged in human rights issues, in particular the UN, have for some time been concerned with the international promotion of the rights of the disabled. The UN in 1993 adopted the 'Standard Rules on the Equalization of Opportunities for Disabled Persons', which set out policy guidelines on promoting equality of opportunities for persons with disabilities and the able bodied. While this provided guidance for the legislative process at national level, it was not legally binding. Given such concern, together with the observation that 'while some countries have enacted comprehensive legislation in this regard, many have not' (UN, 2006), pressure increased to enact a legally binding international convention. Negotiation began in 2001, was adopted by the UN General Assembly in December 2006 and will come into force following formal ratification by twenty members.[5]

The Convention essentially provides a framework of standards and obligations in light of which, states are required to act through their own legislative processes. As well as adopting the language of inclusion and seeking to encourage a cultural shift in terms of how persons with disabilities are perceived, it sets out material measures that include ensuring services, goods and facilities are accessible to persons with a disability. In this sense, it provides a context for the pursuit of disability rights through international development assistance.

5.3   Disabled People's Organizations and sport

As noted above, there has been a sharp increase in the range of so-called DPOs that have engaged in lobbying for the rights of disabled people, both at the level of national policy making and at the level of international negotiation, as in the case of UN Convention.[6] The international mobilization of a range of advocacy groups seeking to promote the rights of disabled people is then, a significant aspect of wider development assistance. The activity of Action on Disability and Development (ADD) demonstrates the strategy adopted by such organizations. Their active lobbying, designed to influence the drafting of the UN Convention on the rights of Persons with Disabilities utilized alliances with other like-minded organizations such as World Vision and the lobbying of state actors. ADD, as with many other DPOs, acknowledge the capacity of sport to support advocacy activity. The choice of Kenyan born British wheelchair racer Anne Wafula-Strike as an ADD Goodwill Ambassador is noteworthy in this respect. The brief of the Goodwill Ambassador is to act as a role model. This, combined with a range of lobbying activities, is designed to encourage states to ratify the UN Convention.

5.3.1   Bringing sport into the frame

Of particular significance to this study is the extent to which these DPOs adopt sport as an aspect of their development strategy. At the same time, sports specific organizations representing people with disabilities continue to increase in number and capacity to influence the wider development agenda. Partnership between sports specific and more general DPOs are also characteristic of the evolving development environment. Table 5.1 presents a small sample of DPOs engaged at some level, in development through disability sport, listing the type of sport-in-development projects that they have initiated or supported.

Finally, as most chapters in this book have mentioned, there is a danger, when addressing the role of sport-in-development to over-emphasize the place of sport in the overall development process.

Table 5.1   Organizations engaged with disability sport-in-development

Organisation	Programme/initiative	Programme/initiative aim
Non-governmental DPO		
Handicap International	*Fun Inclusive*	Production of handbook concerning use of sport in rehabilitation process
Landmine Survivors Network	*Princess Diana Memorial Sitting Volleyball Tournament*	Annual event held in Bosnia, brings together former Croat, Bosnian and Serb adversaries
Action for Disability and Development	*Goodwill Ambassador*	Paralympian, Anne Wafula-Strike: role model and lobbyist for disability rights
World Health Organisation	*(partner)International Paralympic Symposium on Disability Rights*	Identifying key issues relating to disability rights and mechanisms for ensuring equity and inclusion.
World Institute on Disability	*Promoting inclusive education (partners, USAID / OSCE)*	Challenging negative stereotyping of people with intellectual disability, through resourcing Disability Youth Advocacy Teams
International Disability and Development Consortium	*Series of reports and manuals on health related issues (partner WHO)*	Mental Health of Refugees manual (96) provided practical advice to operatives working with displaced people. Reference to use of physical activity to combat stress
Sports NGO		
FIFA	*Kicking Disability Into Touch*	Promoting sport for disabled in Afghanistan
International Paralympic Committee (IPC)	*Disability rights toolkit*	Heighten awareness of the rights of the disabled and advocate creation of UN Convention
Special Olympics	*Athlete Leadership Programmes*	To introduce participation in leadership programmes for people with intellectual disabilities.

Table 5.1   Organizations engaged with disability sport-in-development
– *continued*

Organisation	Programme/initiative	Programme/initiative aim
Special Olympics	*Sportworks (Chad)*	Bringing marginalized groups from host and refugee communities together (Right to Play)[7]
Edusport Foundation, Zambia[8]	*Kicking Aids Out (partner includes UK Sport)*	Heightening awareness of HIV/AIDS
International Wheelchair Tennis Federation (IWTF)	*The Silver Fund*	Facilitating the development of Wheelchair Tennis

Disability sport-in-development does not escape this, particularly where large scale DPOs are attempting to address deep-seated inequities at a societal level and are lobbying for significant policy shifts meaning that there is a tendency to exaggerate the benefits of some of these programmes. However, the current trend toward adoption of sport as part of the delivery framework of such organizations and the significant body of evidence (particularly from medical research literature, which demonstrates the efficacy of sport in the rehabilitation of people with disabilities) provides a platform for the expansion of sport as part of the delivery framework of such organizations.

5.4   Disability sport and international development – emerging challenges

The opportunity for people with disabilities to engage in structured sport and physical activity programmes is a relatively recent phenomenon. While there are records of earlier forms of sport for the disabled (De Pauw and Gavron, 2005), commentators on the development of sport for the disabled, for example Anderson (2003) and Silver (2003) focus on the particular significance of the work of Ludwig Guttmann at the Stoke Mandeville Spinal Injuries unit in the period following World War Two. Speaking on the introduction of disabled sport during that period, Guttmann (1972: 254) notes that it was 'the consideration of the overall training effect of sport on the neuromuscular system which induced me to use the sportive activities of these severely disabled as part of the medical treatment'. He commented, it soon became apparent that; 'sport for these severely disabled has a greater meaning than it has for the able-bodied', proving to be helpful as a 'complementary remedial exercise to the conventional method of physiotherapy' and helping to counteract the adverse psychological impacts of becoming disabled (1972: 254). It was in this context that the use of structured sport and recreation within rehabilitation programmes for war wounded was first developed. Organized competition soon became a feature of these programmes and led to the initiation in 1948, of the Stoke Mandeville Games.[9] These Games were held annually at Stoke Mandeville until 1960 when the pattern of locating the Games directly following the Olympic Games in the host country, was established.

The period following the 1960 Olympic Games was characterized by the gradual development of a number of international disability sports organizations and codification of 'new' sports (DePauw and Gavron, 2005: 89–112). At the same time, increased research into the impact of sport on rehabilitation programmes for disability provided further evidence of its value in a number of contexts including:

- Reducing incidences of rehospitalization
- Reduced reporting of clinical depression
- Improvements in physical competence
- Improvements in self-concept and self-efficacy
- Reduced reporting of loneliness and isolation[10]

Partly in response to such research (see endnote 11) and an increasing interest in sport at a political and social level, a number of country-wide development projects have been undertaken in the past fifteen years. While they are diverse in their organization, objectives and level of resourcing, they share the core aim of enhancing quality of life for people with disabilities and have generally been implemented through a range of partnerships between governmental and NGOs as the following sections illustrate (see, for example, Higgs (2001)).

Finally, the perception that the policies of developed liberal democratic states are relatively enlightened in relation to disability rights and inclusion of the disabled in sporting opportunities, has contributed to a distinct historiography of disability. This has tended to suggest the relative 'backwardness' of other cultures relative to respect for the rights of the disabled. Miles (2007: 1) discusses in particular, the tendency of advisors travelling to African or Asian states to assist in planning disability and rehabilitation services, working on the assumption that there was no 'worthwhile cultural heritage or traditional practice upon which anything "modern" could be built'. This in turn generated anti-thetical myths of golden eras when disabled people were honoured and held esteemed positions in indigenous communities. Both perspectives were, he argues, unhelpful generalizations. It has also been encouraged in part, by commentaries emerging from developing states on contemporary experiences of disability (see, for example, Fattah (2001)). Such perspectives foster the view that it is appropriate for agencies and organizations representing the interests of developed states to drive the development agenda as it relates to disability sport. This presents a particular challenge, given the general acknowledgement that the principle of partnership predicates effective development assistance.

5.4.1 Conflict and rehabilitation: a role for disability sport

The consequences of warfare have increasingly featured as a factor in the development of rehabilitation programmes since the 1960s. Such programmes for injured combatants have reflected heightened expectations for recovery and the subsequent capacity of individuals to function independently. Developments in medicine, prosthesis and rehabilitation programmes, have all contributed to this process, with the focus on recovery from disabling injuries gradually shifted from survival, through increasing levels of independent living, and to more general quality of life issues. By the time of the Vietnam war, for instance, the expectations of survivors was very different from that of survivors from previous conflicts.[11] There was a requirement to consider how disabled combatants could develop a range of life-skills in relation to their new situation. Sport and recreation played an increasingly significant part in this process.

As noted in the introduction, one consequence of contemporary warfare is the significant increase in the number of disabled people. Research carried out by the Landmine Survivor's Network (2007) estimates that 18,000 people are killed and injured from landmines every year. Of these, 80% are civilians, of which fewer than 10% have access to proper medical care and rehabilitation programmes. This reflects the preponderance of victims in developing states and has significant consequences for development assistance programmes. It is noteworthy however that this increasing rate of disability is not just restricted to developing states. The pressure group Veterans for America reports that while the death toll of American service personnel has remained relatively low,[12] the number of Iraqi war veterans receiving disability benefit had, by summer 2007, exceeded 150,000.[13] For many of these, participation in physical activity has the potential to become both an aspect of the rehabilitation process and longer term contributor to enhancing the quality of life of participants. Meanwhile, the resourcing of rehabilitation programmes for Iraqi victims disabled by the conflict, poses a major challenge for the international community in the coming years.

The difficulties facing individuals in developing states, disabled as a result of conflict, are compounded by relatively poor levels of resourcing and support networks. This relates both to medical care in the immediate aftermath of the trauma and to longer term rehabilitation and reintegration of individuals into society. Considerable efforts are being made by a range of international agencies to ensure access to specialist medical care and most recent developments in prosthesis in areas of armed conflict. In September 2007 the WHO, in conjunction with the UN High Commissioner for Refugees (UNHCR), the UNICEF and the World Food Programme (WFP) launched an appeal in response to the 'enormous challenge' faced by governments and NGOs as they grappled with the health needs of Iraqi refugees. This included 'hundreds of Iraqi amputees needing prostheses' in Syria alone.[14] The scale of the challenge remains formidable given the range and complexity of regional conflicts. UN research on the cost of armed conflict estimated world military expenditure in 2005 at US$1.1 trillion. Of that, total UN peacekeeping operations accounted for less than 0.5%. Meanwhile as far back as 1995, the UN General Assembly was reporting that the treatment of land mine victims was 'unfortunately far beyond the capacity of most mine-affected states'. Against this backdrop, the adoption of sport and recreational activities as a conduit to assist the rehabilitation and re-integration of individuals disabled in conflict situations is an increasingly significant dimension of development programmes. At the same time, it is the responsibility of those advocating sport-in-development to retain a sense of perspective regarding what can be achieved in relation to other aspects of the development process.

Certain societies have, because of their history of political instability and conflict, engendered particular interest from the sport-in-development community. The experience of Cambodian society as it emerges from a generation of conflict is one clear example. The high – and growing – numbers of amputees resulting from anti-personnel mines that were a feature of this regional conflict,[15] has attracted the engagement of a number of disability sport programmes. Initially, these were limited to rehabilitation and re-integration efforts. As the activities become established however, interest in elite competitive sport began to emerge. The Cambodian National Volleyball League for the disabled is one such example. Falling within the geo-political sphere of influence of Australasia, it is not surprising that actors from that region, feature prominently in development assistance programmes. The Australian Business Volunteer Programme and the ANZ Royal Bank have for example, been particularly active in this area.

The capacity to respond effectively to the particular circumstances of the development setting, in order to ensure that the development process becomes self-sustaining, both in terms of use of technologies and the establishment of a skills base, determine the efficacy of development assistance programmes. The UK based NGO, Motivation, has since 1991 engaged in fifteen development projects primarily aimed at promoting self-sustaining wheelchair technologies in areas where problems with access to raw material and distribution networks, rendered conventional wheelchairs inappropriate for long term use. In response to requests for simple wheelchair technology in Cambodia, the agency developed the 'Mekong', a wooden three-wheel design which subsequently reached the finals of the BBC Design Awards in 1996. While provision of the wheelchairs provides the potential for enhanced mobility, developing the personal skills to adapt to physical impairment and to effectively use the chair, requires effective counselling and training. It is during such programmes that introducing adapted sport and recreational activities can play a part in developing such skills.

Finally, a heightened interest in the potential for sport to help counter some of the trauma resulting from conflict situations is reflected across a number of sports disciplines. This was recently reflected in the International Council for Sports Science and Physical Education (ICSSPE) *Sport and Post-Disaster Intervention* conference (November 2007). The staging of the conference was the result of the cooperation of a number of international cross-sectoral actors, namely the Federal Ministry of the Interior, Germany (assistance with finance) and with the cooperation of the Fürst Donnersmarck-Foundation and the German Red Cross. The conference combined an assessment of the potential of various occupational therapy models to contribute to re-integration (Donner) with an investigation of the emerging role of sport science as it expands into the area of adapted physical activity (Doll-Tepper) and specialist psychological support (Kirk). At the same time, it is important to recognize the extent of the challenges facing such interventions; in particular the impact of geo-political interests and attendant resourcing issues that will ultimately determine implementation and efficacy.

5.5 Development assistance and competitive sport for the disabled

This chapter has, until now, concerned itself with development led programmes that, in line with the classification outlined in the introductory chapter, are recognizable as plus sport. It is clear however, that assistance with the enhancement of specific sporting forms does constitute another aspect of the sport-in-development frame. The remainder of the chapter focuses on such sport plus activity.

Most forms of competitive disability sport are in their formative years and continue to develop institutionally and expand internationally. Apart from the development of competitive wheelchair basketball in the 1940s, the establishment of most recognized 'disability sports' such as wheelchair tennis and sitting volleyball, took place during the 1970s and 1980s with others such as wheelchair rugby emerging much later. International competition is predicated on significant investment by the relevant federations and affiliated organizations, in order to consolidate recognition of sporting codes and competitive frameworks as well as supporting the general development of the sport through enhanced coaching and administrative support. The suggestion here is that such activity constitutes development assistance since without such transference of resources, there would be great difficulty in establishing these new sporting forms in most developing societies.

5.5.1 From 'diffusion' to 'development assistance' – the dissemination of competitive disability sport

The comprehensive body of literature relating to international diffusion of modern sporting forms provides a valuable resource when investigating the challenges facing contemporary sport development assistance. This is referred to in some detail in the introductory chapter and is articulated by a number of sports historians and sociologists, for example Dunning and Rojek (1992) in their exploration of sport in the 'civilizing process'. The origins of contemporary initiatives seeking to use sport as a conduit for overseas development assistance for disabled persons, are determined by the same social and cultural influences that were apparent during the period when modern sporting forms were going through the process of international transmission and translation. The familiar themes of the social, physical and cultural value of sport have then, underpinned calls for engagement in the development of modern sporting forms since their initiation. As discussed in the introductory chapter, the diffusion and adaptation of new sporting codes continues as an ongoing process. This is particularly the case regarding relatively new disability sports. While reflecting many of the characteristics of earlier records of diffusion, in terms of the development and reach of institutions and the impact of different cultural contexts on the nature of the activity, the process as it relates to disability sport, is increasingly packaged as development assistance as the following case study demonstrates.

5.5.2 Extending the boundaries of competitive sport: development assistance and wheelchair tennis[16]

The challenge of establishing an indigenous infrastructure through which services can be maintained and continue to evolve, has for some time been the central objective of aid organizations. This approach is now clearly articulated in most projects relating to food production and the development of essential services such as establishing and maintaining water supplies. Similar principles have been recognized as essential to the effective long-term development of a range of other provisions, including sport. Such activity is evident in the capacity building of sports that have only recently become established internationally. Wheelchair tennis, like many disability sports, has had a relatively brief existence as a fully codified competitive activity, since it emerged in 1976. The International Wheelchair Tennis Federation (IWTF) was not formed until 1988, yet through successful development it managed to establish itself in less than 20 years as an internationally recognized Paralympic sport.

One significant advantage facilitating the development of wheelchair tennis has been the opportunity to use the existing infrastructure, which has supported the development of tennis internationally. The IWTF was from the onset, fully integrated into the International Tennis Federation (ITF). As in many development situations, the impact of projects is largely determined by the ability of donor organizations to access organizations and agencies within the recipient country, with the capacity to assist its operation. The existence of ITF structures across many developing as well as developed states has provided an important point of reference for those engaged in the administration of a range of IWTF initiatives. In addition to the support of national tennis federation structures, the assistance of Embassy and Consular services, and in the case of Commonwealth Countries, High Commissions, has been significant, particularly in the early stages of the project.

The IWTF regional development project in Sri Lanka was of particular note given the context of continuing conflict within which it was taking place. As a result of the large numbers of young men disabled in conflict between the separatist Tamil Tiger movement and the Sri Lankan authorities, a general rehabilitation programme had been initiated by the Sri Lankan army in collaboration with the Sri Lankan Tennis Association. Under the auspices of the IWTF Silver Fund, the organization was able to provide expert assistance and specialist equipment to an initiative that was significantly under-resourced.

The international success of any initiative is clearly dependent upon the existence of an international infrastructure and network of individuals with appropriate playing and coaching skills. The IWTF have been successful in 'internationalizing' itself in a relatively short time frame, through effective promotion of contacts worldwide and use of that network to disseminate the sport. In this context its organizational objectives have been realized, with reciprocal benefit to partners in recipient states.

5.6   Driving international development through disability sport: the Olympic movement

Since its inception in the late nineteenth century, the Olympic movement has been expanding the idea of engaging sport in the pursuit of wider social and cultural objectives. In this context, an extensive body of literature has explored the ideological framework underpinning the initiation of IOC and its development in the early years. The dynamics of the international political environment and the shifting values reflected in post-colonial thinking have influenced the direction and emphasis of Olympism in terms of wider human development goals. Nevertheless, the ideal of Olympic sport-in-development has remained a central tenet of the Olympics throughout the life of the movement.

The philosophy of internationalism underpinning the Olympic Movement has remained as a key driver in the initiation of development assistance programmes. Most prominent in the emergence of elite sport development were the post-war activities of the Committee for International Olympic Aid and its successor, Olympic Solidarity with the objective to assist the needs of elite athletes in developing countries. In this, they attempted to fulfill the dual role of contributing to the international sporting infrastructure necessary for the development of international competition, as well as providing support for individuals and groups within recipient states. The tacit recognition of the relationship of colonialism to development and the need to address the disparity between developing and developed states, may be interpreted as part of the strategy to secure acceptance of the Olympic Movement as an 'international' phenomenon. Nevertheless, it demonstrated the role that development assistance could play in the development of sport internationally.

Notwithstanding misgivings about the capacity of the movement to deliver, the Olympic development ideal is reflected in the contemporary Olympic Charter (2007) which restates the fundamental principle of Olympism; '...to place sport at the service of the harmonious development of man, with a view to promoting a peaceful society concerned with the preservation of human dignity'. The vision is articulated in the increasing engagement of the IOC within the sport-in-development movement with a range of joint initiatives such as the IOC-UNHCR *Giving is Winning* programme, formal development links with the International Paralympic Committee (IPC) and the expansion of development activities under the auspices of the Olympic Solidarity organization. IPC programmes can then be interpreted as extending this philosophy of attempting to 'internationalize' the movement through engagement with the sport-in-development process.

5.6.1   The Paralympics – an evolving context for sport-in-development

The inclusion of competitive sport for athletes with disabilities within the Olympic Movement is a recent phenomenon. The International Stoke Mandeville Games for the disabled had been initiated quite separately from the Olympic Games. It had been held annually at Stoke Mandeville, until 1960 when the pattern of locating the Games directly following the Olympic Games in the host country, was established. While it was from that point, increasingly associated with the Olympic Movement, the link with Stoke Mandeville remained strong. Indeed it continued to be referred to in much of the documentation, as the 'international Stoke Mandeville Games', reflecting a reluctance among some to accept the term 'Paralympics'.[17]

The development of international sport for the disabled and establishment of the IPC as a key player in the Olympic Movement, has by definition, expanded the sport-in-development remit of the movement to include disabled athletes. The articulation of a vision 'to contribute to a better world for all people with a disability' (IPC Handbook 2003) and implementation of a set of specific initiatives aimed at promoting inclusivity and enhancing the health of people with disabilities in developing states, has mainstreamed the IPC within the sport-in-development frame. Partnerships with key actors such as Right to Play and UNESCO has enhanced the profile of the IPC in sport-in-development, however questions remain concerning the substantive nature of a number of the initiatives currently being promoted by the organization.

Development assistance projects relating to the Paralympics has reflected underlying concerns with equity and inclusion for people with disabilities internationally and a clear need to build capacity and infra-structure in developing states. Most recently, the IPC development assistance strategy for 2007 identifies priorities and the allocation of development assistance resources between 'development grants' and 'Organizational Development Initiatives' (ODI).[18] Grants are awarded to accredited organizations to assist in implementation of programmes designed to enhance athletic performance, quality of leadership and organizational development. ODI on the other hand, focuses on support specifically for National Paralympic Committees to assist with strategic planning and organizational development. The focus on development of organizations in order to enhance capacity of the Paralympic movement internationally, is noteworthy. The level of resourcing from the IPC is however, limited and the movement is dependent upon the development of partnerships internationally.[19] The three-way partnership between Commonwealth Games Canada (CGC), UK Sport and the IPC to provide support and training to increase the capacity of NPCs in the African region is a recent example of such activity.[20]

5.6.2   A particular human development challenge – intellectual disability and the Olympic movement

The particular challenge of responding to the needs of intellectually disabled people in the human development frame is acutely recognized by a number of international organizations and agencies. The rights of people with intellectual disability have been addressed at a number of levels within the UN, subsequent to the 1971 UN Declaration on the Rights of Mentally Retarded Persons. In 2001 the UN General Assembly in resolution 56/115 'urges governments, intergovernmental organizations and non-governmental organizations to provide special protection to persons with developmental and psychiatric disabilities with special emphasis on integrating them into society and protecting and promoting their human rights'. Concern over ensuring appropriate recognition, safeguarding of civil rights and instituting effective support programmes for what in effect constitutes a wide spectrum of intellectual impairment, continues to exercise the minds of legislators and civil liberty groups internationally. Such concerns have implications for a range of international development programmes where support is dependent upon good governance, social inclusion and the protection of civil liberties. Equally however, the tendency to stereotype and stigmatize developing societies as backward in their approach to engaging with people with intellectual disabilities, can have a negative impact on donor – recipient relations and the efficacy of subsequent interventions.

Sport-in-development programmes for people with intellectual disabilities reflect the challenges and dilemmas facing societies generally, when addressing the development needs of this part of their communities. The commitment to provide a framework for competitive sport and the recognition, classification and subsequent support of athletes with intellectual disabilities evolved from a series of sports camps organized in 1962 in the USA. This subsequently led to the first international Special Olympics Games in 1968. The Special Olympics are qualitatively different from the Olympics and Paralympics in that they constitute a network of grass-root organizations that are essentially self-sustaining while feeding into a framework of regional, national and ultimately international Special Olympics events organizations. The stated objective of the movement is to operate as an 'international non-profit organization dedicated to empowering individuals with intellectual disabilities to become physically fit, productive and respected members of society through sports training and competition'.[21] Recent documentation estimates that the movement now draws in excess of 2.25 million participants world-wide (Special Olympics Annual Report 2005).

The establishment of the organization around the theme of advocacy provided a clear rationale for its later engagement with the sport-in-development movement. At the same time however, the decentralized nature of the Special Olympics and limited access to a centralized pool of resources, has placed significant limits on its capacity to engage in sport-in-development initiatives directly. Such activity is heavily dependent upon resourcing by partners – both in the form of key international organizations and agencies as well as a wide range of indigenous organizations. For example, the Special Olympics – FIFA Development project launched in spring 2006 in Tanzania, Namibia and Botswana reflected this particular approach to resourcing development by focusing on the pursuit of a range of social and health objectives through sport. Its principle aim was to, over the period of one year, recruit 500 additional participants to the Special Olympics football regional network and to use the recruitment process as a point of access to provide health screening for this particularly vulnerable group. The operation was dependent upon funding and logistical support from FIFA as well as the support of the National Football Associations from the three recipient countries. The wider stated objective was to tackle the social stigma associated with intellectual disability and in this the heightened profile of Special Olympic athletes in televised 'displays of friendship and unity' with national football team members, become part of a range of symbolic activities that were aimed at contributing to societal change in attitudes toward disability.

Many challenges continue to face sport-in-development efforts in this area. While international agencies and organizations increase lobbying for the rights of people with intellectual disabilities, its move up the human rights agenda has been slow and the response of societies internationally has been mixed. The attendant problem of accessing resources to implement programmes has continued as a particular challenge for organizations such as the Special Olympics. In addition, there are considerable cultural and logistical issues to be addressed in terms of linking competition frameworks for people with intellectual disabilities, to the International Paralympic Movement who are reticent, following the widespread cheating in categories designated for intellectually disabled athletes at the Sydney 2000 Paralympic Games, to shift the parameters of the Paralympics (IPC, 2007). Nevertheless, increasing attention at a domestic level within developed states, to the rights of people with intellectual disabilities, is being translated into an awareness of the need to address this issue in a wider international development context.

5.7   Synthesizing the arguments

As discussed in the introductory chapter, the use of sport as a development tool is part of the process of broadening the activities of the development assistance community in an attempt to engage marginalized groups, including people with disabilities, as it responds to the challenge of the MDGs. The experience in many donor countries, of engaging with sport as a means of achieving a number of social policy objectives in a domestic setting and the interest of a range of sports organizations and agencies in this process provides the rationale for expanding activities into the wider development arena. Such expansion does however require careful re-interpretation of how sport can act as an agent for social change in order to align initiatives to new cultural contexts. This in turn, involves an assessment of what constitutes 'marginalized' and how the experiences of disabled individuals and organizations representing people with disabilities, should inform and direct arguments concerning the universalism of human rights.

The international development of disability sport has been influenced by a number of political, cultural and organizational imperatives. In particular:

5.7.1 The rights of disabled people

The UN Convention on the Rights of Persons with a Disability reflects an attempt to further enhance the principle of the universal human rights through an international legal framework. This provides a context for the pursuit of disability rights through international sport development assistance. In addition, the international mobilization of a range of advocacy groups seeking to establish the rights of disabled people and their heightened expectations concerning a range of quality of life issues, has acted as a catalyst for international sport development assistance.

5.7.2 From domestic to international imperatives

Assumptions concerning the capacity of sport to enhance quality of life in a domestic context has underpinned policy developments and funding priorities at national level in a number of developed states. The concept of disability rights and its establishment as part of the domestic political agenda of Western liberal democratic states has created the imperative for addressing the same issues of equity and inclusion within development assistance programmes. Assumptions concerning the capacity of sport to enhance quality of life in a domestic context have underpinned policy developments and funding priorities at national level. In this context, development of inclusion as a key aspect of the UK domestic political agenda during the late 1990s and reflected in a number of national sports policy initiatives such as in the case of the UK Inclusive Fitness Initiative (IFI), has subsequently been one of the influences on the international development assistance agenda as it relates to sport. The same assumptions are increasingly being transferred into the international arena and are underpinning policy developments at international level, as reflected for instance in the 'Sport for Development and Peace' programme.

5.7.3   Capacity to demonstrate the efficacy of sport-in-development

As explored elsewhere in the book, and in particular by Coalter, a key challenge facing the sport-in-development movement is the imperative to produce a body of evidence that demonstrates how sport can effect change in a development setting. This has become particularly important in light of the trend toward evidence based policy decisions. While the sport-in-development community are constructing mechanisms in response to this challenge, it is important to integrate findings from a range of disciplinary areas. In relation to disability sport-in-development, the existence of a comprehensive body of evidence, developing from analysis of medical data concerning rehabilitation from traumatic injury and linking to sport science investigation, creates a particularly substantive basis from which to develop the argument concerning the capacity of sport to deliver other policy objectives including the areas of health and social welfare. Given the ongoing difficulties in demonstrating the efficacy of sport-in-development, this may well become a particularly significant aspect of decisions on resource allocation.

5.7.4   Conflict, instability and underdevelopment

The endemic political instability and systemic economic weakness in much of the developing world has been presented variously as a product of a process of underdevelopment and the asymmetry characteristic of colonial and post-colonial relations (Frank, 1967; Baran, 1973). Notwithstanding its rationale, such instability has a major impact on the quality of life of individual citizens. Due to the prevalence of disabling illness, civil and ethnic conflict, poverty and relatively poor levels of medical support, the presence of a range of disabilities is for example, a more prominent feature of developing states than of developed states. Changes in warfare technology and increased capacity to inflict disabling injuries on civilian populations and military personnel have contributed to large increases in the number of young disabled in some areas of the developing world. This in turn creates the imperative for enhanced rehabilitation programmes as part of wider development initiatives. Such programmes are increasingly utilizing sport and recreational programmes as a vehicle for development of communication, motor and social skills. While acknowledging that such activity is addressing the symptoms rather than the cause of underdevelopment, they nevertheless can make a meaningful contribution to enhancing quality of life of individuals in such situations.

5.7.5 Development assistance and the establishment of 'new' international sports

Since disability sports are in their formative years, their internationalization requires investment in a range of supporting roles in order to establish these 'new' sporting forms outside their place of origin and to create the basis for international recognition, legitimacy and ultimately for international competition. In these contexts, the diffusion of disability sport reflects many of the characteristics of earlier dissemination of sporting forms (Guttmann, 1994). The experience of disability sport is however noteworthy in that the process of dissemination is generally framed within the wider development assistance process. As part of development assistance, the relationship between disability sport and the wider inclusion and social justice agenda is particularly significant. In that sense, tension exists between the imperative to develop an inclusive infrastructure to enhance opportunities to participate and the concern of international organizations such as the IPC, to develop elite competitive frameworks.

Finally it should be noted that the journey toward full social integration of people with disabilities continues within developed as well as developing states. Such integration requires not just opportunities for people with disabilities – physical and intellectual – to participate and compete, but also to engage in every facet of sport, including leadership, management and development.[22] This has implications for the development community in the sense that traditional 'donors' are engaged in an internal development process that should inform and direct their relationship with the recipients of development assistance. In this sense also, international organizations such as the UN have an important mediating role to play in the establishment of a universal perspective on the rights of people with disabilities.

The challenge of resourcing a sustainable framework of international development assistance initiatives through sport, for people with disabilities, remains formidable. Yet its capacity to contribute to rehabilitation, social integration and personal development is tangible and has been evidenced through a number of programme outcomes. Effective partnership between a range of policy makers and advocacy groups and the commitment to move beyond short term political considerations is the precursor to effective development in the future. Finally, while sport can contribute to the development process, commentators have a responsibility to acknowledge the significance of wider strategic issues such as the international trading regime, the management of regional instabilities and respect for universal human rights, as having a most profound effect on the quality of life of the recipients of development assistance.

Notes

1 The concept of Pluralism is widely used in the field of International Relations. For an early Pluralist commentary, see for example Keohane R. and Nye J. (1974). More recently, many analyses on the nature of world politics, adopt an implicitly Pluralist perspective. For instance Armstrong *et al.* (1996) in their assessment of the role of international organizations in diplomatic discourse. Also, Linklater (1998) in his discussion of community and citizenship in the 'Post-Westphalian era'.

2 WHO Report to the 58ᵗʰ World Health Assembly (14ᵗʰ April 2005) *Disability, including prevention, management and rehabilitation*. The UN, in the preamble to the Convention on the rights of Persons with a Disability, use the figure of 650 million people experiencing some form of disability.

3 The creation in the UK in 2007 of a new body with the title of the Commission for equality and Human Rights to encompass the rights of a number of groups previously represented by separate bodies – namely women, ethnic minorities, gays, the old, the religious, the disabled and the human rights of all Britons, has come under severe criticism from many organizations in the UK. See for instance, commentary in: *The Economist* 30ᵗʰ November 2006, *Snow white and the Sevenisms*.

4 See Linklater (1998) on 'Universality, Difference and the Emancipatory Project'(46–76).

5 http://www.finlandun.org/netcomm/news. In addition to national governmental representation and engagement of NGOs, the EU became engaged due to the principle of shared competencies of the member states, represented through the European Commission.

6 The IPC was one of the disability organizations that lobbied for the development of an international Convention.

7 Please note that as of April 2006, this project was suspended due to safety and security concerns.

8 The Kicking Aids Out initiative involves a partnership of a range of organizations across sub-Saharan Africa – of which the Edusport Foundation is one. The initiative is supported by UK Sport.

9 See for example Cooper (1990).

10 Williams *et al.* (2001) trace a succession of research programmes addressing these areas.

11 Coverage of the lifestyle impact of injuries sustained by combatants is fragmented – however an impression can be gained through reference to a number of papers published in medical journals: for instance Dougherty (2001).

12 Washington Post records the death toll as being 3468 on the 18ᵗʰ February 2007.

13 http://www.veteransforamerica.org In many cases, death had been avoided as a result of body armour protection of the abdomen, however this had left limbs exposed. The impact of the war on the Iraqi civilian population is at

the some time, creating a legacy that will take generations to deal with effectively.

14 UN Daily News Service (18th September, 2007).
15 It is estimated that one person in every 236 in Cambodia is an amputee. UN Documentation Centre. UN Daily News Service (4th April 2006).
16 This case study has been taken from Beacom (2007), pp. 96–98.
17 National Archives – FO 371 / 176045 (November 1964). A report on the 1964 Paralympic Games was forwarded from the British Embassy in Tokyo to the Foreign Office. The term 'Stoke Mandeville games' was used on a number of occasions in the report. The report noted that the games, though relatively small in comparison to the Olympics, had been effectively organized by the Japanese Ministry of Welfare and had been enthusiastically received in Japan. This, despite what was reported as 'deep-seated prejudices against disabled people in that society'.
18 *2007 IPC Development Assistance:* Report by the International Paralympic Committee. http://www.paralympic.org
19 It is noteworthy that the combined funding for the development grants and ODI is US$112,500.
20 http://www.commonwealthgames.ca/site/index_e.aspx?DetailID=1215 This partnership arrangement also includes input from the British Paralympic Association (BPA) and the Canadian Paralympic Committee (CPC).
21 Stated objective of Special Olympics http://www.specialolympics.org
22 The leadership programmes currently offered by Sports Leaders UK reflect this.

Bibliography

Abdul-Fattah, M. (2001) 'The Use of Community-based Rehabilitation as a Model for Integrated Sport Activities', in Doll-Tepper *et al.*, *New Horizons in Sport for Athletes with a Disability: Proceedings of the International Vista '99 Conference (Vol. 2).* Oxford: Meyer & Meyer Sport (UK) Ltd. pp. 791–798.

Action on Disability and Development (2006) *History of ADD.* http://www.add.org.uk/adds_history.asp

Anderson, J. (2003) 'Turned into Taxpayers: Paraplegia, Rehabilitation and Sport at Stoke Mandeville', in *Journal of Contemporary History,* **38**(3), 461–475.

Armstrong, D., Lloyd, L. and Redmond, J. (1996) *From Versailles to Maastricht: International Organisation in the Twentieth Century.* Basingstoke: Palgrave.

Baran P. (1973) *The Political Economy of Growth.* Harmondsworth: Penguin.

Beacom, A. (2007) 'A Question of Motives: Reciprocity, Sport and Development Assistance', in *European Sport Management Quarterly,* **7**(1), pp. 81–107.

Cooper, A. (1990) 'Wheelchair Racing Sports Science: A Review', in *Journal of Rehabilitation Research and Development,* **27**(3), 295–312.

DePauw, K. and Gavron, S. (2005) *Disability Sport (2nd ed).* Champaign: Human Kinetics.

Disability Discrimination Act (1995) Office of Public Sector Information.

Disability Discrimination Act (2005) Office of Public Sector Information.

Dunning, E. and Rojek, C. (eds) (1992) *Sport and Leisure in the Civilising Process.* Basingstoke: Macmillan.

Economist (30th November 2006) *Snow White and the Seven isms.*

Dougherty, P. (2001) 'Transtibial Amputees from Vietnam War: 28 Year Follow-up', in *The Journal of Bone and Joint Surgery*, Vol. 83, 383–389.

Finland's Permanent Mission: UN, New York (2007) *The European Union and the UN*, http://www.finlandun.org/netcomm/news (accessed March 2007).

Frank, A. (1967) *Capitalism and Underdevelopment in Latin America*. New York: Monthly Review Press.

Gereffi, G. (1991) 'Power and Dependency in an interdependent World – a guide to understanding the contemporary global crisis', in Little, R. and Smith, M. (eds), *Perspectives on World Politics*. London: Routledge, 318–324.

Guttmann, L. (1972) 'Development of Sport for the Disabled', in *Sport in the Modern World: Chances and Problems – Papers from the Scientific Congress Munich – Organizing Committee for the Games of the XXth Olympiad Munich*. Berlin: Springer-Verlag, pp. 254–256.

Guttmann, A. (1994) *Games and Empires: Modern sports and cultural imperialism*. New York: Columbia University Press.

Higgs, C. 'Making a Difference – Using Sport and Recreation in the Guyana Project for People with Disabilities', in Doll-Tepper *et al.* (2001) *New Horizons in Sport for Athletes with a Disability: Proceedings of the International Vista '99 Conference (Vol. 2)*. Oxford: Meyer & Meyer Sport (UK) Ltd., pp. 799–814.

Humanitarian Policy Group (February 2001) *Politics and Humanitarian Aid: Debates, Dilemmas and Dissension*. Report of a conference organized by ODI, POLIS at the University of Leeds and CAFOD, London.

International Council for Sports Science and Physical Education (2007) *Sport and Post-Disaster Intervention Handbook*. ICSSPE Publication.

International Paralympic Committee (2007) *IPC Development Assistance*. IPC.

International Paralympic Committee (January 2007) *Position Statement Regarding the Participation of Athletes with an Intellectual Disability at IPC Sanctioned Competitions*. IPC.

Jellinek, J. (2004) Book Review 'History of the Treatment of Spinal Injuries', *Journal of the Royal Society of Medicine*, **97**(3), 148–149.

Keck, M. and Sikkink, K. (1998) *Activists Beyond Borders: Advocacy Networks in International Politics*. Ithaca NY: Cornell University Press.

Keohane, R. and Nye, J. (1972) *Transnational Relations & World Politics*. Cambridge: Harvard University Press.

Keohane, R. and Nye, J. (1974) 'Transnational Relations & World Politics', *World Politics*, **27**(1), 39–62.

Landmine Survivors Network (2007) *Landmine Facts*. http://www.landminesurvivors.org/what_landmines.php

Larsen, K. (October 2002) 'Effects of Professionalisation and Commercialisation of Elite Sport on Sport for All'. Conference Presentation – *9th IOC Sport for All Conference*, Arnhem.

Linklater, A. (1998) *The Transformation of Political Community*. Cambridge: Polity Press.

Loeb, V. (2nd September 2003) 'Number of Wounded in Action Rise: Iraq toll Reflects Medical Advances', in *Washington Post*.

Maguire, J. (2004) 'Challenging the Sports-industrial Complex: Human Sciences, Advocacy and Service', in *European Physical Education Review*, **10**(3), 299–322.

McCullough, B. 'The International Organisation and Structure for Disability Sport and the need to Accelerate the Development of the Regions', in Doll-Tepper *et al.* (2001), *New Horizons in Sport for Athletes with a Disability: Proceedings of the International Vista '99 Conference (Vol. 2).* Oxford: Meyer & Meyer Sport (UK) Ltd. pp. 699–716.

Miles, K. (2007) *International Strategies for Disability-related Work in Developing Countries: Historical, Modern and Critical Reflections.* www.independentliving. org/docs7miles200701.pdf

Noel, A. and Therien, J. (Summer 1995) 'From Domestic to International Justice: The Welfare State and Foreign Aid', *International Organization,* **49**(3), 523–553.

Rains, C. 'The Forgotten Athletes – a critical appraisal of IPC sports competition at world and Paralympic levels', in Doll-Tepper *et al.* (2001) *New Horizons in Sport for Athletes with a Disability: Proceedings of the International Vista '99 Conference (Vol. 2).* Oxford: Meyer & Meyer Sport (UK) Ltd, pp. 493–498.

Silver, J. (2003) *History of the Treatment of Spinal Injuries.* New York: Kluwer Academic/Springer.

Special Olympics (2005) *Special Olympics Annual Report 2005.* Washington D.C.

Special Olympics (2007) *The Mission and Vision of the Special Olympics,* http:// www.specialolympics.org (accessed October 2007).

Tregaskis, C. (2004) *Constructions of Disability: Researching the interface between disabled people and non-disabled people.* London: Routledge.

United Nations (1993) *Standard Rules on the Equalization of Opportunities for Disabled Persons.* UN Documentation Centre.

United Nations General Assembly (6th September 1995) Agenda item 46 *Assistance in Mine Clearance – Report to the Secretary General.* UN Documentation Centre.

United Nations (2006) *Convention on the Rights of Persons with Disabilities.* UN Documentation Centre.

UN Fact Sheet for the International Day of Peace (2006) *Costs of War and Peace.* UN Documentation Centre.

UN Daily News Service (15th September 2007) *UN Agencies launch $85 million appeal to aid 2.2 million Iraqi refugees* (Issue DH/4985).

UN Daily News Service (4th April 2006) *Marking First Ever Mine Action Day, UN Calls for Ban and Clean-up Funds.*

Williams, T. *et al.* 'Sport and Rehabilitation – Patterns of Initial and Continuing Participation in Wheelchair Basketball in the UK and Germany', in Doll-Tepper *et al.* (2001) *New Horizons in Sport for Athletes with a Disability: Proceedings of the International Vista '99 Conference* (Vol. 2). Oxford: R. Meyer Sport (UK) Ltd., pp. 603–614.

World Health Organization (14th April 2005) *Disability: Including Prevention, Management and Rehabilitation.* Report to the 58th World Health Assembly. Geneva: WHO.

6
Dilemmas and Opportunities in Gender and Sport-in-Development

Martha Saavedra

6.1 Introduction

Sport can be a powerful, and potentially a radical and transformative tool in empowering girls and women and affecting gender norms and relations throughout a society. As with able-bodiedness/disability and youth, gender emerges at the intersection of the physical and the social, and this is precisely where sport also resides. The embodied nature of both gender and sport suggests possibilities for intertwining the two for development interventions. Programmes such as the Go Sisters EduSport in Zambia[1] and Moving the Goal Posts in Kenya demonstrate this as they provide physical, psychological, and social benefits, targeted at girls and young women. However, seeking to empower females through sport is somewhat paradoxical given that the world of sport can be a bastion for male privilege and power, an important arena for asserting a particular kind of male dominance over women (and some men), as well as furthering EuroAmerican hegemony *vis-à-vis* the Global South. Indeed, objections to women's general involvement in sport (which varies according to the type of sport and location), often rest on the ways in which 'gender norms' (viewed historically and spatially) are challenged by external forces, which can range from NGOs to the state and to international cultural flows. With variation across settings, there remains a strong link between sport, body practices, gender and sexuality.

While there are many ways that sport, gender and development can intersect, this chapter will consider some of the dilemmas and opportunities posed in the particular use of sport to promote female empowerment, especially in contexts where in the larger world of sport (globally, regionally and locally), women and girls remain marginalized. A case study of an organization in Kenya which uses football in its work with girls and women will illustrate many of these issues as well as the difficulties in affecting and documenting change. The chapter first addresses theory and context for this case study. After a review of relevant theory on gender, and gender and development, an overview of the relationship between gender and sport is provided. Tensions in this relationship are explored seeking points of leverage for, or resistance to, social change and how this affects the possibilities of employing sport for development goals. The chapter then moves to a more explicit discussion of the contemporary sport-in-development movement, and the place of gender in it. Highlighted are ethical issues raised by development practices, aid and global power imbalances. I also contend that one can not presume that the relationship between sport and gender is universal, and as such, any sport-in-development efforts must be grounded in a clear appreciation of local dynamics. The chapter ends with the case study details and analysis. Overall, my approach is as a scholar *and* an advocate, my perspective one of cautionary 'praxis' – theory tied with practice, advocacy with critique.

6.2   Gender and sport

The world of sport remains profoundly gendered, with practices and experiences marked and bounded by sex and sexuality – often exclusively male or female, masculine or feminine. This gendering can be explored via multi-layered analysis of psychological, cultural and social beliefs and practices that plots, explains and predicts stasis and change. Here, gender is taken to mean 'a relationship between the social categories of men and women...' that conceptually 'is a complex and unfixed mix of significant structural and cultural or representational considerations both making and marking social distinctions between those constituted as sexes' (Essed *et al.*, 2004: 4). Admittedly, the concept of gender and the process of gendering can be slippery to follow, especially as developments in feminist theory have undermined earlier renderings of a simple binary with sex as biology (fixed) and gender as culture (mutable), where instead sex is viewed as an artifice, gender is a performance[2] and both are historical constructions (Butler, 1990; Butler, 1993; Schiebinger, 2004; Laqueur, 1992). Hence, for many theorists, the usefulness of the concept of gender in analysing subjectivity[3] and identity may well have reached its end, whereas concepts such as the 'lived body' articulated by Toril Moi serve the feminist project better, and in the case of sport studies, perhaps prove to be extremely valuable (Moi, 2001; Young, 2002: 414).[4] In other words, gender as an analytical tool can be essentialist and has limitations, whereas 'the lived body is a unified idea of a physical body acting and experiencing in a specific socio-cultural context...' (Young, 2002: 415). Historically, gender analysis has also suffered from a bias towards the white, upper middle class experiences of women in the Global North. It is well worth interrogating the conceptual usefulness of gender in analysing lived experiences elsewhere, especially in post-colonial spaces, as Mohanty (1991) and Oyewumi (1997) do. Certainly, attempts to bring a gender analysis to development processes have been highly contested as explicated later.

Following Iris Marion Young's (2002) intervention in this debate however, I would retain the concept of gender for analysing social structures and institutions especially when it comes to sport-in-development. Young argues that in addition to exploring the meaning of lives and the normalizing discourses that can cause suffering, '[f]eminist and queer theories are also projects of social criticism. These are theoretical efforts to identify certain wrongful harms or injustices, locate and explain their sources in institutions and social relations, and propose directions for institutionally oriented action to change them. This latter set of tasks requires the theorist to have an account not only of individual experience, subjectivity and identity, but also of social structures' (Young, 2002: 419). Young goes on to propose three axes of gender structures: a sexual division of labour, normative hetero-sexuality and gendered hierarchies of power (422). These structures are historically and spatially specific and 'condition the actions and con-sciousness of individual persons,' shaping and constraining their choices, opportunities and resources (426). In this study, gender is viewed through these axes in complicated and varied ways to structure individuals' experiences of and relationship to sport. These axes also allow for comparative insights to differentiate between experiences in the Global North and Global South, and help frame the context is which the case study can be viewed.

Leaving aside theoretical complexity, casual acknowledgement of the fact of sport having gendered dimensions is common. This acknow-ledgement comes in the form of front page articles in the New York Times about high school girls in the United States wrestling and beating boys (Lewin, 2007), by Kenyans in the US who in early 2007 were surprised to learn that girls 'back home' are playing organized football, or by ESPN specials on the first NBA player, albeit former player, to come 'out of the closet' (Amaechi, 2007). Why is it that girls anywhere playing football (or indeed rugby, boxing, or wrestling women coaching boys) can still be surprising? Why is it newswoi that a professional basketball player is homosexual? These puzzles, get to the heart of a dilemma – 'Why, if women and girls do engage in sport, are they still marginalized or at best a "special case" in the dominant practices, ideologies and organizations concerned with sport?' (Saavedra, 2005b). Why is it normal for boys to 'do sports', but somehow remarkable for girls to 'do sports'? Why are the sporting boys presumed to be heterosexual? These are simple questions on which much has been written, but questions still persist. And, in the emerging institutionalized practices around sport-in-development, they are only partially addressed. There is a sense of the potential in using sport to address some of the inequalities and injustices faced by girls and women. Less appreciated are the more radical possibilities for altering gender relations, and the risks that may be encountered, especially as global hegemonic sporting structures are permeated with particular norms and expectations about gender.

In directly confronting the puzzle around females and what is perceived as 'normal' in sport around the world,[5] female involvement in sport has the power to upend what is seen/presented as 'normal' and become a major force for social change beyond sport by challenging gender norms. Many find that such changes are positive and to be applauded, even encouraged. Advocacy organizations such as Women Sport International, or various national level associations for women and sport provide incentives, awards and even legal aid. For many, women's sporting achievements are a vindication of a struggle, showing power and presence. In a nice capitalist twist, sports product manufacturers can use images of female athletes to sell products while instantly invoking a connection to a larger narrative of justice and social advancement (Cole and Hribar, 1995). Some will find the puzzle of women in sport uncomfortable because powerful women can be threatening and undermine a seemingly stable order. Indications of discomfort might include ridicule (e.g. the American 'shock jock' Don Imus' rants about the Rutgers University women's basketball team in April 2007)[6] or self-policing (the anti-competitive philosophies of female physical educators in the early 20th century United States).[7] Others simply will deem female athletes to be undesirable, even evil and worthy of opposition. Hence, the Football Association in England banned its affiliates from having anything to do with the 'evil' of women's football from 1921 to 1971 (Lopez, 1997; Williams, 2003). Public displays of athleticism by females can be proof of unwanted influences and the moral failings of a family or community. The popular film 'Bend it like Beckham' explores such sentiments. Girls' involvement in sport elicits reactions at multiple levels of consciousness and behaviour. It can mobilize observers either for or against it 'because they are girls'. Because of this 'power', this decentering effect, female involvement in sport can and has been deployed in the development process where particular changes in the social order affected by gender are sought.[8] As gender norms vary across time and space, this also opens up sport-in-development projects to cross-cultural misunderstandings and complications, a prospect returned to later.

Analysing the intersection of gender and sport is not just about females' involvement in sport. Considerable work has been done on masculinity and sport (Mangan, 2000; McKay *et al.*, 2000; Messner, 1992; Messner, 1990; Messner and Sabo, 1994; Nauright, 1997). In the world of sport-in-development however, 'gender' is usually only invoked when referring to the involvement of girls and women. This chapter would seem to reinforce that by focusing on a case study of an NGO using football for female empowerment. Some projects, such as those of the MYSA in Nairobi, do engage boys in querying existing gender structures seeking to get boys to see girls differently and change their behaviour (Brady and Banu Khan, 2002). Others engage boys in promoting women's health issues, such as a boys' football tournament in Khartoum, Sudan organized to highlight the campaign against female genital cutting (Gruenbaum, 2005). Many sport-in-development projects deal with post-conflict situations where participants experienced violence as victim, perpetrator or both. How much the gendered aspect of the violence and healing is explicitly explored in these projects would be the subject of another paper. I would suggest that attention to the impact of gender structures on the experiences of men and boys in sport would augment any sport-in-development project. For much of the world, though, the perceived normality of male participation sport means that an approach that explicitly and consistently addresses gender structures, for example, by a self-reflexive exploration of the meaning and performance of masculinities in the context of sport, or by engaging in a mixed sex sporting experience that privileges unfamiliar skills, would seem awkward. The work of those who have explored gender and sport suggest one reason for this: questions about sexuality emerge quickly and, for some, uncomfortably.

One of Young's axes, normative heterosexuality, is particularly visible in the realm of sport. The issue of sexuality, sport and behaviour is central, and it runs both along the heterosexual as well as homosexual dimensions, although the greatest concerns have much to do with the particular social moment in question with great variation across time and space. With women's involvement in sport, the sexuality question lurks right below the surface, with sport either making the person less of a woman (risking her fertility), or revealing her as something other (the 'L' word – a lesbian). Interestingly, sport-in-development projects regularly take on reproductive health problems, especially HIV-AIDS, and STIs (sexually transmitted infections). However, few sport-in-development projects as such do not deal with the issue of same-sex relationships, unless one counts the Gay Games and related queer sports teams and leagues since they explicitly invoke the language of change and empowerment. In a wide review of gender and sport projects, Mama Cash catalogued just a few sport projects geared towards lesbians in Belgium, the Netherlands, Brazil and South Africa. (van Beek and Leibman, 2007: 24, 29, 32–33, 35) However, such projects have not been embraced by the mainstream movement that is made visible in the UN/NGO development world. This particular query though jumps ahead of the analysis, which at this point turns in greater detail to the specific mix of gender and sport-in-development.

6.3   Gender and sport-in-development

Elsewhere, I have explored the nexus of gender and sport-in-development more generally, offering some historical background and an overview of activities (Saavedra, 2005b). This chapter is particularly inspired by a case study of one organization, Moving the Goalposts, Kilifi[9] in Kenya, though it is situated in a general context for assessing gender, sport and development. One important element in this analysis is to highlight a larger historicized framework drawing on critical development studies and gender studies. On the practical side, I seek to also evaluate specific programmes and projects, not only by considering 'best' approaches and practices, but also by paying attention to political and institutional location, and the opportunities and constraints created by that location. Admittedly, I am an advocate for women and girls in sport, and I am not an unbiased 'objective' observer. My perspective is also Africa centered, but not limited to the African continent.

The arguments that I want to emphasize are as follows. Undertaking 'gender, sport and development' projects is hard and serious work that occurs within a specific place and context. As such, it requires several areas of knowledge. First, and perhaps most important, is local knowledge, particularly of the local language(s), culture, history, and geography.

Second, sport-specific knowledge is crucial – love of sport is not enough.[10] This involves knowledge of particular sport as well as knowledge of training, coaching and mentoring. Likewise, as sport is paired with other developmental goals, specific knowledge in those areas (health, environment, conflict resolution, *etceteras*) is also required. Organizational, business, managerial and entrepreneurial skills are also required as are 'people skills'. These arguments mirror the seven conclusions that van Beek and Leibman came up with in their review of women-sport-and-development initiatives: 1) professionalize sports projects; 2) employ safety and security measures; 3) map the socio-cultural environment; 4) integrate women's full participation; 5) match sports activities to women's empowerment aims; 6) network; 7) make more data available (van Beek and Leibman, 2007: 3 and 17). Working at the intersection of gender and sport-in-development is inherently political, and thus potentially contentious and risky. As C.L.R. James spelled out in his account of West Indian cricket, sport can mobilize resources in ways that can create change, sometimes painfully (James, 1993). Hence, this is about *power*, and disrupting current distributions of power. At this juncture, some general context is warranted.

6.4   Historical context of gender and sport-in-development

One starting point in analysing the current gender and sport-in-development movement is to realize that it is not a new impulse that sport might be directed towards achieving ulterior social outcomes; rather it is *central* to the history of modern sport. The role of gender in sport as it is understood and practised today is linked with the rise of modern state. In very generic terms, at least by the early nineteenth century, the European state was concerned with the *physicality* of its agents and the general population. It was not only readiness for war that was at issue, but also hygiene and health. Sport has also been central to social movements such as 'muscular Christianity' in the Victorian era, and the establishment of organizations such as the Young Men's Christian Association or the YMCA. Certainly, the history of modern sport in the Global South has been marked by directed purposefulness. In the eras of colonialism and imperialism as emphasized in the Introduction to this publication, ruling powers used sport as a tool of change and 'discipline'. Rulers also sought to control sport to avoid subversion and resistance. Colonial subjects in turn adopted, adapted, modified, ignored, and rejected Western forms of sport.[11]

One small but important point here is that I hesitate to characterize the advent of modern sport in the Global South as the 'dissemination' of modern sport. I would suggest that modern sport was not 'disseminated' so much as there was a parallel emergence as well as some visceral links in the development of global modern sport. This is partly because without colonialism and imperialism there would not have emerged modern industry, and ultimately no global capitalism, important elements in the history of modern sport. How modern sport is understood (e.g., categorized, measured, competed) also developed in reference to the creation of others – and the *others* were not only other classes, but also those in other lands, often subjugated via imperialism. In some case there seems to be strands of a dialectic process underway to take the example of 'modern' high jumping techniques, *gusimbuka-urukiramende* and Ernst Jokl that John Bale elaborates in his 2002 book, *Imagined Olympians*.[12] However, as techniques and perceptions developed, what is true is that what has emerged is an international mode of sport that is dominated and signified by the Global North.

In this context, sport has followed many trajectories such that local influences have impacted the evolution of sport in one place, and may later be re-inscribed elsewhere.[13] Nevertheless, a western hegemony of institutions and structure remains though not without regular and continued contestation. Hence, sport carries historical and cultural baggage especially from its hegemonic core. I argue this is particularly true of the gendered system of sport in the Global North, which can be characterized by a hegemonic heterosexual hyper-masculinity that is situated within a consumerist, individualistic ethos. It is certainly posited against [almost] any homosexual visibility ruling out muscular femininity in a binary and exclusive definition of sexuality. While women's pursuit of sport is possible, it tends to be peripheral and always problematic. It also stands as a challenge to hegemonic norms of sexuality. One question though is whether women's sport *is always* problematic or not. Is this true everywhere? And, if so, why?

Hence, it is reiterated here that it is not new that sport should be used for social, political or economic goals. As highlighted in the introductory chapter, this chapter is concerned that the level of ahistoricism in the current articulation of sport and development reflects an unstated or thinking that sport is inherently 'good'. Alternatively in a more complicated iteration – 'our sport' is good and can be cordoned off from that which is bad. As Giulianotti writes, there are problems in any argument that considers sport *a priori* to be a force of good (Giulianotti, 2004: 356–357). He notes that some approaches are *functionalist* – 'sport meets crucial social needs'. However, it is evident to most, that sport can also be dysfunctional. Giulianotti is also concerned about 'Sport Evangelists' who in a neo-colonial repositioning, are transferring an impulse they developed at home to a very different setting overseas. Further, in his view, the effort seems to be skewed to youth (young men) while ignoring the needs of others, including women and the elderly. He interrogates the cross-cultural politics of sport human-itarianism with several questions. Has there been sufficient dialogue between donors and recipients of aid? Is empowerment of recipients a clear goal? Who 'owns' the projects? And centrally, what are the dynamics of power and meaning behind cross-cultural 'cooperation' between donor and recipients?

Following the work of Mauss (1967), Sahlins (1972), and Bourdieu (1977), Hattori (2003) offers insight to these questions with a useful analysis of development aid in the article, *Giving as a Mechanism of Consent: International Aid Organizations and the Ethical Hegemony of Capitalism*. When aid is given is reciprocity expected? Is there unequal power? Does the aid confirm status on the 'giver'? These questions help to understand the mechanism of consent involved. Hattori asserts that much of international aid serves to affirm the current logic of development assistance and unequal relations. It also infuses capitalist conditions with ethical meaning and allows for moral regulations (Hattori, 2003). And while the distinction should be made between 'gift' and entertainment expenses, it is often not in globally approved corporate accounting standards. Thus, FIFA's humanitarian budget in 2003 was £907,000 (US$1.84 million), while their budget for the FIFA inner circle for six weeks in Paris in the 1998 World Cup finals was £5 million (US$10.13 million) (Giulianotti, 2004).

In the debates on women and development, these struggles over definitions, representation, unequal power, consent and morality are continually waged (Cornwall *et al.*, 2007; Mohanty, 1991). The first wave of development theoretical work that acknowledged gender as a factor emerged in the 1970s. Known as Women in Development (WID), this analytical framework was essentially concerned that moderniza-tion was not only ignoring, but also marginalizing women as develop-ment 'progressed'. Advocates emphasized that women can and do make economic contributions, and they lobbied for women to be included in development projects. Employing a liberal approach of inclusion and equality, limitations were soon felt, and many felt WID did not adequately challenge patriarchy. A more radical approach appeared, Women and Development (WAD), which cautioned on the dangers of integrating women into patriarchy and instead advocated for women-only projects. The WAD approach though lent itself to marginalization and also ignored differences among women. In the 1980s and 1990s, the impact of neo-liberal and structural adjustment policies hit many hard. In response, a new paradigm emerged, Gender and Development (GAD), highlighted unequal power relations around the world between men and women, and focused on empowerment and gender analysis. Race, class, gender and global positioning are intertwined in this approach. Postmodernism has further impacted analytical frameworks leading to explorations of power and difference with close attention to the power of language and discourse that are refracted through global disparities. (Marchand and Parpart, 1995; Connelly *et al.*, 2000; Rathgeber, 1990; Jaquette, 1982).

The struggles over discourse, power, difference and morality are intense where gender meets development. The intimate connections between aid and moral regulation, for instance, are especially pronounced in development programmes that impact women's bodies as witnessed in power struggles over veiling, appropriate dress, female genital cutting, abortion, and family planning. Convictions of righteousness can obscure complexities and marginalize those who do not fit within preconceived categories. Win (2007) poignantly articulates how African middle class women have been 'silenced and erased from the images of development and rights work' (82), in favour of the 'poor, powerless, and invariably pregnant' barefooted African woman (79). This stereotype sells well, bringing in financial resources for aid agencies and ennobling those delivering aid. A beneficiary who wields agency becomes an oxymoron. 'Doing gender' itself has become a way of conferring status on development bureaucrats and organizations as competent and virtuous (Woodford-Berger, 2007: 122). Gender mainstreaming, following in the path of WID, WAD and GAD, has become the widely adopted buzzword for dealing with the 'woman question' in development work since the 1995 Beijing Conference on Women. It heralds the acceptance of a gender critique and diffusion of appropriate policy and practices throughout the development enterprise (Subrahmanian, 2007: 112).[14] Yet, it has morphed into a standardized approach in which all are responsible, yet none are accountable, (Mukhopadhyay, 2007: 140), allowing development actors to check off 'gender' from their to-do list. '...[G]ender is applied as a depoliticized, technical device, generating log frames and statistics, but doing little to challenge unjust gender relations. This is gender analysis denuded so that it ceases to challenge the patriarchal power of the development industry, and instead "adds value" to existing meta-narratives' (Mama, 2007: 153). Unequal relations within and outside of the development industry remain unchallenged and unchanged.

Much of the current rhetoric around the power of sport-in-development is reminiscent of colonial officers musing on civilizing unruly natives or technocrats pining for a 'modernized' (read de-traditionalized/de-tribalized), disciplined worker. Does sport contribute to a future for participants in which their needs are met and they are empowered? Or is sport only serving to develop participants who are more tightly enmeshed in a globalized economy, in which sport is one of many transnational consumptive industries?[15] Analysing the impact of the global commodity and labour chains associated with sport is outside the scope of this chapter. Yet recalling the complicated and contradictory gendered effects of global capitalism, foregrounding this in the analysis of gender and sport-in-development is critical, especially when on the reproductive side, woman are often centrally responsible for managing household consumption, and on the productive side, women's labour is so essential in the sport apparel industry. Here, two of Young's axes, the sexual division of labour in the home and the gendered hierarchies of power in the workplace and global chain, intersect powerfully.

In this context, a reflection on aid in Africa, where an overwhelming number of sport and development projects are located, is relevant. In many global fora the African represents what Hubbard and Mathers have called 'emaciated modernity,' where global capitalism has failed to transform, thus triggering sympathy, a burden of responsibility to care about Africa and contributing to 'the "just" notions of humanitarian aid and the regime of the NGO' (Hubbard and Mathers, 2004: 454). In their convincing analysis of the reality TV show, *Survivor Africa*, they expand on this, while also arguing that it is a particularly American problem:

> Africa is often dismissed in popular media as out of time and a failed project. We assert, however, that Survivor Africa places *an imagined Africa as central to an emerging discourse of a humanitarian American empire*, not a footnote to it, and that the history that makes this neo-liberal utopia possible is located in earlier colonial representations of Africa. Although this empire of the present cites these colonial images, it differs significantly in its mode of operation and ideal subject. *The neo-liberal utopia* that seeks to mediate America's relations with much of the rest of the world is just as *needful of*

discourses of humanitarianism as the empires of the 19th cent\
But while the Europeans sent missionaries and scientists to pave \
way for their commercial enterprises, Americans send NGOs and
development agencies (*emphasis added*) (445).

Even if the approach and historical ties are different, development
aid to Africa remains important throughout Europe, most recently
exemplified by the former British Prime Minister, Tony Blair and his
prioritization of Africa, despite entanglements elsewhere. Another
point of concern relevant to Africa is raised by Darnell who cautions
that current practices and institutions in the sport-in-development
movement may even (re)construct racialized privilege by producing
and constraining 'racial bodies and racial knowledge of Whiteness and
the Other' (Darnell, 2007).

6.5 Gender and sport in the Global South

Certainly with respect to sport and gender, there are powerful external
and global influences. (Note that global is distinct from external and
can be quite local).[16] Global influences include historical trajectories
and power configurations that determine which sporting codes are
practised and rewarded. As dance becomes more 'sportized' for instance,
it is the couples form and competitions, which emerged in Europe and
the Americas, that have gained notice and the moniker of 'World
Championships'[17] and not the competitive group dancing among
women that one finds in West Africa (Heath, 1994).

Beyond the particular sports practised, there are global discourses,
practices and policies that affect gender in both positive and negative
ways. Hence, the English Football Association's ban on women's football, from 1921 to 1971 directly affected the British colonies.[18] More
recently, FIFA and IOC mandates on gender inclusion and targeted
expenditures have affected behaviour and institutions. FIFA's 10% rule
in its Goal programme is one example, where a national football association is required to spend 10% (US$25,000) of aid received from the
programme per year on women's football.

It is clear that across time and space, there are different notions of the
body and mind, their balance, relative values, and gendered manifesta-
tions. The value of physical activity for instance can vary affecting how
the practice of sport by men, women, and children is understood. Here
the axis of gendered hierarchies is important. In China, for instance,
sport was historically not a male preserve. For the Imperial bureaucracy,

elite education emphasized mind over body. Sport was therefore better suited to women and lower-classes (see Riordan and Dong, 1996; Riordan and Jones, 1999; Brownell, 1995; Dong and Mangan, 1998). In contrast, in Darfur in the 1980s, some religious figures preached that women from 'good' Muslim families should not labour in the fields; in Khartoum, women riding bicycles were harassed. In Senegal in the late 1990s, the preferred female body types of the Drianke (socially powerful urban women) and the Disquette (upwardly mobile, young urban women) mitigated against an athletic muscularity for women.

There is an argument that the valences are just different and international success in sport trumps any reluctance to honour women. Thus many accomplished female athletes are heroes/heroines (gender-neutral) in their home-countries. In Nairobi, I was surprised by the casual acceptance and promotion in the media of a recent female boxing extravaganza 'The Africans versus the Americans' in November 2006. Further the *Daily Nation* (newspaper) featured on a regular basis many more articles on women's sports than the average U.S. paper. There were even features on the local Mombasa Women's Football League, in which the to-be-discussed MTG Superteam plays.

Gender is not always the most limiting factor for would be athletes. Education, class, age-group, and marriage status may play important roles. Women from wealthy and politically elite families in Northern Sudan for instance have consistently engaged in tennis and equestrian sports, despite cultural barriers to participation in sport. In various African countries, there are instances of women as referees in male sports, much more than in established male sports in the United States. This is so for basketball, football *and* wrestling in Senegal, and football in Kenya. Women's basketball has been one of most popular spectator sports in Senegal. Likewise, women's volleyball was the second most popular sport in Peru in the 1980s. In specific settings and times, opportunities for female participation in sport and the popularity of women's sport have flourished despite apparent gender barriers and hierarchies.

Nevertheless, this chapter assumes at least some association between sport and masculinity, if only because of the hegemonic presence of the Global North in the sporting world. In this association, there are gendered expectations that privilege male access to the organization and practice of sport in the majority of cases. Given this, one can postulate that female sport continues to be transgressive and potentially 'revolutionary.' It disrupts received notions about gender roles, and allows for new possibilities with positive spillovers for women in other social arenas. Truly, most projects are not just about sport, and have explicit goals outside of sport. They often tackle very specific ('plus sport') local problems, which can include:

1. Poverty, un(der)employment, weak/absent infrastructure
2. Family dislocation/dysfunction
3. Illiteracy and/or Schooling obstacles
4. Sexual violence (rape, incest)
5. Child labour/human trafficking
6. STIs, HIV-AIDs, other diseases
7. Drugs – use and trafficking
8. Limited rights and/or limited knowledge of rights
9. War, famine, environmental degradation, *etceteras*.

Most sport-in-development projects though are not explicitly designed with goals of changing or transgressing existing gender roles and expectations. As of March 2008, the International Platform on Sport and Development identified only thirty of the 264 total projects documented as somehow dealing with gender, and only thirty-four of the 264 as having some component targeted specifically towards girls and women.[19] Table 6.1 provides a sampling of the twenty of these 'gender' sport-in-development projects found in Africa (Twenty-one are categorized as targeting girls and women in Africa). While a full review of these projects is beyond the scope of this chapter, a review of the Platforms database reveals a wide variety of means and goals within these projects. Even among these though a focused gender analysis on the use of sport is not common.

The ILO project in Mozambique for instance does not necessarily involve women directly in sporting activities, but rather, organizes them through the local OlympAfrica sport centre in an income-generating cooperative to produce and sell groceries and school uniforms. (Sport and Development Platform, 2006b, Sport and Development Platform, 2006a). The Finnish funded LiiKe project in Tanzania seeks to improve school attendance of both boys and girls by developing school sport capacity and facilities. The reasoning is that improved facilities attract students and motivate teachers. Their goal is 'to involve every pupil and ensure equal opportunity to participate in sports regardless of *gender ability*.' [emphasis added] (Sports Development Aid, 2002). Kicking Aids Out, an international network of organizations, has developed a program to build awareness about HIV and AIDS through educational games and activities. Training mentors and peers educators is central. Women

Table 6.1   Sample of projects in Africa that have an explicit gender focus

Project	Organizer	Location
Football, social support and peer-led health education for rural teenage girls	Moving the Goalposts Kilifi	Kenya
Education through Sport	LiiKe (Sports Development Aid – Finland)	Tanzania
Go Sisters	Education through Sport (EduSport) Foundation	Zambia
Kicking AIDS Out! (International Network)	Commonwealth Games Canada (CGC)	various
NOC/ADEL Project of Women's Cooperatives in Boane	International Labour Organization (ILO)	Mozambique
Olympic Youth Ambassador Programme (OYAP) – Lesotho	Lesotho National Olympic Committee	Lesotho
Play Soccer	Play Soccer	Ghana, Senegal, South Africa, Zambia
Synergy and capacity building through sport and culture in Western Kenya	Danish Gymnastics and Sports Associations (DGI)	Kenya
U-Go-Girl	Sports Coaches' Outreach (SCORE)	Namibia, South Africa, Zambia
Women in Paralympic Sport (WIPS) Development Initiative	UK Sport	various countries in Africa

Source: Sport and Development International Platform project database, sportanddev.org, accessed April 5, 2006.

and girls are very involved, and the research of two graduate students on gender and sport in Africa is highlighted on their web site.[20] However, a focused gender analysis *per se* is not apparent in the online materials. In practice, when working with women and girls, the implementing organizations may have more directly confronted the nexus of gender and sport, undertaken analyses, articulated policies and lived the realities.

One could very well take a gender critical stance when working to include females in sports projects or even when working only with boys and men. A conscious, pro-active approach to gender is most obvious though in the projects that exclusively focus on girls and women, such as the WIPS Initiative, U-Go-Girl, Go Sisters and Moving the Goalposts where the language of empowerment and change is clear.

With all these sport-in-development projects the point is to *mobilize* people and resources through sport in a way that presumes the sporting experience will be a mechanism to change. Projects seek to create or take advantage of various modes of intervention, including:

1. Awareness via themed tournament and other events
2. 'Captive' audience for add-on events
3. Capacity building through organizing sport
4. Life skills through practice of sport
5. Health benefits through practice of sport
6. Demonstration effect – *Tunaweza!*[21]

The demonstration effect is especially valuable in changing essentialist perceptions and assumptions about gender, able-bodiedness, caste, class, *etceteras*. It is fitting that the motto of Moving the Goalposts is *Tunaweza* – Kiswahili for 'We can do it'. The organization employs multiple ways to build skills and capacity, and to ultimately demonstrate to the community and themselves alternative and powerful ways for women and girls to be socially engaged. In this lies the potential for change along Young's three axes of gender structures: the sexual division of labour, normative heterosexuality and gendered hierarchies of power.

6.6 Case study: moving the goalposts, empowering girls and changing gender structures

In late 2006 I visited the project, Moving the Goalposts, Kilifi, Coast Province Kenya, north of Mombasa. Its mission is 'to improve the social, economic and health status of women and girls' through involvement with football (Owuor, 2007: 5). In addition, I have been in communication with project staff for nearly two years on various details of their work. Their web site (www.mtgk.org), reports, newsletters and other publications have also contributed to my understanding of this organization. Moving the Goalposts is an intriguing organization, committed to developing a 'transparent and self critical organizational culture' while tackling difficult problems in a rapidly changing environment (van Dam, 2008; Owuor, 2007: 6).[22] Eventually, it will be the focus of extensive studies and ethnographic narratives. In the meantime, my encounter with MTG has led me to better understand the impact of a project combining gender, sport and development in a comparatively poor region, especially as I compare it with what I am familiar with in Senegal and Sudan as well as my own sporting experiences as an athlete, trainer, coach and single mother of two athletically inclined sons in the United States.

Kilifi is a district as well as a town in Coast Province. It is one of the least developed districts in Kenya, while Coast Province is itself one of the poorest provinces in the country and in which overall poverty has increased from 43.5% to 69.7% from 1992 to 2005/2006 (Hoorweg, 2000; Obwocha, 2006; KNBS, 2007).[23] Around 8% of the population is infected with HIV/AIDS, a higher than national average. 66% of the population lives below the poverty line (Belewa, 2005). The population is mostly Mijikenda, a cluster of people from discrete groups who politically came together in the 1930's, but there are also Swahili and other ethnic groups (Middleton, 2000: 103). Christianity, indigenous religions and Islam are all present. As a whole, Coast Province has a high degree of socio-cultural heterogeneity. This combined with a history as a British protectorate, opened it up to alienation of land and resources by absentee landlords and 'up-country' Kenyans, creating a form of internal colonization (Wolf, 2000: 132). The Mijikenda, have been particularly vulnerable to this and women carry much of this burden. With respect to the axis of gendered hierarchies, the situation is relatively stark. Kilifi's Gender Development Index is in the bottom 20% of districts in Kenya (36th out of 45) (Belewa, 2006: 2; Holte-McKenzie *et al.*, 2006: 366).[24] Within the Mijikenda, family power lies at intersection of patriarchy and gerontocracy. The Mijikenda tend to be patrilocal with polygyny possible.[25] Wives move in with their husband's extended family on a homestead, leaving their own families and networks. Senior male elders control major resources which include land, trees, and household property. Hence, married women are under direct control of both patrilineage elders and their wives. Women do have usufructuary rights[26] to land and some tree crops, but this is increasingly circumscribed by scarcity and adoption of individualizing principles of national land tenure reform (Ciekawy, 1999).

The region is a holiday destination for foreigners and wealthy Kenyans. Tourism and agriculture are the mainstay of the economy, but agricultural production does not generate nearly enough income.

'Traditionally', women were mainly engaged in agricultural labour. Now most households are reliant on wage income of young and middle-aged men. Struggles between men of the different generations are common. The conflicts are often deflected onto women, especially younger women who have married into the group. Women's cash income options are limited. Rural based women have few opportunities to earn cash income, and many have adopted rural-urban 'straddling' strategies. Those without education sell vegetables or palm thatch in market, become maids, do construction, or resort to prostitution (Ciekawy, 1999). In the current conditions of poverty, there is increased stress on families. They can become dislocated, disintegrated, and dysfunctional. There is a pervasive sense of precariousness of survival. This stress may account for the reported extensive domestic and sexual violence, as well as for alcohol related abuse.

Regarding education, Kenya made a bold move in 2003 by abolishing primary school fees. Nevertheless, families must pay for books, uniform, food, and transportation. Secondary school is not free, and most are boarding schools. The cost is out of reach for many families even if girls do pass exams with sufficiently high scores.

Women's power is circumscribed. The acute gender hierarchy combines with a sexual division of labour that leaves women particularly vulnerable in a stressed economy. Early marriages and teenage pregnancies are common for young women. Teenage girls show the highest rates of new HIV infection in Kenya. Poor women in Kilifi District have the lowest rates of both literacy (26.8%) and school enrollment (54.4%) in Kenya (Belewa, 2005; Holte-McKenzie *et al.*, 2006: 366) There are very few women leaders and decision makers in Kilifi. Girls are particularly culturally disempowered (Holte-McKenzie *et al.*, 2006: 371–374). Women do voice their complaints and can use gossip and divination among other means to address their concerns. There is also a strong historical female role model in Mektalili, a diviner and leader of 1914 Giriama war against the British colonialists (Ciekawy, 1999).

With respect to Young's axis of normative heterosexuality, it is important to recognize that local norms around sexuality are not the same as norms in the Global North (and even there, there is much diversity). Still, in Kenya, heterosexuality is assumed, homosexuality is illegal, and there is an overall dismissiveness towards the possibility of homosexuality. I have little knowledge of what space there may be for alternative sexualities in Kilifi District. Nevertheless, sexualities which go against the norm do exist in Kenya. A few scholars have written on this topic, and there are activist groups in Kenya (Amory, 1997; Barasa,

2007). The topic also periodically emerges in the media, such as at a provincial meeting in Mombasa on adolescence in April 2006, when the Health Minister Charity Ngilu said she was 'shocked by revelations that homosexuality among teenagers was rampant in Coastal towns,' and would refer the matter to the Cabinet (Ringa, 2006). In other parts of Africa in the realm of sport for women, vocalized concerns have not so much about sexuality and the possibility of homosexuality – although those are increasing[27] – as much as they have been about the effect on fertility, i.e., that athleticism might hurt fertility or conversely that participation in sport will increase the chances of an unwanted pregnancy (Saavedra, 2003). As indicated above, teenage pregnancy is a particular problem in Kilifi District and results from difficulties girls and women face on all three axis – the sexual division of labour, gendered hierarchies and a particular kind of normative heterosexuality. In the United States, studies indicate that girls' involvement in sport reduces the chance of teenage pregnancy (Sabo *et al.*, 1998). As a result of a high rate of teen pregnancy in Kilifi District, officials are keen to lower it. Involvement in sport may be a way to do this, but it will take changes along all three axes.

6.6.1   History of Moving the Goalposts

The organization, Moving the Goalposts (MTG), was established in 2000 by Sarah Forde Owuor and local educational and development officers. It expanded from one to five staff members in 2005, including a project coordinator, Margaret Belewa, who has extensive development experience. There is significant volunteer work from a local advisory board, UK based supporters and most importantly, from the participants themselves. MTG has received funding from the Ford Foundation, Plan International and Alistair Berkley Trust among others. The stated focus of MTG is:

1. Mobilizing and empowering girls and women through football
2. Developing their self-esteem, confidence, teamwork and organization skills
3. Peer education on reproductive health and problem solving
4. Capacity-building in community through developing skills of individuals

Major problems identified by girls in informal conversations include: paying for school fees; the necessity of bringing home income to share with family; and eating – figuring out where a meal will come from as they lack the cash to eat out or provide for themselves when participating in football activities. Issues raised by participants during MTG monitoring and evaluation (M & E) visits to schools also include STI's, wife beating, rape, and incest.

MTG's programme is centered on football organized in an extensive grassroots effort with over 150 teams for nearly 3000 girls and women that play in tournaments (MTGK, 2008). There are two more formally organized leagues with on-going play, one for open age with 25 teams and another league for under-twelve-year-old players with 29 teams (Belewa, 2006). Girls' committees organize teams, leagues, tournaments and commemorative events. They also undertake the training of referees and coaches. Peer education and mobile video shows are central components of their method in tackling poverty and for empowering girls. Peer education topics covered include: reproductive health (adolescence menstruation, HIV-AIDS and STIs), decision making, assertiveness, problem-solving, girls' rights and gender-based violence. Girls develop skits, poems and raps to deliver messages. MTG provides training in public speaking. MTG also stresses community involvement, including volunteering at orphanages and working with other organizations in the community on events such as World AIDS Day. In early 2008, MTG participants most who are very poor themselves, took clothes, sanitary pads, blankets, and food they collected to the Red Cross for distribution to those internally displaced after the post-election violence (Owuor, 2008c). A new collaborative project addresses a major barrier for girls and women – affordable and hygienic sanitary protection. Lacking this, girls and women miss days of school and work and are less likely to participate in sport. MTG has teamed with The Kids League in Uganda (www.kidsleaguefoundation.org), and a secondary school in Marsabit, Kenya, to work with Dr. Moses Musaazi of Makerere University in Uganda to produce affordable sanitary pads out of local papyrus reeds. At the feasibility stage now, they aim for this social enterprise to help girls attend school regularly, play sports and provide income and employment (Owuor, 2008b; Isingoma, 2006).

True to an emphasis throughout the development industry, MTG has taken seriously a programme of monitoring and evaluation (Holte-McKenzie *et al.*, 2006). For MTG, this is a participatory endeavour with an emphasis on process, though outcome is also important. A volunteer team collects and analyses information on 'the football experiences of girls; the impact of football on their life skills; and the sexual and reproductive health needs of girls' (Owuor, 2007: 4). The girls on the volunteer team gain important life skills and experience through the development of the M & E tools, data collection and evaluation. The M & E process also provides for quick feedback and adjustments in the implementation of *programme* components, such as a modification to the selection method for best player from match reports to team mate votes (Owuor, 2007: 15). Another part of MTG's M & E *programme* is a Life Stories project encouraged by the Ford Foundation Nairobi office and conducted by Sarah Forde Owuor with several girls over a two year period.

An emerging area of conscious focus for MTG is the development of organizational, business, and management skills. MTG seeks out and offers training in peer education, office and computer skills, and curriculum development. Participants also gain work experience through volunteering with MTG in the field and in office. MTG has just begun a new process of educational support, by assisting a former staff member now attending university.

6.6.2 Outcomes for MTG

A major outcome is that MTG has survived eight years and has grown significantly. They have increased the number of players and teams, sustained league play and tournaments, formed open age and under 12 super teams, gained media exposure, produced a newsletter, developed a web-site (www.mtgk.org), raised funds successfully, and developed a robust governing structure and volunteer network. Two hundred and thirty-seven girls have been trained as coaches, 136 as referees, 33 as first aiders, 82 as peer educators and 100 girls in other leadership roles. Ten girls have recently been trained as counsellors. The open age 'Superteam' has competed successfully in several tournaments in Mombasa and Nairobi. In 2007, the 'MTG United Under 16s won the national Mombasa Show tournament and 8 players from MTG were selected for the Coast Province girls' football primary schools team which won the national finals in Nairobi' (Owuor, 2008a). One player was selected as one of two young athletes to represent Kenya in a youth forum at the All-Africa Games in Algeria (Owuor, 2008c). As indicated above, an extensive participatory and self-defined M & E process is currently underway to assess the impact of specific *programmes* (Owuor, 2007). MTG has also networked nationally and regionally, sending staff members to learn from other organizations around the continent and elsewhere. With their collaborative sanitary pad project and a project to advocate nationally and regionally for women's football, they are also finalists in a 2008 global Internet competition to find the best projects using sport for 'a better world' (Owuor, 2008b).

What is less clear is how significantly their work has moved them along the three axes or other structures around them. Other girls' teams have formed in nearby towns and villages – is this part of the demonstration effect from MTG? Or are they all a manifestation of or convergence with other processes such as FIFA's encouragement of women's football globally? Can other changes in the local area be attributed to MTG's work? The best answers will be likely to come from the on-going M & E process within MTG. However, as discussed in Coalter's chapter in this publication, measuring social change is inherently difficult. Furthermore, as the political crisis in early 2008 in Kenya makes plain, particular institutions (overly powerful executive, weak legislature) and social structures (wide gap between masses and wealthy elite) can severely limit the efficacy of individuals and groups. Worse, the failures of such structures can eliminate gains in an instant.

6.6.3   Challenges and obstacles

It is often the mundane experiences encountered while working with current infrastructure of the regions which consume time, funds and ingenuity. As I found for female athletes in Dakar, Senegal, transportation is a major issue for the girls and the organization. Lack of reliable affordable and safe transportation creates regular difficulties in carrying out daily activities, practices, games, and peer education. In their 2006 M & E assessment, transport problems were raised repeatedly (Owuor, 2007). In that report, another quotidian concern emerged – lunch. In the 2006–2007 season, when the superteam travelled to games, lunch was not provided. Players were not only hungry, but discontented with their coaches. There was discomfort in their relationship with their parents from whom players have to beg for money (Owuor, 2007: 26).

The difficulty of melding the girls into teams is also not to be discounted. Using participatory rural appraisal techniques (e.g., fact sheets and problem trees) in visits with several teams, the M & E team discovered a key problem for the football teams: players were not turning up for practice. While external issues such as difficulties at home, too much school work and lack of money or permission constitute some of the reasons, internal team dynamics are reportedly a greater cause of no-shows. These internal factors include a lack of football skills or a coach, and disagreements, poor attitudes and a lack of respect for each other. Some drop out either because they finished at the school where the team was based or they became pregnant (Owuor, 2007: 14 and 27). Another problem which annoyed team mates was that some girls used football as an excuse to dodge other duties and expectations from their families.

Communication among and with girls is also problematic. By sharing experiences they are gaining confidence locally and among themselves, but not necessarily in other settings. It is hard for them to assert themselves with presumed authorities. Even among themselves, when encouraged to participate fully, power relations functioned such that younger girls and those with less education would defer to others (Holte-McKenzie *et al.*, 2006: 371). There is also the stumbling block of their expectations on outsiders and those perceived with more power, which sometimes takes on the feel of a dependency syndrome.

The football infrastructure in the country is also a major obstacle. For the past few years and particularly in late 2006, the Kenyan Football Federation (KFF) has been in disarray. Suspended by FIFA, disbanded by the government, with factions, accusations, court cases, corruption rampant, the likelihood of much organized assistance from the larger football community is unlikely any time soon, though a local Mombasa based league with a corporate sponsor helped, but only for the 2006–2007 season. The MTG Superteam finished second in that league in January 2007. The league was important for the girls and the organization gave them exposure. A few of the girls and one in particular have been noted in the media as being good enough for the national team. However, with the current KFF dysfunction, there will be few options for girls who desperately want to continue with football. Despite efforts of various advocates for women's football since the 1980s, the lack of will and continuity from year to year in regional and national leagues stands as a major discouragement. On the axis of gendered hierarchy, the football establishment is such that women and girls are almost entirely locked out of the formal structures in Kenya. MTG however, is not shying away from this and has stepped in to take a leadership role to seek change directly in KFF.

Another question is what will happen when other NGOs, some with deep pockets and international stature, albeit without as much local experience, enter the district, promoting women's football. The ideal would be for them to collaborate and build on each other's strengths. An organizational clash of cultures though is likely along the way. With the popularity of sport-in-development such projects will continue to appear. Like the KFF leagues though, without commitment to the use of sport and all the mundane work that goes into supporting a dedicated sporting operation combined with development goals, sustainability in the long run is questionable. Sport-in-development may be like many other development fads that come and go.

6.7 Conclusion

Undertaking gender and sport-in-development projects is hard and serious work. Elsewhere I have discussed general considerations in such efforts (Saavedra, 2005a; Saavedra, 2005b). Theoretically and practically, there is much to navigate. While being familiar with contemporary theories and debates on gender and development is useful, here I will emphasize again the importance of integrating four areas of knowledge. The most important is local knowledge, particularly of the local language(s), culture, history, and geography. Also required is knowledge of sport, of the particular development sector targeted and of organizational management. It is a given, though maybe under-appreciated, that working at the intersection of sport, gender and development is inherently political, and thus potentially contentious and risky. Invoking C.L.R. James again, sport can mobilize resources in ways that can create change, in ways that create and challenge structures of power.

Understanding the praxis of gender, sport and development will continue to evolve. Further evidence from this and other projects must be collected and evaluated. The work of the Moving the Goalposts M & E team will in time be one of the best sources for evaluating the efficacy of this sort of work. That it will be produced by the girls themselves is one of the best outcomes anticipated.

Notes

1 Go Sisters 'aims at empowering girls by training them to become youth peer coaches and leaders, involving them at all levels of planning and implementation, providing them with EduSport school and college scholarships etc' (Mwaanga, 2004: 5). The EduSport website, www.edusport.org.zm, had been down for several months at the end of 2007 to 2008, apparently while the NGO was undergoing reorganization, though the organization is still active.
2 '...[G]ender is not a noun', but 'proves to be performative...constituting the identity it is purported to be. ...[G]ender is always a doing...There is no gender identity behind the expressions of gender; that identity is performatively constituted by the very 'expressions' that are said to be its results' (Butler, 1990: 24–25).
3 The term 'subjectivity' is used in many ways. My meaning here refers to how a person's experiences and perceptions of the world influence her understanding of self and place in the social world.

4 Moi's work in her 2001 collection *What is a Woman and Other Essays* is an attempt to move beyond the poststructuralists' critique of the Anglophone feminists' sex-gender binary. She finds that the critique creates confusion about sex, gender and the body. Her alternative concept of the 'lived-body' draws on the work of Simone de Beauvoir. Her concern is very much with theory that helps people understand and describe their experiences so as to deal with lived problems. Following de Beauvoir, she emphasizes that 'one of the many possible answers to the question 'What is a woman?' is 'a human being,' (Moi, 2001: 8).

5 I do not presume that the relationship between sport and gender is the same every around the world, and have written against this assumption elsewhere (Saavedra, 2005a).

6 Don Imus, a well-known American shock jock, had a long-running talk show, *Imus in the Morning,* on New York's WFAN radio station. It was syndicated by CBS and simulcast on MSNBC television across the United States. During the 2007 NCAA Basketball Championships, he called the Rutgers women's team, who had made it to the finals, 'nappy-headed hos'. The racist and sexist comment and the conversation as a whole stirred a controversy that resulted in CBS firing him. Rutgers lost the final to Tennessee. The incident led to a national debate on race and speech; there was much less interrogation of the meaning of the remarks with respect to female athletes.

7 In the early 20th century, women physical education professionals developed a philosophy and *programme* for women's sport that sought a space and value system for women's sport separate from men's sport, deemed to be corrupt, commercial, aggressive and elitist. From within white, middle class institutions, the emphasis was non-elitist, minimally competitive, and advocating sports-for-all. Activities were 'appropriate' for girls and avoided 'mannish' tendencies. I have summarized an account of this in my chapter, 'Sport' in *A Companion to Gender Studies* (2005a). For more in depth accounts, see Cahn (1994), Hult (1994), Festle (1996) and Guttmann (1991). An insightful analysis of the impact of these US based physical education teachers on the struggle over 'girl's rules' in basketball in Western Canada can be found in Job and Vertinsky (2008).

8 Indeed, it is also the other way around. In a major 2007 publication on women and development practice, the contradictions inherent in practices and policies is represented on the front cover by a picture of young women in Islamic dress in an urban alley holding footballs. Nowhere in the text though is the issue of women, sport and development addressed (see Cornwall *et al.*, 2007).

9 For details see www.mtgk.org.

10 I find troubling some tour companies who offer a working vacation where one can 'give' to a poor community through sport, but 'You don't need any qualifications to coach sports, just a knowledge of the game', (www.travvellersworldwide.com/13-kenya/13-kenya-sports-diani.htm) accessed 16/2/07.

11 There is a vast literature on the history of modern sport and a growing literature on the history of non-Western sport. In addition to Mangan and Mujumdar's work cited in the introduction, examples of some of this literature

include, Alegi (2004), Arnaud (1998), Baker and Mangan (1987), Bale and Sang (1996), Darby (2002), Deville-Danthu (1997), and Hargreaves (1997).

12 As what became labeled as the modern technique of high jumping was developed in Europe, sport scientists such as Jokl were simultaneously investigating the physical culture of others, including 'jumpers' in what is now Rwanda and Burundi. Bale's work suggests this juxtaposition was not a coincidence, but part of a coherent process of defining modern technique.

13 An example is the influence of South American players on Italian and Spanish soccer in the mid-20th Century. See Chapter 3, 'The South American Artists' in Lanfranchi and Taylor (2001).

14 It follows earlier approaches starting in the 1970s with 'women in development' followed by 'women and development' and then 'gender and development'.

15 Some may argue that these are not mutually exclusive.

16 Local actors for instance can be the agents of global influence as they serve as exchange points for goods, ideas, idioms, fashions and practices that flow in and out of a community. 'Locals' may also operate transnationally to provide support for the continuation of locally defined practices.

17 I am likely outside my element and speak of something I have only observed briefly. There appear to several organizations vying for primacy (as in boxing and commercialized wrestling). And perhaps if I searched more carefully I would find a category of World Championships in African dancing.

18 I found a quote once on a very direct effect in Port Harcourt in Nigeria in the 1920s, but I have since lost the source. England's FA supposedly just recently (February 2008) apologized for the 50 year ban, though some have their doubts about the nature of the FA's statement (Doyle, 2008).

19 http://www.sportanddev.org/en/projects/index.htm, accessed 19 March 2008.

20 Mwaanga (2003) and Maro (in progress). See http://www.kickingaidsout. net/5-3_body.htm. Accessed 19 March 2008.

21 Kiswahili for 'We can do it'.

22 The fact that they are so transparent, sharing so much information in person and online, has made it possible for me to learn so much more about Moving the Goalposts than I would have been able to if I were relying solely on my two-week visit. One of the problems in the development industry is the 'parachuting-in' model of accruing knowledge. Short visits and lots of reading, do not an expert make. Ultimately, I am sure I am still misconstruing aspects of MTG and its work. I trust the participants themselves will produce the definitive record of MTG's story and contributions.

23 Another publication puts the poverty incidence in Coast Province at 57.6% in 2006. (Central Bureau of Statistics *et al.*, 2006).

24 The Gender Development Index follows the same dimensions and indicators as the Human Development Index but adds the difference in achievements between men and women. A lower GDI relative to HDI indicates a higher level of gender disparity. In Kenya as a whole the GDI is 0.521 and is equal to the HDI. This means that on the average there is relative equality at a national level between men and women. However, Kenya's HDI places it 148th out of 177 countries with data available. (UNDP, 2007).

25 'Patrilocal' is an anthropological term that refers to the wife relocating to her husband's family home. Also, in Coast Province, 8.7% of marriages are

polygamous, the second highest among provinces. Northeastern Province had a higher incidence of overall poverty (73.9%) as well as a higher rate of polygamous marriages (13.2%) in 2005/2006 (Obwocha, 2006, pp. 14 and 40).

26   Usufructuary rights mean that they have the right to access the land for certain uses, but they do not have complete control over the disposition or use of the land.

27   For example in 2005 in South Africa, a clash took place in the media between a female football official and the captain of the national women's football team, Banyana Banyana. The official questioned the 'femininity' of the team while the captain shot back that whether they were lesbians or not did not matter. What they needed was support for their playing. See Saavedra, 2005.

Bibliography

Alegi, P. (2004) *Laduma!: soccer, politics and society in South Africa*. Scottsville, South Africa: University of KwaZulu-Natal Press.

Amaechi, J. (2007) 'John Amaechi Busts Out; Excerpt from "Man in the Middle"'. *ESPN The Magazine*. 26 February 2007, http://sports.espn.go.com/nba/news/story?page=espnmag/amaechi&campaign=rss&source=ESPNHeadlines (accessed on 28th February 2007).

Amory, D.P. (1997) '"Homosexuality" in Africa: Issues and Debates'. *Issue: A Journal of Opinion*, 25(1), 5–10.

Arnaud, P. and Riordan, J. (1998) *Sport and international politics*. London and New York: E & FN Spon.

Baker, W.J. and Mangan, J.A. (1987) *Sport in Africa: essays in social history*. New York, Africana Pub. Co.

Bale, J. (2002) *Imagined Olympians: body culture and colonial representation in Rwanda*. Minneapolis: University of Minnesota Press.

Bale, J. and Sang, J. (1996) *Kenyan running: movement culture, geography, and global change*. London and Portland, OR: F. Cass.

Barasa, L. (2007) 'Kenya: Gays And Lesbians Step Out to Demand Rights'. *The Nation*. Nairobi, 26 January 2007. http://allafrica.com/stories/200701251091.html (accessed on 1 March 2008).

Belewa, M. (2005) 'Annual Report'. Kilifi, Kenya, Moving the Goalposts.

Belewa, M. (2006) 'Annual Report – Tunaweza'. Kilifi, Kenya, Moving the Goalposts. January–December 2006.

Bourdieu, P. (1977) *Outline of a Theory of Practice*. New York: Cambridge University Press.

Brady, M. and Banu Khan, A. (2002) *Letting Girls Play: The Mathare Youth Sports Association's Football Program for Girls*. New York: Population Council.

Brownell, S. (1995) *Training the Body for China: Sports in the Moral Order of the People's Republic*. Chicago: University of Chicago Press.

Butler, J. (1990) *Gender Trouble: Feminism and the Subversion of Identity*. New York: Routledge.

Butler, J.P. (1993) *Bodies that Matter: On the Discursive Limits of 'Sex'*. New York: Routledge.

Cahn, S.K. (1994) *Coming on Strong: Gender and Sexuality in Twentieth-Century Women's Sport*. New York: Free Press.

Central Bureau of Statistics, The World Bank, SIDA & SID (2006) 'Geographic Dimensions of Well-Being in Kenya: Who and Where Are the Poor? A Constituency Level Profile, Volume II'. Nairobi, p. 80.

Ciekawy, D. (1999) 'Women's Work and Witchcraft Accusations'. *Women's Studies International Forum*, **22**(2), 225–235.

Cole, C.L. and Hribar, A. (1995) 'Celebrity Feminism – Nike Style Post-Fordism, Transcendence, and Consumer Power'. *Sociology of Sport Journal*, **12**(5), 347–369.

Connelly, M.P., Li, T.M., MacDonald, M. and Parpart, J.L. (2000) 'Feminism and Development: Theoretical Perspectives', in Parpart, J.L., Connelly, M.P. and Barriteau, E. (eds) *Theoretical Perspectives on Gender and Development*. Ottawa, International Development Research Centre, pp. 51–159.

Cornwall, A., Harrison, E. and Whitehead, A. (2007) *Feminisms in development: contradictions, contestations and challenges*. London and New York, New York, Zed Books; Distributed in the USA exclusively by Palgrave Macmillan.

Darby, P. (2002) *Africa, Football, and FIFA: Politics, Colonialism, and Resistance*. London and Portland OR: F. Cass.

Darnell, S.C. (2007) 'Playing with Race: 'Right to Play' and the Production of Whiteness in 'Development through Sport', *Sport in Society*, **10**(4), 560–579.

Deville-Danthu, B. (1997) *Le sport en noir et blanc: du sport colonial au sport africain dans les anciens territoires français d'Afrique occidentale (1920–1965)*. Paris: L'Harmattan.

Dong, J. and Mangan, J.A. (1998) 'Gender Relations in Chinese Sports: Continuity and Change in Traditional Gender Culture'. *International Sociological Association (ISA) Annual Conference*. 26 July–1 August 1998.

Doyle, J. (2008) 'FA Apologizes for its Sexism and Homophobia? Really?' *From A Left Wing*. London. http://fromaleftwing.blogspot.com/2008/02/fa-apologizes-for-its-sexism-and-.html (accessed on 1 March 2008).

Essed, P., Kobayashi, A. and Goldberg, D.T. (2004) 'Introduction', in Essed, P., Kobayashi, A. and Goldberg, D.T. (eds) *A Companion to Gender Studies*. London: Blackwell Publishing, pp. 1–25.

Festle, M.J. (1996) *Playing Nice: Politics and Apologies in Women's Sports*. New York: Columbia University Press.

Giulianotti, R. (2004) 'Human Rights, Globalization and Sentimental Education: The Case of Sport', *Sport in Society: Cultures, Commerce, Media, Politics*, **7**(3), 355–369.

Gruenbaum, E. (2005) 'Bumps on the Road to Freedom from Female Genital Cutting', *Civil Wars in Sudan: Casualties, Displacements, and Injustices, 24th Annual Meeting of the Sudan Studies Association*. York University, Toronto. 18 August 2005.

Guttmann, A. (1991) *Women's Sports: A History*. New York: Columbia University Press.

Hargreaves, J. (1997) 'Women's sport, development, and cultural diversity: the South African experience', *Women's Studies International Forum*, **20**(2), 191–209.

Hattori, T. (2003) 'Giving as a Mechanism of Consent: International Aid Organizations and the Ethical Hegemony of Capitalism', *International Relations*, **17**(2), 153–173.

Heath, D. (1994) 'The Politics of Appropriateness and Appropriation: Recontextualizing Women's Dance in Urban Senegal', *American Ethnologist*, **21**(1), 88–103.

Holte-McKenzie, M., Forde, S. and Theobald, S. (2006) 'Development of a participatory monitoring and evaluation strategy', *Evaluation and Program Planning*, 29(4), 365–376.

Hoorweg, J., Foeken, D. and Obudho, R.A. (2000) *Kenya Coast Handbook: Culture, Resources and Development in the East African Littoral.* Münster: Lit Verlag.

Hubbard, L. and Mathers, K. (2004) 'Surviving American empire in Africa: The anthropology of reality television', *International Journal of Cultural Studies*, 7(4), 441–459.

Hult, J.S. (1994) 'The story of women's athletics: Manipulating a dream 1890–1985', in Costa, D.M. and Guthrie, S.R. (eds) *Women and Sport: Interdisciplinary Perspectives.* Champaign IL: Human Kinetics, pp. 83–106.

Isingoma, J. (2006) 'Makapads: Makerere University Makes Affordable Sanitary Pads', *UG Pulse: The Pulse of Uganda.* 16 December 2006. http://www.ugpulse.com/articles/daily/homepage.asp?ID=549 (accessed on 17 February 2008).

James, C.L.R. (1993) *Beyond a Boundary.* Durham: Duke University Press.

Jaquette, J.S. (1982) 'Women and Modernization Theory: A Decade of Feminist Criticism', *World Politics*, 34(2), 267–284.

Job, C. and Vertinsky, P. (2008) 'Order on the Court: Vancouver Girls Rule', in Bandy, S.J., Hofmann, A.R. and Krüger, A. (eds) *Gender, Body and Sport in Historical and Transnational Perspectives.* Hamburg: Verlag Dr. Kovač, pp. 105–118.

Kenya National Bureau of Statistics (KNBS)(2007) 'Kenya Facts and Figures'. Nairobi. http://www.cbs.go.ke/downloads/kff2007.htm?SQMSESSID=5b515544d4d17c39114b88cef9a0e6d0 (accessed on 16 February 2008), pp. 1–92.

Lanfranchi, P. and Taylor, M. (2001) *Moving with the Ball: The Migration of Professional Footballers.* Oxford; New York: Berg.

Laqueur, T.W. (1992) *Making Sex: Body and Gender from the Greeks to Freud.* Cambridge, Mass.: Harvard University Press.

Lewin, T. (2007) 'In Twist for High School Wrestlers, Girl Beats Boy', *New York Times.* National ed. New York. February 17, 2007. pp. A1, A13.

Lopez, S. (1997) *Women on the Ball: A Guide to Women's Football.* London: Scarlet Press.

Mama, A. (2007) 'Critical connections: feminist studies in African contexts', in Cornwall, A., Harrison, E. and Whitehead, A. (eds) *Feminisms in Development: Contradictions, Contestations and Challenges.* London; New York, and New York, Zed Books; Distributed in the USA exclusively by Palgrave Macmillan, pp. 150–160.

Mangan, J.A. (2000) *Making European Masculinities: Sport, Europe, Gender.* London and Portland OR.: Frank Cass.

Marchand, M.H. and Parpart, J.L. (eds) (1995) *Feminism/Post-modernism/Development.* London and New York: Routledge.

Maro, C.N. (in progress) 'Gender difference on cognitive, motivational and affective responses within Tanzanian PE context. An achievement goal approach'. PhD Thesis, Norwegian University of Sport and Physical Education (Norges Idrettshøgskole). Oslo.

Mauss, M. (1967) *The Gift: Forms and Functions of Exchange in Archaic Societies.* New York: Norton.

McKay, J., Messner, M.A. and Sabo, D.F. (2000) *Masculinities, Gender Relations, and Sport.* Thousand Oaks Calif.: Sage Publications.

Messner, M.A. (1990) 'When bodies are weapons: Masculinity and violence in Sport', *International Review for the Sociology of Sport*, 25(3), 203–220.

Messner, M.A. (1992) *Power at Play: Sports and the Problem of Masculinity*. Boston: Beacon Press.

Messner, M.A. and Sabo, D.F. (1994) *Sex, Violence & Power in Sports: Rethinking Masculinity*. Freedom CA: Crossing Press.

Middleton, J. (2000) 'The Peoples', in Hoorweg, J., Foeken, D. and Obudho, R.A. (eds) *Kenya Coast Handbook: Culture, Resources and Development in the East African Littoral*. Münster: Lit Verlag, pp. 101–114.

Mohanty, C.T. (1991) 'Under Western Eyes: Feminist Scholarship and Colonial Discourses', in Mohanty, C.T., Russo, A. and Torres, L. (eds) *Third World Women and the Politics of Feminism*. Bloomington and Indianapolis: Indiana University Press, pp. 51–80.

Moi, T. (2001) 'What is a Woman? Sex, Gender, and the Body in Feminist Theory', *What is a Woman and Other Essays*. Oxford: Oxford University Press, pp. 3–120.

MTGK (2008) 'Our Projects: Football, Leadership and Life Skills Project'. http://mtgk.org/pro_fll.html (accessed on 10 October 2007).

Mukhopadhyay, M. (2007) 'Mainstreaming gender or 'streaming' gender away: feminists marooned in the development business', in Cornwall, A., Harrison, E. and Whitehead, A. (eds) *Feminisms in Development: Contradictions, Contestations and Challenges*. London; New York, and New York, Zed Books; Distributed in the USA exclusively by Palgrave Macmillan, pp. 122–135.

Mwaanga, O. (2003) 'HIV/Aids at risk adolescent girls empowerment through participation in top level football and Edusport in Zambia'. *Sport and Exercise Psychology*. Masters Thesis, Norwegian University of Sport and Physical Education (Norges Idrettshøgskole). Oslo, pp. 1–139.

Mwaanga, O. (2004) 'Project Document'. Lusaka, EduSport Foundation 3 April 2004. http://www.globalgiving.com/pfil/1647/projdoc.doc (accessed on 29 February 2008), pp. 1–8.

Nauright, J. (1997) 'Masculinity, Muscular Islam and Popular Culture: 'Coloured' Rugby's cultural symbolism in working-class Cape Town c. 1930–70', *The International Journal of the History of Sport*, 14(1), 184–190.

Obwocha, H.O. (2006) 'Key Findings on the Socioeconomic Characteristics and on Poverty Estimates from the Kenya Integrated Household Budget Survey (KIHBS) May 2005–May 2006'. Nairobi, Ministry for Planning and National Development. http://www.cbs.go.ke/speeches/minister/pdf/Launch%20of%20 KIHBS%20Basic%20Report.pdf?SQMSESSID=3d855668454e60a8ea251ba1d22 62566 (accessed on 15 February 2008), pp. 1–64.

Owuor, S.F. (2007) 'Monitoring and Evaluation of MTGK Strategic Plan 2006'. Kilifi, Moving the Goalposts. January 2007. http://www.globalgiving.com/ pfil/1696/projdoc.doc (accessed on 1 March 2008), pp. 1–46.

Owuor, S.F. (2008a) 'MTG Annual Report for Global Giving – Highlights of 2007'. Kilifi, Moving the Goalposts. January 2008. http://www.globalgiving. com/pfil/1696/MTG%20Annual%20Report%202007%20for%20GG.doc (accessed on 1 March 2008).

Owuor, S.F. (2008b) 'Tunaweza (Kiswahili: We Can Do It!)', in Ashoka Changemakers (ed.) *Entry in Sport for a Better World Competition*. http://www.change-makers.net/en-us/node/2672 (accessed on 20 January 2008).

Owuor, S.F. (2008c) 'Updates from the Field to Global Giving'. Kilifi, Moving the Goalposts. January 2008. http://www.globalgiving.com/pr/1700/proj1696d. html (accessed on 1 March 2008).

Oyewumi, O. (1997) *The Invention of Women: Making an African Sense of Western Gender Discourses*. Minneapolis: University of Minnesota Press.

Rathgeber, E.M. (1990) 'WID, WAD, GAD: Trends in Research and Practice', *The Journal of Developing Areas*, 24(4), 489–502.

Ringa, M. (2006) 'Kenya: issue of homosexuality among Coastal youths', *The East African Standard*. Nairobi. 16 December 2006. http://myafrica.wordpress. com/2006/12/16/kenya-issue-of-homosexuality-among-coastal-youths/ (accessed on 1 March 2008).

Riordan, J. and Dong, J.X. (1996) 'Chinese women and sport: Success, sexuality and suspicion', *China Quarterly*, 145, 130–152.

Riordan, J. and Jones, R. (1999) *Sport and Physical Education in China*. London; New York: E & FN Spon.

Saavedra, M. (2003) 'Football feminine – Development of the African game: Senegal, Nigeria and South Africa', *Soccer and Society*, 4(2), 225–253.

Saavedra, M. (2005a) 'Sport', in Essed, P., Kobayashi, A. and Goldberg, D.T. (eds) *A Companion to Gender Studies*. London: Blackwell Publishing, pp. 437–454.

Saavedra, M. (2005b) 'Women, Sport, and Development'. *Sport and Development International Platform*. http://www.sportanddev.org/data/document/document/ 148.pdf

Sabo, D., Miller, K., Farrell, M., Barnes, G. and Melnick, M. (1998) *The Women's Sports Foundation Report: Sport and Teen Pregnancy*. East Meadow, New York: Women's Sports Foundation.

Sahlins, M. (1972) *Stone Age Economics*. Chicago: Aldine.

Schiebinger, L.L. (2004) *Nature's Body: Gender in the Making of Modern Science*. New Brunswick, N.J.: Rutgers University Press.

Sport and Development Platform (2006a) 'Local Socio-Economic Development through Sport, Boane, Mozambique'. http://www.sportanddev.org/en/ projects/ mozambique/local-socio-economic-development-through-sport-boane- mozambique.htm (accessed on 19 March 2008).

Sport and Development Platform (2006b) 'NOC/ADEL Project of Women's Coop- eratives in Boane'. http://www.sportanddev.org/en/projects/mozambique/noc/ adel-project-of-women-s-cooperatives-in-boane.htm (accessed on 19 March 2008).

Sports Development Aid (2002) 'Annual Report of Activities Done in 2002'. http://www.liike.fi/sda/doc/SDAreport02.pdf (accessed on 16 February 2006).

Subrahmanian, R. (2007) 'Making sense of gender in shifting institutional con- texts: some reflections on gender mainstreaming', in Cornwall, A., Harrison, E. and Whitehead, A. (eds) *Feminisms in Development: Contradictions, Contest- ations and Challenges*. London; New York, and New York, Zed Books; Distri- buted in the USA exclusively by Palgrave Macmillan, pp. 112–121.

UNDP (2007) 'Kenya Country Fact Sheet: 2007/2008 Human Development Report'. 27 November 2007. http://hdrstats.undp.org/countries/country_ fact_sheets/cty_fs_KEN.html (accessed on 16 February 2008).

van Beek, M. and Leibman, D. (2007) '(she's into sports) Report on sport as a tool for empowerment'. Amsterdam, Mama Cash. May 2007. http://www. mamacash.org/uploads/File/she%20has%20news/publicaties/Shes_into_sports _18-05-07_web.pdf (accessed on 1 March 2008), pp. 1–40.

van Dam, C. (2008) 'National network to develop girls and women football in Kenya', in Ashoka Changemakers (ed.) *Entry in Sport for a Better World Competition*. http://www.changemakers.net/en-us/node/4276 (accessed on 17 February 2008).

Williams, J. (2003) *A Game for Rough Girls: History of Women's Football in Britain*. London: Routledge.

Win, E.J. (2007) 'Not very poor, powerless or pregnant: the African woman forgotten by development', in Cornwall, A., Harrison, E. and Whitehead, A. (eds) *Feminisms in Development: Contradictions, Contestations and Challenges*. London; New York, and New York, Zed Books; Distributed in the USA exclusively by Palgrave Macmillan, pp. 79–85.

Wolf, T.P. (2000) 'Contemporary Politics', in Hoorweg, J., Foeken, D. and Obudho, R.A. (eds) *Kenya Coast Handbook: Culture, Resources and Development in the East African Littoral*. Münster: Lit Verlag, pp. 129–156.

Woodford-Berger, P. (2007) 'Gender mainstreaming: what is it (about) and should we continue doing it?', in Cornwall, A., Harrison, E. and Whitehead, A. (eds) *Feminisms in Development: Contradictions, Contestations and Challenges*. London; New York, and New York, Zed Books; Distributed in the USA exclusively by Palgrave Macmillan, pp. 122–135.

Young, I.M. (2002) 'Lived Body vs Gender: Reflections on Social Structure and Subjectivity', *Ratio*, **15**(4), 410–428.

7

On the Backs of Peer Educators: Using Theory to Interrogate the Role of Young People in the Field of Sport-in-Development[1]

Sara Nicholls

7.1 Introduction

Young people in all countries are both a major human resource for development and *key agents for social change*, economic development and technological innovation. *Their imagination, ideals, considerable energies and vision are essential for the continuing development of societies in which they live.* The problems that young people face as well as their vision and aspiration are essential components of the challenges and prospects of today's societies and future generations.[2]

In February 2006, during the XX Winter Olympic Games, the use of sport-in-development[3] was thrust into the spotlight in North America after Clara Hughes, a Canadian speed skater, and American speed skater Joey Cheek both pledged their support to Right to Play, a non-profit athlete driven organization that trains coaches to deliver sport and health programmes in Asia and Africa (Right to Play, n.d.). Both athletes spoke eloquently and passionately about the use of sport to create an environment for young people to access health education and leadership development. These actions created a long-sought connection between sport and development goals that was tangible for the average citizen to grasp and understand.

The use of sport as a tool for development has until recently, occupied a place of relative obscurity in North American consciousness. The ways in which sport can be used in an attempt to foster leadership, good citizenship and self-esteem, particularly for young people, are commonly understood, but the use of sport towards achieving development and social change goals, such as the promotion of HIV/AIDS education, has been outside of many dominant understandings of sport's role in society (despite the use of sport historically for social change as outlined in the introductory chapter). Specific sport-in-development programmes have existed informally for many years, harnessing the convening power of sport to address social, health and development issues. Although popular, the often informal nature of the movement has challenged development professionals, the sporting world and grassroots implementers to define terminology, showcase results and to build the evidence base to highlight the success of sport as a tool for social development (Nicholls and Giles, 2007).

As noted in the introductory chapter, sport-in-development aspires to build local capacity to harness the power of sport to foster community-based change. Such development efforts are being facilitated by young peer educators tasked with leading sport activities and mentoring peer to peer discussion groups on issues such as HIV/AIDS health education, environmental sustainability, peace building and gender equality. It could be argued that sport-in-development is largely occurring on the backs of young people through peer education,[4] as they carry the responsibility for achieving a large majority of sport-in-development objectives. The focus of this chapter is to better understand why policy and programming relating to sport-in-development appears to lack meaningful contributions from young people, while arguing for options to challenge and reshape this trend.

The UN (1995) has acknowledged the important role that young people play in influencing the conditions of their own lives. The UN (1995) further notes that participation must move beyond young people's mere involvement in token decisions, but instead be viewed as critical to realizing the rights of young people in shaping their future. The time has come for the field of sport-in-development, which is clearly tied to youth issues to take up this challenge. The space created by the use of sport as a tool for development can create a strong link between the knowledge held by Southern youth and the ability to act as a catalyst for change, but this must be consistent and include long term consideration at all levels of programme and policy development.

What follows is a discussion of the contribution of 'young leaders' (meaning the young peer educators who facilitate grassroots activities) to the field of sport-in-development, using theory to highlight how and why their voices, actions and narratives have tended to be ignored within this environment. This chapter outlines the importance of peer leadership and by using some examples, will engage with theoretical principles drawn principally from Michel Foucault's (1975, 1980) work on power, discourse and subjugated knowledge. Feminist considerations, postcolonial analysis and empowerment theory will be considered to link aspects of Foucauldian power and knowledge to the field of sport-in-development and subsequent interaction with young people. Lewis and Mills (2003: 1) note that postcolonial theorists often engage with feminist constructs as both disciplines are often 'essentially about challenging existing boundaries'. In a world where behavioural boundaries and social normative processes are shaped by hegemonic, patriarchal and oppressive situations, a feminist perspective is critical when using an interlocking analysis to consider issues of race, gender and culture to examine power and knowledge processes within programmes aimed at both young men and women.

Considerations of power and knowledge centre on concerns that the sport-in-development movement tends to be dominated by a 'vertical hierarchy', which affects donor-recipient and North-South relationships. At present, young people tend to be at the bottom of such vertical hierarchies, delivering programmes, but rarely involved in the policy or programme development process and far removed from financial or long term planning. This chapter contends that the vertical hierarchy and resulting power relationships should be challenged to move to a more 'horizontal' approach between peer educators, their organizations and the donors who work with these organizations, thus creating opportunities for all parties to influence the sport-in-development process. By disrupting dominant colonial (and postcolonial) 'North-South' binaries, a horizontal approach would seek to value the knowledge held by young people, reflect their contributions in policy and programme development, therefore making it possible to re-imagine the role that young people can play in advocating for stronger, more effective policy and programmes.

7.2   Setting the stage to read sport-in-development through theory

The field of sport-in-development is a casualty of broad universal claims as to the value of sport. Sport has been claimed to 'serve as an effective tool for social mobilization, supporting health activities such as HIV/AIDS education and to be of vital importance to the development of young people' (United Nations, 2003: v), but supporting academic evidence does not abound. Brady's (1998) work speaks to the breadth of investigations pertaining to general social benefits that can be accrued through sport participation, but found negligible research which has investigated the use of sport to create an environment conducive for reproductive health education. Brady (1998: 82) states, 'the scope of sports and education experiences for adolescents in the developing world appears to be significant, yet to date, remains essentially undocumented'. Schwery (2003) has also lamented the lack of attention to unearthing the potential for sport to contribute to social development, noting that the small number of evaluations on sport-in-development programming in Africa does not create an understanding of the key factors that lead to successful interventions with populations at high risk. In chapter three of this publication, Coalter takes up the challenge of evaluation related to sport-in-development. Empirical evidence is important in building acceptance and understanding of any concept, but organizations such as the MYSA and the Zimbabwe Sport and Recreation Commission (both considered in Coalter's case studies) who have been implementing sport-in-development programmes for over fifteen years have considerable 'evidence' that could benefit academic study. Although few grassroots practitioners have access to the language or the opportunity to publish in academic journals, this does not mean that their practical understanding of how sport development works should be any less valid (Nicholls and Giles, 2007). As the sport-in-development community seeks to enhance the accountability and efficacy of their programmes, the provision of a conduit for youth expertise to contribute to peer-reviewed academic literature could add significant value.

The role of the peer educator is further complicated in understanding power relationships as young people are often, by nature of their status in organizational hierarchy, removed from a position of authority. One set of relationships tends to exist between the donor and the organization to develop programmes and another separate relationship exists between the organization and the peer educators to deliver programming. The position as the implementer is far removed from strategic visioning or consultation, creating a distance that unless consciously considered, can impede the flow of knowledge. While evidence as to the impact of sport-in-development initiatives is few and far between, the necessary privileging of peer educators' contribution makes it possible to develop a rich and mutually beneficial understanding of the value of sport-in-development, which could meet the needs of academics, practitioners and communities within the Global South. This cannot occur without unpacking of the pervasive power relations and colonial history that provides the frame of reference for the sport-in-development community and does not systematically consider the needs and contributions of peer educators to the global movement.

Reading sport-in-development through theory will illustrate barriers to the flow of information from the grassroots to policy makers and begin to illuminate how connections with young people are critical to challenging dominant systems. Peer educators' experiences and input must be heard in real and meaningful ways if the efficacy of sport-in-development initiatives is to be enhanced. These challenges are not new to development. The failure of development professionals to recognize the privileging of Northern knowledge and the subsequent colonial subjugation of Southern knowledge creates a cycle of dominance that ignores grassroots practitioners' – such as peer educators' – valuable contributions to the strengthening of development practices (Elabor-Idemudia, 2002).

7.3 Reading sport-in-development through theory: Foucault, power and discourse

The adoption of theoretical constructs provides analytical tools for developing a clearer appreciation of the role of peer educators. The interdisciplinary nature of sport-in-development, and subsequently the role of peer educators within this movement, can pose a challenge to theoretical examination as many theories could potentially be employed. Feminist (Weedon, 1987, 1999), post-structural (Foucault, 1975, 1980), and post-colonial (Said, 1979) theories are amongst those that hold potential to serve as catalysts for social change by acting as a checkpoint to examine existing knowledge and its subsequent production (Maguire and Young, 2002), and therefore will be the main focus of this analysis.

A feminist post structural perspective informs aspects of this chapter, as feminist readings of theory and research are essentially feminist not only in their focus on the marginalization of women, but in the challenge of dominant practices (Reinharz, 1992). Through connection with feminist theory, which recognizes the intersection of feminist thought with postcolonial development theory, it is understood that there is 'no one truth, no one authority, no one objective method which leads to the production of knowledge' but there is instead an understanding that 'the experience of all human beings is valid and must not be excluded' (Spender, 1985: 5). Participatory processes that encourage grassroots contributions are also critical to feminist analysis and discussed in order to better understand the creation of space for dialogue between Northern and Southern practitioners using sport as a tool for development.

A Foucauldian reading of the role of peer educators' related to sport-in-development challenges practitioners to think differently about what is known, how it is known and how new processes for change can be mutually constituted. Central to Foucauldian theory is the notion of discourse and the ways in which power is transmitted through discourse (Rail, 2002). Discourse can be defined as a system of ideas or knowledge linked to specific text which is used to identify and legitimize the privileging of power of one person over another (Fairclough, 2003) or, alternatively, 'a body of language use that is unified by common assumptions' (Abercrombie et al., 2000: 99). It is within discourse that meanings are developed and power realized (Rail, 2002). Discourse is the method by which power relations are reified and reinforced, including, for example, those generated through colonialism. Within a Foucauldian approach, it is necessary to acknowledge that there never exists just one relationship or one discourse, but instead numerous relationships and discourses (Foucault, 1975).

Feminist, poststructural and postcolonial theory can be linked to sport-in-development through an examination of subjugated knowledge (Foucault, 1980). The subjugation of (neo-) colonized people's knowledge is a key ingredient in the 'colonial project', subsequently forcing local knowledge into the margins (Cassidy et al., 2001). When youth in developing countries are subjected to homogenizing discourses and conceptualized as 'poor', 'disempowered', 'illiterate' and in need of 'development', any contribution peer educators could make to furthering understanding the use of sport-in-development is instantly discredited, and therefore subjugated.

Colonial discourses privilege white, patriarchal Northern knowledge and deem inferior the knowledge stemming from the non-white South (Cassidy et al., 2001; Chakrabarty, 2000). Mohanty (1988: 61) notes, 'colonisation has been used to characterize everything from the most evident economic and political hierarchies to the production of a particular cultural discourse about what is called the 'Third World''. This definition of colonization implies structural domination, meaning a system of control and discursive oppression whereby dominant discourses continue to propagate practices of subjugation within marginalized populations (Mohanty, 1988). Indeed, local knowledge is a casualty of the colonization process as it is not considered a valuable contribution to the colonial project (Cassidy et al., 2001). The use of theory to interrogate colonization and its ensuing discourses can create a space for change as the 'colonized' challenge grand meta-narratives and traditional discourses of their inferiority (Giles, 2005).

Colonialism, subjugated knowledge and peer education are inter-connected. Colonialism has created a situation in which local knowledge is subjugated and, by extension, peer educators' knowledge is further repressed as their contributions are ignored or considered insignificant. Sport-in-development is not unique in lacking engagement of youth expertise. Frequently, manuals are written to educate youth, but with little youth involvement. Trainings are devised to 'build youth capacity,' but youth are rarely consulted on what capacity is needed and to what end. The use of participatory research, especially with these theoretical perspectives, is critical in reshaping the relationship between local knowledge and the growing global discourse of the use of sport-in-development, as this methodology is 'designed to create social and individual change by altering the role of the relations between people involved in the process' (Elabor-Idemudia, 2002: 232). By creating a forum to discuss the production and valuation of knowledge, participatory practices can 'represent the most direct assault on hegemonic knowledge' (Elabor-Idemudia, 2002: 232) and therefore create opportunities as the contributions of peer educators move from the silent margins of discourses on sport-in-development to the active and vocal centre.

The need for this shift to make an active contribution to shaping both policy and programmes related to sport-in-development is essential in that peer educators have been exposed to both the challenges and successes of implementing sport-in-development agendas. As such, peer educators have vast and valuable stores of information that could strengthen the movement of sport-in-development (while at the same time responding to the call of academics who recognize the dearth of 'valid' 'empirical' data on the impact of sport-in-development), but do not have the space to share their contributions. Understanding how peer educators contribute to and shape sport-in-development within a collective of various meanings and understandings, allows for both socio-political analysis and cultural critique (Rail, 2002). More needs to be known about what peer educators do to engage their peers in a sport context as well as what kind of on-going support and training is needed for peer educators to be effective. This information must be provided by the peer educators themselves. Analysis and critique of sport-in-development practices can be used to question the hegemonic, patriarchal practices which are prevalent in sport-in-development, evidenced by the lack of understanding of the contribution of peer educators.

The exclusion of young people from the creation of resolutions, academic literature and policy documents related to sport-in-development continues to obscure the contributions of those who live this work on a daily basis. The omission of youth input in knowledge production is unlikely to be a conscious exclusion, or with any malicious intention, but an intersecting analysis that considers issues of race, class and gender could bring to light issues that are keeping their contributions firmly on the margins. If youth contributions are to be systematically considered, shifting the focus from valuing grand policy narratives to grassroots contributions, makes it possible to re-envisage the sport-in-development agenda in such a way that it will meet peer educators' needs and strengthen the quality of programme delivery.

7.4 Acknowledging the place of young people in the world

As stated in the *World Programme of Action for Youth to the Year 2000 and Beyond* (UN, 1995), apart from the statistical definition of youth as defined by the UN as the age cohort from 15–24 years, definitions of youth vary widely in different countries, contexts and communities in response to fluctuating political, economic and socio-cultural circumstances. Widely understood as a transitional concept, 'youth' is viewed as the specific stage between childhood and adulthood, when young people navigate complex personal and socio-economic changes to move from dependence to independence, and assume control of their lives and actions (UNESCO, 2004).

Today's generation of young people is the largest in history, with nearly half of the world under the age of 25 (UNFPA, 2005). Statistics on the effects of poverty, unemployment, illiteracy and disease paint a startling picture and build a strong case for investing in youth. UNFPA's recent report on the world's 1.6 billion youth (2006) calls for young people's needs to be integrated into National Poverty Reduction Strategies. The report further acknowledges that the international community's failure to invest in young people's health and education in developing nations will 'further entrench poverty for generations' (UNFPA, 2006: 10).

Amongst these startling statistics, most shocking is the rate at which young people are being infected with HIV/AIDS. This epidemic is sweeping not only across the continent of Africa, but is having a devastating impact worldwide. Globally, of the world's 1.6 billion youth aged 15–24, 10 million are estimated to live with HIV (UNFPA, 2005). Sadly 6,000 youth are infected everyday with the HIV virus (UNFPA, 2005). Every 15 seconds, a young person between the ages of 15 and 24 is infected with HIV (UNICEF and UNAIDS, 2005). Estimates state that approximately half of all people living with HIV/AIDS becoming infected before the age of 25 and die before the age of 35 (Whiteside and Sunter, 2000). It has been estimated that by the year 2010 in sub-Saharan Africa alone, more than 18 million children – more than all the children in the United Kingdom – will have lost at least one parent to AIDS (UNICEF and UNAIDS, 2005), leaving young people to head households, care for siblings and literally forfeit their childhood. AIDS is redefining the very meaning of childhood for millions and depriving children of many of their basic human rights (UNICEF, UNAIDS and WHO, 2002). Peer educators in the field of sport-in-development are making valiant contributions to the fight against HIV/AIDS as they work to spread information on prevention and breakdown barriers resulting from pervasive stigma and discrimination (Jakobsen, 2004), but there must be constant consideration of the magnitude of the task and the recognition that small scale interventions can only do so much up against pervasive socio-cultural challenges.

Peer to peer discussion groups, peer facilitated workshops and peer coaching are common methodologies in the use of sport-in-development in regards to HIV/AIDS prevention. HIV/AIDS education through sport is a consistent theme due to the immense impact of the disease in Southern Africa. A search of the International Platform of Sport and Development regarding the number of projects involving HIV/AIDS education returned over 800 responses. Although not all programmes and projects mentioned in this search are delivered by peer educators, youth are the primary target and delivery mechanism for these messages (Swiss Academy for Development, n.d.). HIV/AIDS is a highly complex disease, with a myriad of social and cultural factors that influence its spread. The young people who deliver sport and HIV/AIDS education programmes have valuable first hand experience as to how to make this connection and also how to navigate the subsequent challenges. As a result, there must not only be increased youth involvement in creation of these initiatives, but also a concomitant increase in attention given to the quality of delivery, as with such complexity comes the potential for misinformation and the feeding of stigma and discrimination.

Stigma and discrimination around HIV/AIDS, health and gender issues cannot be ignored in utilizing peer education as a methodology. Kerrigan (1999) has found that trusted peers can have a strong influence over the behaviour of peers. This influence over behaviour can be fluid and it is important to continue to revisit the information being delivered by peer educators in order to ensure that information is accurate, of the highest quality and would make positive contributions to peer learning environments. Clark *et al.* (2006) have found that peer education does not only occur through a 'formal' peer education process, but that youth who are exposed to programming then tend to informally share what they have learned with youth in their networks. In short, diffusion of innovation can occur as education spreads outside of the intended audience, as the information from the primary contact continues to diffuse via peer to peer interaction.

7.5   The role of the peer educator

Peer education is becoming an increasingly significant aspect of development strategies. Although young people often informally share information (Milburn, 1995), recently particular attention has been focused on the contribution of peer educators to broad development goals. In Lesotho for example, young leaders, typically aged 15–25, are trained through the OlympAfrica Youth Ambassador Programme (OYAP), an initiative of the Lesotho National Olympic Committee. Ambassadors are exposed to a rigorous leadership training schedule involving facilitation and building of life and health skills. Once they have received the necessary training, OYAP Ambassadors are then tasked with mentoring Basotho youth, facilitating daily sport and physical activity programming as well as providing leadership development opportunities. These Ambassadors also offer informal opportunities for participants to access health and life skill information outside of traditional school structures (Commonwealth Games Canada, 2005), which is critical in a country with a high proportion of out of school youth. OYAP operates on the principle that peers can be an important conduit of information, and is making a major effort to connect with out of school youth.

The empowerment model builds skills and the belief in self that is necessary to combat negative social and economic conditions that exist in communities. The term 'empowerment' has been employed by feminists and postcolonial theorists at various points in history who have sought to theorize and mobilize action in response to increasingly hegemonic, patriarchal and oppressive trends. Though widely used, the term is subject to a great deal of uncertainty as to what it 'really' means and how it can be 'really' applied (Ristock and Pennell, 1996). Empowerment theory is difficult to define, but problematizes the lack of control over one's destiny (Kerrigan, 1999) and creates space for individuals to acknowledge the lack of control and to take action to change the situation.

Peer education has developed through the use of participatory or empowerment models of education to theorize the lack of power at the community level and the ability of community members or 'peers' to challenge and combat negative social or economic community conditions (Kerrigan, 1999). Noted education theorist Paulo Freire (1970) found that empowerment occurs through the full participation of the people affected by a given problem to recognize the issues and to plan an appropriate response. Dialogue within the affected community is essential to collectively plan and implement a response to the challenge in question, resisting a solution created by the North or outside 'experts' (Kerrigan, 1999). Peer educators can play an effective role in creating empowering environments, since youth often turn to each other for advice, and behaviour validation (Milburn, 1995). With effective training, it is possible for peer educators to connect with each other and form networks of information and support, but it is critical that this training be comprehensive and repeated over time.

Empowerment theory raises numerous questions, highlighting doubts about the sustainability of empowerment against powerful socio-cultural realities and the necessary criteria to assess when one has been 'empowered'. Empowerment processes involve a shift in self perception as individuals reflect on the social conditions that oppress their ability to create their own destiny and take action. It is in the move towards action that empowerment and peer education intersect to contribute to positive community based change. This combination of action and reflection is generally referred to as praxis (Freire, 1970), and when illuminated by theory offers a powerful tool to understand how young people benefit from the empowerment process and contribute to social change. Empowerment projects, such as those facilitated by the EduSport Foundation in Zambia, seek to create a forum for young girls to build leadership and life skills, with the hope that as they become 'empowered' and equipped to deal with the challenges of life, subsequently reducing their vulnerability for exposure to issues such as HIV/AIDS (Mwaanga, 2004).

7.6   Participatory development practice

According to Frisby *et al.* (2005), participatory programme development or participatory research seeks to understand the lived experience of those involved in or excluded from interventions while aiming to improve the human condition. Imperative to the success of participatory programme development is the involvement of participants in the knowledge production process. If participatory practices are ignored, the diversity of Southern nations (Diawara, 2000) is marginalized and can contribute to an increasing homogenization of problems such as poverty and HIV/AIDS. This homogenization can result in the oversimplification of quick fix solutions. As the field of sport-in-development grows there must be a concerted effort to recognize that homogenization of 'Africans', 'youth', and 'the poor' is embedded in knowledge production as increasingly manuals and training courses are created outside of local contexts, devoid of essential socio-cultural contexts to provide universal solutions. Participatory development practices can create space to discuss these issues and, if used creatively, can ensure that peer educators' voices are heard. Local knowledge includes practical and theoretical knowledge, but also encompasses the cultural and social interpretations that are connected to this knowledge (Diawara, 2000). Understanding this process can cause challenges for donors who are unfamiliar with the local context of their partners' lived experiences. It is essential that development projects inspire dialogue between community members and donors (Diawara, 2000), because 'universalistic approaches based on global strategies of problem-solving can only succeed if they are mediated by local knowledge' (Diawara, 2000: 370). This serves as a warning to the international movement of sport-in-development to continue to seek out knowledge from the local level and maintain a commitment to avoiding the reproduction of colonial practices, while encouraging the use of participatory practices (Nicholls and Giles, 2007).

Although participatory techniques have become prominent in development practices (Parpart, 2002), techniques that aim to privilege knowledge from community members, in light of donor/recipient, North/South, knower/known binaries, are not common practice in the field of sport-in-development (although section 7.7 documents one example of this). Policy-related acceptance of sport-in-development for example, is occurring mainly in multilateral organizations or in the Global North, which point frequently to the 'power of sport' to make change in the global South (The Sport and Development for Peace International Working Group, 2006). Interestingly, it has been recognized that 'sport and physical education are absent from the agendas of the African Union and the New Partnership for African Development (NEPAD)' (The Sport and Development for Peace International Working Group, 2006: 15). This difference in policy level acceptance highlights a fundamental disconnect between the developed/developing world and priorities of the geographical North/South in using sport-in-development. A possible reason for this difference between the North and South may be due to the very nature of sport-in-development. As many sport-in-development activities happen informally, facilitated by youth who are rarely seen as legitimate contributors of knowledge or 'experts', donors can work directly with grassroots organizations, and do not necessarily have to work in partnership with Southern governments. This highlights the need for informal sport-in-development initiatives to work within formal development structures to ensure that the contributions at the local level connect to national and regional agendas, recognizing that this vertical approach must also be mediated by complimentary horizontal consultation.

7.7   Peer education as participatory practice in action

The key to successful peer education is in the horizontal dialogue that enables participants to plan as equals and to take a course of action that is contextually and culturally sound (Kerrigan, 1999). This horizontal approach must be encouraged through local organizations and the relationship of local organizations with donors. Research is beginning to demonstrate that 'peer education is an appropriate means to promote behaviour change or modification' (Hughes-d'Aeth, 2002: 399) and that youth-centered activities, such as sport groups, drama, games and music, serve as powerful venues for behaviour change (Hughes-d'Aeth, 2002).

Research demonstrates that possessing life skills may be critical to young people's ability to positively adapt to and deal with the demands and challenges of life (Ad Hoc Working Group for Youth and the MDGs, 2005). Life skills are behaviours that enable individuals to adapt to and deal effectively with the demands and challenges of life. There are many such skills, but core life skills include the ability to do the following: make decisions, solve problems, and think critically and creatively; clarify and analyse values; communicate, including listen, build empathy, be assertive, and negotiate; cope with emotions and stress; feel empathy with others and be self-aware (Ad Hoc Working Group for Youth and the MDGs, 2005). UNICEF (2007) has endorsed an approach that recognizes the importance of developing life skills as an important component of educating youth about health-related issues including preventing the spread of HIV/AIDS. The life skills approach is an interactive, educational methodology that not only focuses on transmitting knowledge, but also aims at shaping attitudes and developing interpersonal skills. The main goal of the life skills approach is to enhance young people's ability to take responsibility for making healthier choices, resisting negative pressures and avoiding risk behaviours. Sport offers an innovative environment within which to build these skills as there is an opportunity to interact with others, deal effectively with conflict and build self-confidence.

Peer education networks in sport-in-development do exist. The Kicking AIDS Out network for example, is an international network of organizations that uses peer educators to facilitate discussion around HIV transmission as well as a tool to fight the stigma and discrimination attached to the disease in a sport context. Since 2001, peer educators from Europe, Africa, Asia and the Eastern Caribbean have accessed training to integrate HIV/AIDS education into their country's existing youth sport programming. Interestingly, 60% of Kicking AIDS Out peer leaders are female, offering an opportunity for young women to access much needed information on HIV/AIDS, which disproportionately affects young women (UNAIDS, 2006). The network is very aware of the importance of quality in peer education and is working to create a network of learning between peer educators for communication, sharing and problem solving. The Secretariat has recently made an attempt to decentralize its work. Previously all Secretariat staff were based in Oslo, Norway, but now a full time position is staffed in Cape Town, South Africa, making it easier for the Secretariat to facilitate communication between leaders and respond to their needs in a more timely manner. Change will not happen quickly, and youth are not always involved in the shaping of the direction of the network, but positive change is occurring as the network realizes its responsibility to peer educators who access Kicking AIDS Out training. '[P]eer education is an appropriate and effective strategy if used within a complex of mutually supportive activities' (Turner and Shepherd, 1999: 401) and Kicking AIDS Out is committed to creating mechanisms for continued learning and support.

To ensure that peer educators are armed with the tools for success, training must be adequate, youth-centred and sustained. Kerrigan's (1999) extensive study on peer educators' needs, which vary from situation to situation, has brought to light the importance of appropriate, repeated and accurate training. In order to increase the potential for impact, the international sport community needs to support peer educators and their continued learning. Peer educators benefit a great deal from the opportunity to share learning and to build support networks (Kerrigan, 1999). Articulating a commitment to continued learning creates a forum for the mastery of skills and thus a higher probability of delivery of accurate information, resulting in higher quality sport-in-development initiatives.

A popular method of programme delivery in sport-in-development, 'train the trainers' techniques are resulting in significant numbers of peer educators and coaches receiving training and being tasked with creating a community learning environment for community members. The Kicking AIDS Out network for example, operates on a three tier model. Master trainers, or Leader Level Twos (who are deemed to have exceptional facilitation skills and well-rounded knowledge of HIV/AIDS) are tasked with training the Leader Level Ones (who have strong facilitation skills and knowledge of HIV/AIDS) who then train the peer leaders. This mentoring environment when managed appropriately can facilitate a learning continuum to foster critical life skills which can be applied to negotiating sexual relationships, to developing leadership attributes and making life path decisions that maximize one's potential. Nevertheless, it must be recognized that necessary support to peer educators is not always available in the resource poor and donor driven world of sport-in-development. Certainly, there are very real challenges posed by shortages of resources, and limited capacity to provide long-term support at an organizational level, which results in some peer leaders merely being trained once, and not being connected to a wider vision or strategy for leadership development, resulting in a large and unwieldy pyramid of trainers with an unstable base.

7.8   Conclusion

'...as the world's issues are increasingly youth related, sport is an attractive vehicle for providing young people with the opportunity to shape their own lives. It is a tool that can outreach, engage, inspire, motivate and empower young [people] into the leaders of tomorrow' (Commonwealth Advisory Board on Sport, 2006: 1).

Theoretically-informed considerations of the role of peer educators in sport-in-development offers analytical tools to acknowledge the pervasive power relations that result in the subjugation of knowledge in the global South. The global South is not one homogenous entity, but a vibrant, intricate and diverse combination of nations, languages, values and ideology. The same can be said for the young people who are working to foster positive change in their communities through sport. The contributions of young people are varied and complex and should be treated as such. The use of postcolonial and feminist theory allows for not only an acknowledgment of this diversity, but also a move towards action in a reflexive, action oriented manner. Foucault's (1975, 1980) work on power and knowledge offers tools to challenge dominant discourse and therefore re-imagine the role that young people can play in advocating for stronger, more effective sport-in-development.

Colonial discourses which are prevalent in development practices are increasingly being challenged as development scholars and voices from the South ask questions that bring to light the exaggeration of Northern 'expertise,' which can create a false dependence on the North and the dismissal of Southern knowledge (Marchand and Parpart, 1995). Considerable levels of Southern expertise reside with peer educators in the use of sport-in-development, as referenced in the examples provided in this chapter. They are however, silenced, excluded and ignored as the field produces new reports, resolutions and continues to call for more 'evaluation' in the absence of collaboration with the main implementers of sport-in-development: young peer educators. Peer educators have vital contributions to make and as forums are created for youth to articulate their needs, only then can action be taken to create positive change. Through inclusion of subjugated knowledge in the re-shaping of North-South relationships, policy development and programme creation, it becomes possible to re-imagine a vision for sport-in-development that is grounded in lived experiences and not merely well intentioned but disconnected rhetoric. It is not for this article to specify how young people should be included in the policy creation, research development and programme planning process, but it would be promising for policy makers, donors and local management to solicit the input of young people to understand how they feel that they can best contribute to the field. By continuing to maintain sustained connection with the theories outlined here, it is hoped that a mutually beneficial process for collaboration can be determined.

With another Olympic Games on the horizon (and completed by the publication date of this book), global citizens will again be exposed to athlete endorsement of the role of sport to achieve social development goals, as done by Cheek and Hughes in 2006. This platform may create the necessary momentum for the international community of sport-in-development to recognize that youth are not merely the beneficiaries of sport-in-development, but a driving force. The contributions of young people need to be not only recognized, but celebrated, and their challenges not only acknowledged, but also addressed with clear and comprehensive strategy of long-term support. The current situation demands an alternative vision for sport-in-development that narrows the gap between the international movement and the young people who deliver sport-in-development, visioning the North and South working in long-term, sustainable partnerships to share the weight, the burdens and the successes of the use of sport to achieve global development goals.

Notes

1 I would like to thank Dr. Audrey Giles for her mentorship and support in the development of the work that helped to shape this submission. My sincere thanks as well to Dr. Roger Levermore and Dr. Aaron Beacom for their critical and thoughtful edits. Most importantly, I extend my heartfelt thanks to the young people that I have met over the course of the last five years who continuously inspire, motivate and challenge me through their passionate embrace of the use of sport as a tool for development. I truly hope that the time comes when your contributions are actively sought out as you have such a rich and valuable 'expertise'.

2 World Programme of Action for Youth to the Year 2000 and Beyond. United Nations 1995; as taken from: UNESCO's contribution to empowering youth through national policies. UNESCO (2004), p. 35, *emphasis added.*

3 The terminology 'sport-in-development' has been adopted by the editors and is used throughout this publication to promote consistency. The original format of this paper used the terms sport for development and development through sport to recognize that sport is not always embedded 'in' a development framework and that in certain contexts, development can occur within a sport framework.

4 Peer education is often broadly defined, but 'typically involves the use of members of a given group to effect change among other members of the same group' (Kerrigan, 1999: 7).

Bibliography

Abercrombie, N., Hill, S. and Turner, B.S. (2000) *The Penguin Dictionary of Sociology.* London: Penguin Books.

Ad Hoc Working Group for Youth and the MDGs (2005) 'Youth and the Millennium Development Goals: Challenges and Opportunities for Implementation: Final Report of the Ad Hoc Working Group for Youth and the MDGs', accessed 30th November, 2007, http://tig.phpwebhosting.com/ themes/mdg/ YouthMDG.pdf.

Brady, M. (1998) 'Laying the foundation for girl's healthy futures: Can sports play a role?', *Studies in Family Planning,* **29**(1), 79–82.

Cassidy, B., Lord, R. and Mandell, N. (2001). 'Silenced and forgotten women: Race, poverty and disability', in Mandell, N. (ed.), *Feminist issues: Race, class and sexuality (3rd ed.).* Toronto: Pearson Education Canada Inc, pp. 75–107.

Chakrabarty, D. (2000) *Provincializing Europe: Postcolonial though and Historical Difference*. Princeton: Princeton University Press.

Clark, T., Friedrich, G.K., Ndlouvu, M., Neilands, T.B. and McFarland, W. (2006) *An Adolescent-Targeted HIV Prevention Project Using African Professional Soccer Players as Role Models and Educators in Bulawayo, Zimbabwe*. AIDS Behaviour. Center for AIDS Prevention Studies, University of California, San Francisco.

Commonwealth Advisory Body on Sport (2006) 'Report January 2006', last accessed December 10, 2007 http://www.thecommonwealth.org/Shared_ASP_ Files/UploadedFiles/8968898F-E9FD-4616-BA52-95476503C182_CABOS ReportforSportsMinistersmeeting-14-3-06.pdf.

Commonwealth Games Canada (2005) 'International development through sport: OlympAfrica Youth Ambassador Program', last accessed: December 5, 2007. http://www.commonwealthgames.ca/site/index_e.aspx?DetailId=93,

Diawara, M. (2000) 'Globalization, development politics and local knowledge', *International Sociology*, **15**(2), 361–371.

Elabor-Idemudia, P. (2002) 'Participatory research: A tool in the production of knowledge in development discourse', in K. Saunders (ed.) *Feminist Post-Development Thought*. London: Zed Books Ltd, pp. 227–242.

Fairclough, N. (2003) *Analysing Discourse: Textual Analysis for Social Research*. London: Routledge.

Foucault, M. (1975) *Discipline and Punish: The birth of the prison*. Translated from the French: Alan Sheridan. New York: Vintage Books.

Foucault, M. (1980) *Power/Knowledge: Selected Interviews and Other Writings, 1972–1977* (ed.) Gordon, C. Translated from the French Colin Gordon. New York: Pantheon Books.

Friere, P. (1970) *Pedagogy of the Oppressed*. New York: The Continuum International Publishing Group.

Frisby, W., Reid, C.J, Millar, S. and Hoeber, L. (2005) 'Putting "participatory" into participatory forms of action research', *Journal of Sport Management*, **19**, 367–386.

Giles, A.R. (2005) 'A Foucauldian approach to menstrual practices in the Dehcho region, Northwest Territories, Canada', *Arctic Anthropology*, **42**(2), 9–21.

Hughes-d'Aeth, A. (2002) 'Evaluation of HIV/AIDS peer education projects in Zambia', *Evaluation and Programme Planning*, **25**, 397–407.

Jackobsen, E. (2004) 'Kicking AIDS Out! Using Sport as a tool in the fight against HIV.AIDS', last accessed November 15, 2006, http://www.kickingaidsout.net/ 0/EliJakobsenArticle.pdf

Kerrigan, D. (1999) *Peer Education and HIV/AIDS: Concepts, Uses and Challenges*. Washington: Horizons/Population Council.

Kerrigan, D. and Weiss, E. (2000) *Peer Education and HIV/AIDS: Past Experience, Future Directions*, Population Council, Horizons Project, Washington. Last accessed 15th November, 2007, http://www.popcouncil.org/pdfs/peer_ed.pdf.

Lewis, R. and Mills, S. (2003) (eds) 'Introduction', in *Feminist Postcolonial Theory: A Reader*. New York: Routledge, pp. 1–21.

Maguire, J. and Young, K. (2002) 'Introduction: "Back to the future": Thinking sociologically about sport', in Maguire, J. and Young, K. (eds) *Theory, Sport and Society*. London: JAI, pp. 1–22.

Marchand, M.H. and Parpart, J.L. (eds) (1995) *Feminism, Postmodernism, Development*. New York: Routledge.

McDonald, M.G. and Birrell, S. (1999) 'Reading sport critically: A methodology for interrogating power', *Sociology of Sport Journal*, **16**, 283–300.

Mohanty, C. (1988) 'Under western eyes: Feminist scholarship and colonial discourses', *Feminist Review*, **30**, 62–88.

Milburn, K. (1995) 'A critical review of peer education with young people with special reference to sexual health', *Health Education Research Journal – Theory and Practice*, **10**(4), 407–420.

Mwaanga, M.K.O. (2004) 'Confronting HIV/AIDS through sport' – a paper on the EduSport Foundation's 'Go Sisters!' programme, International AIDS Conference Abstract, 15, no. WePeE6843, July 11–16.

Nicholls, S. and Giles, A.R. (2007) 'Sport as a tool for HIV/AIDS education: A potential catalyst for change', *Pimatisiwin: A Journal of Aboriginal and Indigenous Community Health*, **5**(1), 51–85.

Park, P. (2001), 'Knowledge and participatory research', in P. Reason and H. Bradbury (eds), *Handbook of Action Research: Participative Inquiry and Practice*. London: Sage, pp. 81–90.

Parpart, J.L. (1995) 'Deconstructing the development "expert": Gender, development and the "vulnerable groups"', in Marchand, M.H. and Parpart, J.L. (ed.) *Feminism Postmodernism Development*. London: Routledge, pp. 221–243.

Parpart, J.L. (2002) 'Rethinking participatory empowerment, gender and development: the PRA approach', in *Rethinking Empowerment: Gender and Development in a Global/Local World,* Parpart, J.L., Rai, S.M. and Staudt, K. (eds). Routledge: Warwick, pp. 165–181.

Rail, G. (2002) 'Postmodernism and sport studies', in Maguire, J. and Young, K. (eds) *Theory, Sport and Society*. Oxford: JAI, pp. 179–207.

Reinharz, S. (1992) *Feminist Methods in Social Research*. Oxford: Oxford University Press.

Right to Play (n.d.) *What We Do; About Right to Play,* last accessed: 6th November, 2006, http://www.righttoplay.com/site/PageServer.

Ristock, J.L. and Pennell, J. (1996) *Community Research as Empowerment: Feminist Links, Postmodern Interruptions*. Oxford and Toronto: Oxford University Press.

Said, E.W. (1979) *Orientalism*. New York: Vintage Books/Random House.

Schwery, R. (2003) 'The potential of sport for development and peace', *Bulletin 39*, last accessed 10th December, 2006, http://www.icsspe.org.

Spender, D. (1985) *For the Record: The Meaning of Feminist Knowledge*. London: Women's Press.

Sport for Development and Peace International Working Group) (2006) *Sport for Development and Peace: From practice to policy – Preliminary report of the Sport for Development and Peace International Working Group*. Toronto, Canada.

Swiss Academy for Development (SAD) (n.d.) 'Sport for Development and Peace International Platform', last accessed, 9th January, 2007, http://www.sportand-dev.org.

Swiss Agency for Development and Cooperation (SDC) (2005) *Sport for Development and Peace*. Zurich: Swiss Agency for Development and Cooperation (SDC).

Turner, G. and Shepherd, G. (1999) 'A method in search of a theory: Peer education and health promotion', *Health Education Research*, **14**(2), 235–247.

UN; United Nations (1995) 'World Programme of Action for Youth to the Year 2000 and beyond', last accessed 21st November, 2007, http://www.un.org/events/youth98/backinfo/ywpa2000.htm.

UNAIDS; Joint United Nations Programme on HIV/AIDS (1999) *Peer education and HIV/AIDS: Concepts, uses and challenges*. Best Practices Series. Geneva.

UNAIDS; Joint United Nations Programme on HIV/AIDS (2005) *AIDS in Africa: Three Scenarios to 2025*. Geneva: Visual Media Services.

UNAIDS; Joint United Nations Programme on HIV/AIDS (2006) *2006 Report on the Global AIDS Epidemic: A UNAIDS 10th Anniversary Special Edition*. Geneva.

UNESCO; United Nations Educational, Scientific and Cultural Organization (2004) *Empowering youth through national policies, UNESCO's contribution*. Paris, last accessed 15th November, 2007, http://unesdoc.unesco.org/images/0013/001345/134502e.pdf.

UNFPA; United Nations Population Fund (2005) 'State of the world population 2005 – The promise of equality: Gender equity, reproductive health & the MDGs', last accessed November 4th, 2007, http://www.unfpa.org/swp/2005/index.htm.

UNFPA; United Nations Population Fund (2006). *Moving young: State of the world population – Youth supplement*.

UNICEF (2007) 'Life skills', last accessed 10th December, 2007. http://www.unicef.org/lifeskills/index_4105.html.

UNICEF; United Nations Children's Fund (2006) *Adolescent development: Perspectives and frameworks*. Adolescent development and participation unit. Learning series No. 1.

UNICEF and UNAIDS (2005) *Youth and HIV/AIDS Factsheet: State of World Population 2005*. Available online at http://www.unfpa.org/swp/2005/presskit/factsheets/facts_youth.htm

UNICEF, UNAIDS and WHO (2002) 'Young people and HIV/AIDS: Opportunity in crisis', last accessed: 5th January, 2008 http://www.unicef.org/publications/files/pub_youngpeople_hivaids_en.pdf.

United Nations Inter-Agency Task Force on Sport for Development and Peace (2003) 'Sport for Development and Peace: Towards achieving the Millennium Development Goals', United Nations, New York, accessed 5th May 2006, http://www.sportanddev.org/data/document/document/13.pdf.

Weedon, C. (1987) *Feminist Practice and Poststructuralist Theory*. Oxford: Basil Blackwell.

Weedon, C. (1999). *Feminism, Theory and the Politics of Difference*. Oxford: Basil Blackwell.

Whiteside, A. and Sunter, C. (2000) *AIDS: The challenge for South Africa*. Cape Town: Human & Rousseau and Taffleberg.

World Health Organization (WHO) (n.d.) 'WHO and HIV', last accessed 14th December, 2006. http://www.who.int/hiv/en/.

8

Getting to Know You: Using Sport to Engage and Build Relationships with Socially Marginalized Young People

Tim Crabbe

8.1 Introduction

Core aspirations concerning the capacity of sport to deliver a range of social objectives in a community development context worldwide, are shared by the architects of domestic (UK) development initiatives and by those engaged in the policy process who wish to use sport within international development assistance programmes. This chapter is concerned with the extent to which lessons learned in the domestic (UK) arena, are applicable to the wider development community. To do this, it will focus on the findings of ongoing research from the UK Home Office funded Positive Futures Case Study Research Project which is focused on case study projects using sports based activities to engage 'hard to reach' and socially marginalized young people. It will consider the relationship between project activity and 'the Positive Futures approach' articulated in the *Cul-de-sacs and gateways* strategy document, which outlines what might be seen as a discrete and alternative perspective that breaks with more conventional sporting and youth justice models of development:[1]

> The Positive Futures programme has been built up around young people's involvement in sporting activity but it is not concerned with the celebration, development or promotion of sport as an end in itself. Nor does it merely attempt to use sport as a simple 'diversion' or alternative to time spent engaging in drug use and crime. Positive Futures is a relationship strategy based on the principle that engagement through sport and the building of mutual respect and trust can provide cultural 'gateways' to alternative lifestyles (United Kingdom Government, Home Office, 2003: 8)

8.2 Power of sport

In recent times the notion of the 'power of sport' to do social good has increasingly come to prominence on social policy agendas, as noted in the introductory chapter, but also within sports management and marketing strategies (see Hallinan, 2007). Whether it be the perceived regenerative potential associated with the staging of 'mega events' such as the Olympic Games (discussed in more detail in Chapter 4) or the need to engage young people in purposeful activity in local neighbourhoods, belief in the wider benefits of sport continues to be strongly advocated. Indeed, there remains a widespread tendency within sporting, political and popular discourses to regard sport as an entirely wholesome activity for young people to be involved in; an activity that is conferred with a whole series of positive attributes to the exclusion of the social ills facing wider 'society'. There is of course nothing new about this approach. As articulated in the introductory chapter, organized modern sport arguably owes its very existence to the 'Victorians' attempts to influence and shape attitudes within British public schools and to service the needs of the Empire through the concept of 'Muscular Christianity'. More pertinently to this chapter, during the nineteenth century 'sports were to play a major part...in the creation of a healthy, moral and orderly workforce' and in shaping the values and behaviour of working class youth (Holt, 1989: 136). More recently this mantle has been taken up by international development agencies including the UN which have explicitly emphasized the role that sport can play in improving the lives of individuals and communities, particularly children and young people.

Without necessarily seeking to do so, such social considerations of sport have tended to be framed by this kind of 'functionalist' perspective which emphasizes what sport does *to* people and *for* 'society' (see Blackshaw and Crabbe, 2004). In keeping with this position a number of North American studies have over the years provided some theoretical and empirical support for the notion that participation in sport serves as a deterrence to delinquency and 'deviance' (Hastad *et al.*, 1984; Purdy and Richard, 1983; Buhrmann, 1977; Schafer, 1969). Nevertheless, there remains little definitive evidence of a direct causal relationship between involvement in sports, moral outlook, criminal or deviant behaviour and indeed broader social development (Long and Sanderson, 2001; Coalter, 2007).

Whilst Long and Sanderson (2001: 201) 'are persuaded that there is sufficient cause to believe that community benefits can be obtained from sport and leisure initiatives' they recognize that these may be small scale, exclusionary and isolated. Furthermore, in terms of the specific relationship between sport and crime, whilst there are reasons why sport and leisure activity might influence levels of criminality (see Nichols, 1997), the objectives and rationales of these projects have rarely been made clear, leaving the measurement of outcomes an uncertain exercise (a concern raised by most chapters in this edition). Indeed, paradoxically, while it could be argued that conventional images of sport may be policed through societal expectations which stress its wholesome and socially cohesive nature, for the participant it is precisely sports' legitimation of 'deviance' which is often most compelling (Blackshaw and Crabbe, 2004). For sport provides environments in which acts of violence, confrontation and drug use are licensed in ritualized fashion and given meaning through their association with the hegemonic masculine ideals of toughness, heroism and sacrifice. The bloodstained shirts of rugby players, the pain killing injections given to football players, the high speed crashes faced by Formula One racing drivers all adding to sports ultimate attraction.

As such, sporting activity itself does not necessarily seem to offer the most appropriate means for *challenging* 'deviant' or socially disruptive behaviour. As Lasch (1978: 100) argued, '[g]ames quickly lose their charm when forced into the service of education, character development, or social improvement'. Nevertheless, perspectives that support the use of sport to tackle youth deviance retain their authority in many sporting, popular and political arenas (although there has recently been some re-assessment of the centrality of this role to sports policy bodies such as Sport England) and had a key influence on the support given to the UK Positive Futures initiative which will provide the focus for the remainder of this chapter.

Positive Futures is a UK sports-based social inclusion programme managed until April 2006 within the UK Government Home Office Drug Strategy Directorate which aims to have 'a positive influence on participants' substance misuse, physical activity and offending behaviour.' Launched in 2000, it is now entering its fourth phase of development and is currently delivered through 108 local partnership projects throughout England and Wales. However, the subsequent growth of the programme reflects its *distinction* from, as much as its association with, more conventional 'diversionary' and morally laden models of sports intervention.

As such, rather than focusing on 'outcomes' and 'impact' measures this chapter is concerned to explore the attempts of individual Positive

Futures projects to *engage* their target groups, build *relationships* and achieve meaningful social *development*. In doing so it will consider the extent to which projects are able to act as 'cultural intermediaries, providing gateways between what are often seen as alien and mutually intimidating worlds' (United Kingdom Government Home Office, 2003: 9). This will involve consideration of how participants are targeted, how local geographic, demographic and cultural contours are navigated, the style and delivery of project activities, their appeal to particular target groups and the characteristics and approaches of project staff. Crucially, this will provide a basis for consideration of the extent to which the model has since been mobilized in the context of the Global South and the tensions involved in this transmission process.

8.3 Talking tactics: issues of methodology and method

This chapter draws upon research conducted for the national Positive Futures Case Study Research Project commissioned by the UK Home Office. The two year research programme was focused on seven case study projects located across England and Wales which reflected the diversity of organizational and delivery styles within the wider programme. It was commissioned with a view to assessing, at different stages of individual projects' development, the impact, organizational and process elements associated with their interventions.

One of the points of departure of the research from the focus of many other investigations of sports based social interventions was the contention that a meaningful evaluation requires a methodological strategy that goes beyond simple quantitative analysis (an issue addressed by Coalter in this publication). The evaluative frameworks adopted by funding bodies and partners in the Positive Futures programme such as Sport England had previously tended to stipulate quite prescriptive performance indicators with associated quantitative measures. However, the fundamental principle which guided this study was to ensure that the voices of the young participants, local residents, community groups and involved professionals were at the heart of the research.

The research then was underpinned by a commitment to a Participatory Action Research (PAR) approach. PAR provides a family of research methods united by a set of principles and a style (Estrella and Gaventa, 1998). It is 'cyclical', moving between practical actions and critical reflection and seeks to bring together action, theory and practice, in participation with those who are closest to the area of investigation, in the pursuit of practical solutions to issues of concern to them. It aspires to empower participants through this collaboration, by promoting the acquisition of knowledge to achieve social change, whilst attempting to circumvent traditional hierarchies associated with researcher/researched dichotomies.

A variety of methods of enquiry were mobilized, located predominantly around the actual lived experiences of project staff and the participants and residents in the selected areas. Extensive participant observation was conducted by members of the research team who, over a two year period, spent two days a week in the company of project workers on housing estates; at training sessions, matches and competitive tournaments; on trips and 'residentials' away from the estates; in project offices and the more informal 'social' locations inhabited by project staff, participants and residents; as well as in policy forums and conferences.

In each of the case study locations we identified a sample of participants, groups and activities which were tracked through the course of our research. Whilst the nature of the young people who were engaged by the programme led to a certain level of fluidity and turnover of participants, a combination of intermittent life history interviews as well as group qualitative interviews and discussions were conducted with those who remained in contact. These interviews were themselves augmented by the use of a range of participative techniques which sought to engage participants and residents in the research process in more innovative and self determined ways. These included the use of a range of visually based methods, such as maps, photo-diaries, disposable cameras and mock TV talk-shows. Through the use of these approaches we sought to establish how a variety of individuals and social groups talk about the place of sport within their lives and to account for the 'taken-for-granted' assumptions about how 'facts' and 'realities' come to be represented and the different ways in which communicative resources are used (Atkinson, 1990).

With additional surveys of local archive sources these approaches enabled us to produce detailed 'thick' descriptions (Geertz, 1973) of the contexts in which the work was situated, the engagement strategies employed, particular sporting practices and the social worlds that surround them. This material was used to locate the place of sports based social interventions within the social ecology of the areas and to explore sport's relationship with particular regional histories and notions of neighbourhood. In this way we hoped to achieve a certain latitudinal 'breadth' and longitudinal 'depth' in the study which is only partially reflected in the selected testimony and narrative description offered here.[2]

8.4   Looking for trouble: identifying participants and spaces

Despite its status as a national programme, the organization of Positive Futures is essentially a locally negotiated enterprise embodying a variety of management approaches which have given rise to a diverse and distinct set of project management styles. As such whilst there is a clear national strategy which articulates a particular Positive Futures approach (UK Home Office, 2003), there is less consistency in terms of its application. Indeed, in relation to the initial engagement of participants, we can identify something of a bifurcation between what might loosely be characterized as 'instrumental' and 'organic' approaches.

The 'instrumental' approach reflects a more conventional 'top down' method which identifies those young people who are perceived as problematic in the eyes of welfare institutions who then direct them towards some form of correctional programme. However, in many ways this mode of operation, which has been most readily associated with statutory local government and criminal justice agency led projects, conflicts with the approach identified in Positive Futures own strategy document which suggests that:

> In each area the problems and opportunities faced by marginalised groups of young people themselves provide the template for the development of work plans, with non judgmental and culturally appropriate local opportunities for personal development emerging organically on the basis of what engages effectively (United Kingdom Government Home Office, 2003: 10).

In effect the document espouses a non prescriptive approach driven by the need to effectively engage with the target audience rather than strictly interpreted models of delivery. The support for this 'organic' approach is currently better reflected in the style which is more typically, though not exclusively, adopted by projects led by community based voluntary sector agencies. When one of our case study projects, which fits this categorization, begins a new session they usually start with a phase of outreach activities in the area, utilizing an 'anywhere that we know young people congregate' approach, doing street work as well as going into schools and shopping centres, as the project co-ordinator 'Kate' explained:

> One of the main things we do is outreach, where we go out on the streets with flyers and use our charm tactics. We speak to the young

people on the street and we tell people what we do. We tell them what's on offer for them, we give them a flyer and a phone number and hope that they get along. For more targeted work it's a lot more one to one. We meet with them regularly to build the relationship first (Interview, 23rd March 2005).

A crucial distinction is identified here in the sense that there is recognition that identification and targeting cannot be conducted independently of *relationship* building. Rather than personalized calculations of 'risk' (Beck 1992) being made at a distance, that provide the general public with tangible targets of dangerousness, the neighbourhood setting is seen to produce potential participants, who in many circumstances then turn out to be the very young people who would otherwise need to be coerced into attendance by referral agents. Rather than providing any mystical revelation, the engagement of young people in this way is ultimately revealed as more straightforward and less stigmatizing since attendance at sessions is voluntary and tied into less formal modes of relationship building as revealed in the following narrative field description from the Positive Futures research project relating to an incident from the 25th October 2004:

Kate seemed disappointed with the attendance at the session. She was worried that the football club coaches who were coming the next day would be disillusioned if they only had a few kids to work with. Rather than sit around and worry about it she decided to get out and see who was about, see if there were any kids hanging around the streets who she could be encouraged to come along. Driving around the area it was not the day to be rustling up support for a 'sports day'. The pouring rain had put paid to street corner society as those who were brave enough to face the elements or had no other options made for what shelter they could find. A couple of hardy souls crunched up under the hoarding of a newsagent were similarly struggling for punters willing to offer reward for their rather poorly improvised effigy of Guy Fawkes. Spotting the opportunity Kate stopped and walked over.

Rather than a coin she handed them a flyer and asked if they wanted to come down.

'Its better than sitting out here in the rain'.

Spotting that one of the kids was carrying a crutch the offer was re-inforced.

'Its ok if you're injured cos there are x-boxes and other indoor activities that you can get involved with'.
'I'm not injured it's for whacking people with', he smirked as he smashed the stick against the metal shutter boarding up the shop next door for effect.

Kate, utilizing her local knowledge ignored the bravado and turned to his mate; 'I know you' she said, asking how his mum was. He was soon on board and ran off home to get his Mum to sign the form. Looking to make his excuses the kid with the stick asked:

'Is it where the Pitz is? That's miles away. I'm not goin' there. I'd have to get a bus.' When his mate returned Kate took the form off him and told the boys that it was on all week so they should just come along. As we got back into the car to rustle up some more would-be participants Kate waved at the lads mum who was walking down the street.

There were several more at the session the next day.

This account reflects the project's understanding of the dynamic nature of the engagement process and the need to take account of individual circumstances rather than relying on existing referral pathways, which has clear implications for the role of sport in development strategies more generally. Indeed, even at those projects, which are focused on more targeted approaches, whilst *on paper,* the referrals process can be quite rigid and formulaic, it is more often operationalized by front line staff in a much more flexible manner. As a youth worker explained:

I have had people ask me 'how do you reach the hard to reach young people?' I say, 'well, knock on their door'... Of my core 50 some of them are very hard to reach. Although I might know them and have their date of birth and address it is not always that easy to engage them because you can get to their door and they tell you to F off, or they could come. Of the 50 there are at least 15 who I would say are the hardest to reach, that I find difficult... I will try and arrange a meeting at their school, so they feel comfortable with their teachers there... I'll go to their houses and talk to their parents and try to get the parents on board and we'll all try to talk to them together, if they are involved in the YOT [Youth Offending Team] we can arrange a meeting with the YOT and them so they feel comfortable there, and if all that fails then I'll just knock on their door and say 'can I speak to blah blah please' and then I just make the project sound so fantastic. But there are some who are not engaged and that can be through fear of other young people. They have various reasons as to why they won't come... some of my core group have been severely bullied in school and for that reason they find it difficult to be in group settings (Interview, 21st April 2005).

In some ways this perspective transforms the conventional image of the 'hard to reach'. Instead of this being a label attached to young people, the staff at this project subverted the outlook. They recognize that there are reasons why a young person may be difficult for a worker to make contact with. As such, being designated 'hard to reach' is not seen in terms of a broad behavioural category but in relation to an individual's situation. In this context the emphasis is on the need to work harder at combating the reasons why young people might not be able to access the project. This is a critical point in relation to wider considerations of the potential for sport-in-development globally since what it articulates is an approach which is not tied to a specific set of circumstances but is flexible in terms of both cultural and personal circumstance, whether that be tied to the relative poverty of life on a London housing estate or living with HIV/AIDS in southern Africa.

If part of the attraction of Positive Futures is that it offers something 'different' to participants, this is also related to its capacity to achieve transcendence and escape from those situations. This can be related to its use of venues or activities which convey 'glamour', in order to attract and retain participants. There is no doubt that football, which is the principle activity delivered by Positive Futures, has a glamorous position in many young people's lives both in relation to this programme but also in developing countries which can itself present problems for community sports practitioners who may be seeking to counter the superficiality of over-commercialized sport. However, two of the projects included in the study make strong use of their partnership with English Premiership football clubs and have been able to exploit their glamour effectively in terms of initial engagement. The pictures of players on publicity leaflets and the club strip that the coaches wear along with access to stadium tours and the opportunity to watch matches for free if they assist in the clearance of rubbish before and afterwards are factors in attracting young people to the projects, particularly where young people are supporters of the clubs concerned.

Although the young people are never told that involvement in the projects might lead to them being spotted and finding stardom in the Premiership, it is clear in talking to some of them that they still like to imagine this might happen. In turn though, as one project worker illustrated in the following testimony, there is recognition of the ways in which broader possibilities or progression routes *can* open up from these activities.

> It's, you know, that's what we get, that's what kind of interests them. 'Okay, wow, it's free first of all, I can get in the studio, I can lay down my demo if I'm interested in becoming an artist, I can do that, and it's a starting point for me.' Also, 'if I wanted to become a professional footballer I can start off here, this is a good route and I can get training.' 'I can become a coach at the same time.' And these are the kind of things that keep them interested, and they come in twos, we provide them with as much as we can (Interview, 21st April, 2005).

Similarly, young South Africans are being given the opportunity to benefit from this approach through the Positive Futures Cricket Project launched at the Forest Heights High School, Eersteriver in September 2007, when South African cricketer Jacques Kallis attended as the guest of honour. Developed and funded by UK Sport and the British Consulate General in Cape Town the project provides the first example of the Positive Futures model being used outside the UK. Cricket is used as a means of building trust with young people from marginalized communities, encouraging contact with community leaders and activities with essential life skills training and messages, which are ultimately intended to contribute to reduced drug use, crime and gang activity in the community. Those over 15 years who display leadership skills are being given the opportunity to become peer mentors since for the Youth Development Manager responsible for the project it:

> offers an opportunity to focus on the child and not just the anti-social behaviour, and to work with the underlying issues, which is where change can truly happen (Interview, 15th September 2007).

Both in the UK and elsewhere then Positive Futures is concerned with more than simply offering a 'youth club' where there is access to a free pool table and a place to 'hang out'. Several of the projects utilize a range of unusual, special, 'cool' activities including BMXing, snowboarding, dance, climbing, film special effects and others which stretch the definition of the programme as a sport based social inclusion strategy. These activities stand out and reflect the contemporary appeal of more individualistic 'lifestyle' or 'extreme' sports (Wheaton, 2004). However, whilst their 'currency' can make them very attractive to young people, in an individualistic society there is also the danger that their appeal may prove to be transient as participants search for 'highs' rather than helping to build reciprocal forms of cooperation and collectivity. This is because such activities take place in what Lyotard (1988) calls 'open space-time', in which the selves of the individual participants are only ephemerally transformed in the performativity of the activities themselves (Blackshaw and Crabbe, 2004: 145). As such Positive Futures has identified its staff, and front line workers in particular, rather than 'sport', as the crucial factor in ensuring the development of sustainable progressive pathways for participants. Indeed this is reflected in the use of a wide range of sporting practices in different geographical and cultural contexts which are referred to in this collection and which reinforce the point that the critical factor is not the specificity of the activity but the approach adopted towards development.

8.5   'One of us': styles of delivery, staff roles and cultural capital

Focusing on the approach of staff, rather than on the activities offered, it is clear that projects adopt flexible methods which is dynamic and alive to individual personalities and circumstance as the following excerpt from the first interim Positive Futures Case Study Research Report, *Getting to Know You* reveals:

> The minibus journey to the Shenley School is invariably deafening, with Gemma and Judy talking to the young people about what they have been up to since the last session. The group members seem to have a closer relationship with Gemma than with Judy, due to Judy's role as worker responsible for organizing and delivering transport and administration. This frees Gemma up to knock on doors on the estates if the young people are not waiting when the mini bus arrives and to join in the play and talk to the young people when they break from activities.
>
> Dressed in her usual kit of tracksuit bottoms and hoodie, Gemma who has just turned 21, is keen to show off her 'dead cool' new

trainers. She bounces around, calling everyone 'dude', telling people that they are 'gnarly'. Much to the group's delight sharing transport with her means having to listen to Britney and as they get off the bus and wait for the session to begin, they chat with her about their plans for the evening, some give her a hug and urge her to play.

The activities are led by Robbie who has been running the sessions since September. Robbie knows the area well, and knows some of the young people and is himself a former Shenley pupil. He also still works locally, as a gym instructor, after having previously spent time in the Forces. He is physically imposing, and when someone spills a catch or people collide, his laugh booms across the gym, and the laugh is infectious. He explains the rules of the game, splits the group into teams and encourages players whilst he referees or bowls.

The participants are playing their favourite game, Kwik Krikkit which is sold on the back of the staff's enthusiasm. Gemma whips the group up on the minibus so they are raring to go when they arrive. Robbie delivers bowling to suit each batter and Jeff hurls himself around the pitch fielding. When Paul is caught out by a fielder, he throws down his bat and storms off. Jeff follows him and the two of them sit down, talking about why he is so agitated today. Later, Paul returns to the game.

Jeff is an ex football pro and loves showing off his sporting skills and the young people enjoy watching his tricks. He is very vocal, encouraging players to run, telling the captains to organize their field and get batters in line. When something kicks off, it is Gemma who takes each of the two lads outside, in turn, and speaks to them about their behaviour, reminding them of the Code of Conduct which they have signed up to. Gemma's natural bubbly nature means that when she is suddenly straight faced and moved to take people outside of the session, participants know that they have transgressed and will be banned from that session, and subsequent ones, if they continue to misbehave (Crabbe, 2005: 101–102).

In this example and others, whilst misbehaviour is sometimes met with sanctions and the withdrawal of privileges, there are no fixed disciplinary regimes. Instead the work is about the use of individual, adaptable approaches, which are 'true' to each of the different workers' outlooks and which avoid a 'top down' authoritarian approach. One project worker, 'Serena' described the surely universal necessity of establishing trust with young people before attempting to question particular patterns of behaviour:

> If a young person doesn't gain your trust then they're not going to take that any further and they're not going to try and go any further with a relationship with you. So I mean before you can even – like if you had to pull up a young person for swearing or anything that's not beneficial to them or anyone else, you have to establish a relationship with them first before you can turnaround and say, because they'll turn around and say 'well, who are you, I don't know who you are, you know, you can't be coming to me and telling me that I shouldn't be doing this, I shouldn't be doing that.' So in the first instance when you're signing up with them, even when you're outreaching, introduce yourself, let them know who you are, what you do if you can and then take it from there basically. See them again, it's down to a simple hi, a simple hand gesture in the road when you see them, that keeps the relationship going. If they feel that you were too hard on them and you had to tell them off or tell them that they were doing something wrong, go back to them, explain yourself, if you have to apologise, apologise, but explain that, you know, 'this is the reason why I've done that,' so always give reasons why and explain yourself (Interview, 14th April, 2005).

Here 'Serena' clearly illustrates the essential two-way nature of the relationship between the young person and worker, where the power balance may be unequal but is made more equitable through negotiation, explanation and, if necessary, contrition. Whilst facilitated by the liberal democratic context in which the programme is delivered this approach is entirely consistent with the non-judgmental framework and ability to read and adapt to the alternative social realities of participants through which the staff operate.

Considering the applicability of this approach in other social and cultural contexts, it is worth recognizing that even within the context of the Positive Futures programme there is no such thing as an archetype 'community sports coach'. Rather, projects employ a disparate array of staff with distinct skills and backgrounds who can nevertheless be related to a series of Weberian 'ideal types' embodying certain character types such as the 'boss', 'buddy', 'teacher', 'joker', 'cool dude', 'geezer' and 'expert' (see Crabbe, 2005). Whilst workers may play to or utilize different aspects of these characters or even occupy a number of positions simultaneously depending on the group they are working with, each of the projects is characterized by their employment of staff from a variety of working backgrounds. However, what seems to be emerging is a stronger identification amongst participants with members of staff who are from their area than those who are not. Although the local rootedness of staff is not the only factor at work here, those staff who have a deep knowledge of the history of their areas, who have or had a similar social background to participants, that is those who have similar 'cultural capital', seem able to make stronger connections with the young people and to command more respect.

This point relates to the late French sociologist Pierre Bourdieu's (1962) argument that all humans inherit dispositions to act in certain ways. In this sense they possess an inherited concept of society or *habitus*, which they then modify, according to their own specific local conditions and experiences. For Bourdieu then, the ability to absorb appropriate actions is the key for individuals to be at ease with themselves and others. Equally the cultures of individuals and groups are seen as the tokens by which they make 'distinctions' in order to position themselves and establish group identities (Bourdieu, 1984). The usefulness of these concepts here relates to the point that the ability of Positive Futures workers to engage with participants is connected to their own biographies and embodied selves and the degree to which they are acknowledged and valued in these locales. 'Serena' elucidated the point:

> So, you know, streetwise is where I'm from, you know, from ... which is local, you know, I lived in Jamaica for some time, that helps with the young people that I come into contact with that are from Jamaica and don't have, you know, don't have a clue where to start when they come here, so that has helped me to relate to them a lot. And just general kids, I can relate to them all the time, because, you know, I understand where they're coming from and what's going down and what's not and what's in and what's out and you know. Yeah, we can always chat like normal and they don't feel like they have to be different around me they can be themselves and I can be myself around them as well. And that's how you gain a lot of respect. I think my background definitely helps, it always does. That is what I always take them back to, I show them where I'm coming from and they're like 'wow.' Well, I can do this too.

It is important to note then that each of the character types we have identified reflects a particular social class and gender *habitus*. A working class male might be perceived to perform the 'geezer'[3] role much more proficiently and 'easily' than a woman or middle class man could. Indeed it is this 'easiness' that defines the role. Equally the 'buddy' is a character that is frequently gendered as feminine. Nevertheless in one of the case study locations where the work has proven to be by far the most challenging, locality, social class identifications and outlook have come to the fore, enabling gender and racial distinctions to be suspended. Those staff who share some of the life experiences of those they are working with, having been brought up in deprived neighbourhoods and not initially flourished in a formal educational setting, have shown the greatest commitment to giving the young people who attend activities a second chance. Embodying the 'geezer' persona, they seem to understand the local culture, the values in the community and how young people from the area are perceived.

8.6   Sport-in-development and the role of the cultural intermediary

Within projects of this type then and perhaps regardless of their location, it is the staff's capacity to achieve this level of connection that itself constitutes success, since it is in the nature of the work, the relations formed and the level of access achieved where the battle for legitimacy is largely fought. At their most effective Positive Futures projects straddle two increasingly different worlds and act as interpreter for each. In this respect the programme's success lies in its position as a 'cultural intermediary', providing gateways between what are often seen as alien and mutually intimidating worlds. This concept has elsewhere been most readily applied following Bourdieu (1984) and Featherstone's (1991) use of the term as a way of understanding the emergence of a 'new middle class' which has helped to collapse some of the old distinctions between 'popular' and 'high' culture. However, in the context of this research, the term is used in relation to a quite different cultural axis and focus on the potential for projects to help generate a class of professionals who are able to collapse the barriers between the socially 'excluded' and the 'included'.

The predominant focus of the plethora of social interventions associated with the 'social inclusion' and, in some ways, the broader international development agenda, with their emphasis on social capital and communitarian ideals, has been to encourage 'us' (policy makers, University lecturers, community development initiatives) to determine what is appropriate for 'them' (the poor), despite the rhetoric of community led initiatives. Our research suggests however that successful Positive Futures coaches are often seen in different ways to many of the other agents associated with social inclusion policies such as teachers, police officers, probation officers and youth workers. Part of the reason for this is that when considering what are often regarded as 'alien' social groups such as those engaged with Positive Futures, conventional policy 'speak' merely seeks to 'translate' their ways of living and thinking into its 'own' language. What effective Positive Futures projects are concerned to do is to *understand* people on their own terms through reference to more personal experience rather than policy led language games. The cultural intermediary then becomes more than just a communicator with the wherewithal to open 'information channels between formerly sealed off areas of culture' (Featherstone, 1991: 10). Rather, they act as both an interpreter and a go-between.

In this sense they are regarded as opening up possibilities, providing guidance and demystifying mainstream society rather than asserting some kind of repressive or overly directive authority. The credibility of a sports background coupled with empathy amongst staff for the condition of those they work with has encouraged many young people to engage with projects and in some instances to become qualified as coaches themselves, whilst others have been influenced to go back to school, on to college or into jobs. Some may have fallen by the wayside but rarely are they ignored, demeaned or denied access because of the likelihood that they will be troublesome or lose interest. In this sense part of the appeal of Positive Futures to *participants* may be that staff are not usually seen as 'teachers' and do not enforce the rules participants would associate with youth clubs or traditional youth work settings.

Youth workers differentiate between their role and that of teachers, or police officers, in that the relationships they have with young people are voluntary and informal and founded on trust and understanding. In deprived housing estates when workers are also peer role models, this can be even more effective. In this respect 'Jeff' is viewed by his colleagues as 'a good lad', a young but experienced and skilful community worker, comfortable working with females and males across a range of activities. His outreach skills, as well as those he brings to his sessional work, are highly valued by his colleagues. His background as a professional sportsman means he has sporting expertise, but this is not translated in his work into competitive demands for high levels of skill; he stresses fun and enthusiasm when he plays. Described by one female participant as 'lush,' a group of young women told the project co-ordinator that they would only go on a residential if 'Jeff', the project worker was coming along. He told the girls he'd love to take part in the residential, but that they would only be able to go if they continued to attend sessions and to demonstrate that staff could trust them by being punctual, behaving well *etceteras*... When the young women responded positively to his guidance and came on the residential, rather than maintaining a hierarchical imbalance he was an enthusiastic participant in a mud fight with some of the participants, unafraid to indulge in 'frivolous' behaviour in order to achieve an engagement with the activities being offered.

Nevertheless when away from sessions, demonstrating his own understanding of the participants, he has spoken of his frustration at not always being able to transmit to strategic staff the need to work in a flexible, non output driven way with some young people. He feels that there is something of a reality gap between project managers who drive initiatives at the local level, and those who deliver and are the 'subjects' of them:

> [The managers] want sessions that meet targets. We try to explain to the kids that doing this and that will get them a certificate, but it's impossible to do some of the stuff they ask us to... Some of them have done the minimum amounts of practical work and then they're making policy, setting targets.

Whilst the programme's national strategy has long advocated the style of work that 'Jeff' employs he has identified the desire of senior agency staff to impose ways of working and a search for outcomes which does not necessarily 'speak' to those involved in the projects. He attempts to interpret the strategic messages for the young people he works with, but within a working style which sees him behave in a way which is far removed from the rigid way he sees initiatives on paper. However, in his status as a sessional worker, 'Jeff' does not take part in Positive Futures team meetings and currently appears to have no channel through which to make his feelings and those that he works with known to strategic staff. In this context then, rather than realizing their potential as cultural intermediaries the workers are forced back into the position of one-way 'translator'.

For the political and social theorist Antonio Gramsci the role of the cultural intermediary, or what he referred to as the 'new intellectual', is necessarily broader than this if they are to realize the capacity for effecting change:

> The mode of being of the [cultural intermediary] can no longer consist of eloquence, which is an exterior and momentary mover of feelings and passions, but in active participation in practical life as constructor, organizer, 'permanent persuader' and not just simple orator (Gramsci, quoted in Joll, 1977: 93).

At the time of writing, whilst imprisoned by Mussolini's Fascist dictatorship, Gramsci was centrally concerned with the issue of realizing the revolutionary potential of subordinated workers and was in essence talking of trade union 'shop stewards' in his discussion of the new intellectuals. In a context where work has now become far less central to the processes of contemporary identity formation, social organization and progressive politics, programmes like Positive Futures offer the potential for an alternative means of organizing and realizing the potential of socially marginalized young people by engaging in a similar orientation towards agitation and action. Equally, when carried through to the broader demands associated with sport in development in the international context, we might extrapolate from these findings the weaknesses associated with the imposition of well meaning but culturally unfamiliar approaches brought in from 'abroad'. The cultural intermediary must always be able to face both ways, whilst retaining their credibility.

8.7 'Us and them': consumption, social control and the myth of emancipation

The difficulty with such an emancipatory vision is that in the era of 'liquid modernity' (Bauman, 2001), rather than social inequalities being defined through resistance and state repression they are now navigated through the market place. Consumers are now seen as bound into the social by seduction – driven by the images of 'perfect', sexy bodies emerging from commercial gyms, the dreams of football superstardom peddled to youngsters at soccer summer camps and the celebrity sports stars adorning the covers of lifestyle magazines. As such rather than emancipation from want, disease, squalor, ignorance and idleness that underpinned the creation of the British Welfare State, the welfare services, and by extension social inclusion programmes, now ultimately reveal the horrors of non-participation in the consumerism of the free market.

In this sense sporting interventions are more popularly *believed* to work because they continue to be seen to provide relief from a criminogenic environment. With the 'scallies', 'chavs' and 'hoodies'[4] residing on Britain's housing estates dismissed as 'the objective of aesthetic, not moral evaluation; as a matter of taste, not responsibility' (Bauman, 1995: 100) a romantic fiction of modernist sporting certainties is reproduced which is associated with the conventional functionalist interpretation of sports as inculcating a sense of self-discipline, routine and personal responsibility (Crabbe, 2000). Now enhanced by the seductive glamour and performativity of the celebrity version, sport represents a metaphor for the positively imbued social values that the 'healthy' *majority* claim as their own and which are wheeled out to the zones of exclusion in an effort to alter the behaviour and consciousness of 'risky' populations.

More recently, this seductiveness of sport alongside the demands of the corporate social responsibility agenda has led to a proliferation of interest amongst corporate enterprises who are increasingly looking to extend the reach of this approach to a wider international constituency.

One such scheme, Goal, which is promoted by the bank Standard Chartered (as distinct from FIFA's Goal programme), has taken this approach to India, one of its main operational centres. Goal is represented as a multi-stakeholder community programme which aims to empower young women to become leaders and social activists in their communities using netball as a vehicle for social inclusion. Initially developed in three disadvantaged communities in Delhi, the programme is built upon the kind of developmental approach espoused by Positive Futures. The extension of these principles to an international development programme on the basis of the corporate objectives of a global bank emphasizes the ways in which community sport programmes can then be mobilized as a product of a 'western' mainstream rather than a celebration of the cultural achievements of the disadvantaged. Whilst Positive Futures itself may have been introduced relatively straightforwardly to the South African context, this is again on the basis of a Western model of sport funded and developed by UK led institutions, albeit in conjunction with Lifeline/Childline Western Cape and the Western Province Cricket Club.

For all its positive contributions, there is the very real danger that even those community sports programmes which adopt a developmental approach might be seen to provide a means of educating the 'flawed' or 'illegitimate' consumers in 'our way of doing things'.

Emphasizing the legitimate rules of western consumer society have often proven beyond the community youth worker, probation officer, educational welfare officer or international development worker who lack the cache of social and cultural capital that goes with contemporary sport. What this kind of social intervention might be seen to represent for its sponsors then is an extension of the seductive appeal of its own consumer society which might itself be seen to lie at the heart of divisions from the Global South.

In this sense, despite the best efforts of the Positive Futures programme and individual projects, part of the attraction of these forms of community sports work to the mainstream is their lack of any ideological critique of the corporate sponsored consumerism which contributes both to young people's and impoverished societies 'ghettoization'. Indeed the offer of a 'passport' or gateway 'out' is premised upon the mediated appeal of one of the most rabidly commercialized industries on the planet.

As such, the funding representatives or agents of those who are 'legitimate' members of consumer societies, the socially 'included', are happy to sponsor the endeavours of community sports agencies because of their presumed capacity to 'reach' and 'manage' constituencies of the 'excluded' who, have proven increasingly troublesome for more traditional interventionist and development agencies.

Notes

1 Sport development has conventionally been understood as an approach based upon specific skills development rather than a more holistic personal development approach. Equally the use of sport within youth justice models has conventionally been associated with the use of 'diversionary' rather than developmental approaches.
2 The full research reports emerging from this project can be accessed online at http://www.substance.coop/publications_knowing_the_score.
3 An informal term used in the UK to mean a man and in this context, a man who is accepted by this social group.
4 Derogatory terms used in the UK to describe (often perceived to be unruly) young people.

Bibliography

Atkinson, M. (1990) *The Ethnographic Imagination: Textual Constructions of Reality.* London: Routledge.
Bauman, Z. (2001) *Community: Seeking Safety in an Insecure World.* Cambridge: Polity Press.

Bauman, Z. (1995) *Life in Fragments: Essays in Postmodern Morality*. Oxford: Blackwell.

Beck, U. (1992) *Risk Society: Towards a New Modernity*. London: Sage

Blackshaw, T. and Crabbe, T. (2004) *New Perspectives on Sport and Deviance: Consumption, Performativity and Social Control*. London: Routledge.

Bourdieu, P. (1984) *Distinction: A Social Critique of Judgement and Taste*. London: Routledge.

Bourdieu, P. (1962) *The Algerians*. Boston, MA: Beacon Press.

Buhrmann, H. (1977) 'Athletics and deviance: An examination of the relationship between athletic participation and deviant behaviour of high school girls', *Review of Sport and Leisure*, 2, 17–35.

Coalter, F. (2007) *A Wider Role for Sport: Who's Keeping the Score?*. London: Routledge.

Coalter, F. (1989) *Sport and Anti-Social Behaviour: A Literature Review*. Edinburgh: Scottish Sports Council.

Collins, M. (2002) *Sport and Social Exclusion*. London: Routledge.

Crabbe, T. (2005) *Getting to Know You: Engagement and Relationship Building*, First Interim National Positive Futures Case Study Research Report, http://www.substance.coop/publications_knowing_the_score.

Crabbe, T. (2000) 'A Sporting Chance?: Using Sport to Tackle Drug Use and Crime', *Drugs: Education, Prevention and Policy*, 7(4), 381–391.

Estrella, M. and Gaventa, J. (1998) *Who Counts Reality? Participatory Monitoring and Evaluation: A Literature Review*. Brighton: Institute of Development Studies.

Featherstone, M. (1991) *Consumer Culture & Postmodernism*. TCS, London: Sage.

Geertz, C. (1973) Deep play: Notes on the Balinese cockfight, in Gertz, *The Interpretation of Cultures. Selected Essays*. New York: Basic Books, pp. 412–453.

Hallinan, C. (ed.) (2007) Special Issue on: 'Cultural Diversity and Identity Issues in Sports Organisations', *International Journal on Sport Management and Marketing*, 2(1/2).

Hastad, D., Segrave, J., Pangrazi, R. and Peterson, G. (1984) 'Youth sport participation and deviant behaviour', *Sociology of Sport Journal*, 1(4), 366–373.

Holt, R. (1989) *Sport and the British*. Oxford: Oxford University Press.

Joll, J. (1977) *Gramsci*. Glasgow: Fontana.

Lasch, C. (1978) *The Culture of Narcissism: American Life in an Age of Diminishing Expectations*. New York: Norton.

Long, J. and Sanderson, I. (2001) 'The social benefits of sport: where's the proof'?, in C. Gratton and I. Henry (eds) *Sport in the City: The Role of Sport in Economic and Social Regeneration*. London: Routledge, pp. 187–203.

Lyotard, J.-F. (1988) *Peregrinations: Law, Form, Event*. New York: Columbia University Press.

Morris, L., Sallybanks, J. and Willis, K. (2003) *Sport, Physical Activity and Antisocial Behaviour in Youth*. Australian Institute of Criminology Research and Public Policy Series No. 49. Canberra: Australian Institute of Criminology.

Nichols, G. (1997) 'A Consideration of Why Active Participation in Sport and Leisure Might Reduce Criminal Behaviour', *Sport, Education and Society*, 2(2), 181–190.

Purdy, D.A. and Richard, S.F. (1983) 'Sport and Juvenile Delinquency: An Examination and Assessment of Four Major Themes', *Journal of Sport Behaviour*, 6(4), 179–183.

Robins, D. (1990) *Sport as Prevention, The Role of Sport in Crime Prevention Programmes Aimed at Young People*. Centre for Criminological Research, Oxford University.

Schafer, W. (1969) 'Some sources and consequences of interscholastic athletics: the case of participation and delinquency', *International Review of Sport Sociology*, **4**(1), 63–79.

United Kingdom Government Home Office (2003) *Cul-de-sacs and Gateways: Understanding the Positive Futures Approach*. London: Home Office.

Wheaton, B. (2004) *Understanding Lifestyle Sports: Consumption, Identity and Difference*. London: Routledge.

9
Southern Perspective on Sport-in-Development: A Case Study of Football in Bamenda, Cameroon

Jude Fokwang

9.1   Imagining sports and development

Much of the material in this book addresses sport-in-development as it is constituted through the overwhelming flow of resources from 'Northern' donor states to 'Southern' recipient states. In that sense it presents sport-in-development as part of the classical development assistance process. As the introductory chapter indicates (and strongly echoed in Nicholl's chapter in this publication) however, alternative perspectives on development are evolving, which question the efficacy of development assistance based on such resource transfer. Such perspectives variously concern themselves with the cultural specificity of development settings, the need for empowerment of indigenous communities in the development process and the recognition that knowledge transfer from South to North can contribute to some of the development dilemmas faced in a number of Northern contexts. By focusing on the engagement of Youth Associations in Bamenda, Cameroon, this chapter introduces to the book, a 'Southern Perspective' that is illustrative of such debate.

Clearly, the debate on sport-in-development, although diversified is informed largely by an ethos that places so-called Third World countries at the receiving end of development assistance. This chapter will demonstrate how erroneous such thinking is. Indeed, little focus has been placed on institutions or organizations in 'poor' countries that have evolved local grassroots mechanisms for self-help, often by-passing the state or local government.

In many countries, particularly in those that this chapter refers to as being in the 'Third World', it is frequently argued that sport tends to play a decisive role in national integration (Hess *et al.*, 1988: 572), which is critical to the development process. This assumption is indeed true of postcolonial Cameroon where the national football team has tended to unite Cameroonians more than any cause, ideology or institution.[1] Undeniably, support for the national football team among Cameroonians is almost universal, despite concerns that the government often takes advantage of the national team's victories for its own political agenda (Vidacs, 2003: 175). Football is Cameroon's foremost sport and commands immense prestige on a national and continental scale, especially after Cameroon's fantastic performance at the World Cup Finals in Italy in 1990.[2] Football, unlike other genres of sport in Cameroon has proven to be a key force in imagining the nation[3] and serves as a potential basis for alternative development channels or practices.

Universal enthusiasm for football in the country is apparent in the organization of the 'national championship and the Cup of Cameroon which helps make the abstraction of Cameroon as an idea, as a unit, real in the minds of the people' (Vidacs, 2003: 178).[4] Even though football has been employed in some countries as a form of resistance against repressive rule (Kuper, 2003; Ntonfo, 1994, 1998), in Cameroon it tends to play a central role in imagining the nation. At the international level for instance, it plays a role in the 'invention of national community' by providing a forum where 'national community can be symbolically represented' (Sundeen, 2001: 255).

This chapter aims to illustrate the debate on sport-in-development with the case study of a Bamenda-based youth association involved in self-help activities focused on the moral transformation of local society and the material development of the neighbourhood in which it is based. Subsumed under this objective is a desire to explore the relationship between sport and non-state entities (such as local communities and formal associations) by posing questions such as: how are local communities and identities influenced by sport? What role does sport play in the 'invention' of community and the creation of identities and what prospects are there for local development through sport?

The chapter approaches this question by exploring the assumption that involvement in sport and physical education can potentially contribute to transforming the lives of marginalized groups such as inner-city youths plagued by unemployment and poverty (Lawson, 2005; Sandford *et al.*, 2006) as also outlined in the Nicholls and Crabbe chapters in this publication. This chapter argues that despite the ambiguous role of sport (in the context of this study the focus will be on football) in mobilizing young people in pursuit of group objectives and the construction of identities, it remains a strategic vector through which development initiatives are conceptualized and accomplished. Drawing on ethnographic research from the neighbourhood of Old Town in Bamenda in Cameroon, the chapter shows that sport embodies and articulates the aspirations, tensions and contradictions in the Ntambag Brothers Association (NBA), a local organization of young men involved in sport and community development. It demonstrates that whereas football serves as a crucial vehicle for the attraction and retention of members in the NBA, it is also the object of intense contestations that have occasionally threatened the survival of the association. Despite these apparent contradictions, this chapter argues that sport contributes to the shaping of local identities and the emergence of new sociabilities and that the activities of associations such as the NBAs, offer fresh prospects for contributions by donors and development actors determined to explore alternative avenues and partners for development.

Indeed, the experience in Bamenda is by no means unique nor is it peculiar to communities in developing states. However, the organizational framework developed by local associations, their capacity to set their own agenda, respond to and negotiate internal crisis reveal insights not only about local development initiatives and processes, but also about the place of 'sport' in sport-in-development.

9.2   Sport and football in Cameroon

In order to appreciate this case study, an understanding of the place of sport and football in particular in Cameroon is necessary. Sport is tremendously popular with young people in both rural and urban Africa. As a matter of fact, athleticism is considered essential for survival by most rural residents (Vasili, 1995: 57), a perspective that contrasts sharply with claims expressed by colonial literature about the absence of 'games' and 'physical exercises' in pre-colonial African societies (Kemo Keimbou, 2005: 451), a denial that falsely credits colonialism with the introduction of sport (see Chapter 2, on the Eurocentricity evident in literature regarding development generally and sport-in-development more specifically). Today, many African schools maintain sport and physical education in their curricula and often treat it as a compulsory subject.

Clearly, colonialism shaped the development of sport curricula through the introduction of formal education. During the colonial period, for instance, schools were considered as the nurseries of aspiring footballers and the first destination of clubs looking for promising new players (Vasili, 1995: 57). As discussed in the introductory chapter, compulsory sports also fulfilled the material needs of colonial regimes partly because modern sports were expected 'to treat, to preserve, to discipline the body, regarded as a work 'instrument', the key element for producing wealth in the colonies' (Kemo Keimbou, 2005: 451). Thus young men were often the target of sport curricula, considered as robust actors in the development of the colony – an assumption that still informs the combination of sport and youth ministries in some African countries.[5]

While young Cameroonians have embraced different genres of sport, football remains the most cherished and popular among young men. Indeed it is noteworthy how football dominates sport-in-development throughout the African continent. Football was first introduced in Douala, a coastal town in Francophone Cameroon in the 1920s by the French and gradually spread to other parts of the then French colony (Clignet and Stark, 1974: 409; Vidacs, 2003: 170). Despite its spread to other parts of the country, Yaounde and Douala, Cameroon's administrative and economic capitals respectively, are the principal cities where football remains deeply entrenched. It is probable that football was introduced in the British Southern Cameroons from French Cameroon.[6] However, few Africans had enough resources to support a team and tended to rely on the colonial government for the sponsor of teams, which were organized predominantly along occupational lines (Clignet and Stark, 1974: 409).[7]

Despite the poor state of infrastructure and limited resources, football is played with great zeal throughout the country. In many towns and villages, football matches often accompany social, cultural, political and religious functions. This is equally true of many West African countries (Sarro, 1999; Ntonfo, 1998). In Cameroon, particularly during the long summer vacation (June–August), formal and informal associations (often with the financial assistance of prominent personalities)[8] organize football tournaments popularly known as *inter-quarter competitions*.[9] Prizes for such tournaments range from 50,000CFA to 1 million (US$200 to US$2500) and some teams tend to take on foreign names, a trend that appears to date to the colonial era. Some teams are named after European titles such as Arsenal, Manchester United, Juventus, and Liverpool. This phenomenon is far from new – possibly an indication of young people's association of modernity with Western formations (cf. Nyamnjoh and Page, 2002). Evidence from the colonial period reveals that the French frequently discouraged local Cameroonian teams from adopting European jerseys, an opposition which extended even to the titles of local teams (Clignet and Stark, 1974). For instance, initially named after the leading team in Marseille, the Olympic of Douala was compelled to change its name to Oryx Club during the French colonial period. Clignet and Stark (1974) maintain that the French tended to discourage the borrowing of European club models in order to affirm French pre-eminence not only in the game of football but also as a political power (Clignet and Stark, 1974: 23). Today, European-borrowed names often co-exist with locally created ones such as Chamba Lions and Menchum Eagles, coined occasionally after the teams' ethnic origin or manager. During fieldwork for this project, a local football team was named Pipelines after the team's patron who allegedly, had worked with the World Bank sponsored Chad-Cameroon Pipeline project.

Since 1990, the year that marked a turning point in Cameroonian football at the international level, professional and informal football schools have emerged throughout the country, attracting an ever-growing number of young men. Most of these football academies have been established by local entrepreneurs or corporations such the national brewery, Les Brasseries du Cameroun. A few foreign-based Cameroonian football players have also invested in this sector, although with little encouragement from the national government.[10] The fact that the post-1990 era has seen a significant increase in the recruitment of African footballers, some of whom have performed exceptionally well in some of the major teams in Europe appears to further legitimize football in the eyes of many young men as a pathway of choice to success in life. Today, Cameroonian-born players are professional footballers in Europe, the Middle East and increasingly in Asia.[11] Thus, for a growing number of young men, football appears to be a viable and prosperous career option, especially abroad (Darby, Akindes, and Kirwin, 2007), this, despite the growing body of literature that questions the contribution of such a route to the longer term development of sport in developing societies. Indeed such critical commentary tends to be borne out by the small numbers of young men who actually make it to the professional level. For most young men in rural and urban neighbourhoods, football is simply a recreational game to be enjoyed with friends and other athletes, partly for physical exercise, while also increasingly being viewed by regional and national administrators, as a potential tool for local development (Baller, 2007). Such is the case with the NBA, which incorporated football into its range of activities as a secondary item but which eventually became one of the most salient of associational activities.

9.3 Sport and football in Old Town

While conducting fieldwork between 2005 and 2006 on associational life among young people in Bamenda, I observed that football was an important leisure activity in young men's associations despite the fact that most tended to portray their associations as 'social' clubs rather than athletic associations.[12] Although incorporation of sport is unquestionably central to male associational life in Cameroon, its precise nature and implications have received very little academic attention. It is important then, to explore the various facets of sport, its role and developmental implications with respect to associational objectives.

Central to this chapter is the NBA, an exclusive male association of young men between 25 and 35. This association of about 40 members (at the time this study was carried out) consisted mostly of young men with varying levels of education and socio-economic backgrounds. In general, most of them had attended secondary school and a few had completed university studies. A majority of them were unemployed and lived with parents or relatives and occasionally, were involved in the informal economy. Unemployment was more widespread in the NBA than in the two female associations[13] included in the broader study (but not covered in this chapter) – suggesting a double crisis; that of the 'protraction' of their youth as well as a crisis of masculinity exacerbated by poor economic conditions.

The study employed the anthropological method of participant observation which entailed prolonged observation of associational activities as well as intensive open-ended interviews with selected participants.

9.4 Origin and objectives of sport in the NBA

Sport was introduced into the NBA soon after the association came into existence in the summer of 2004. Although founders of the NBA initially conceived the association as a social group, they also expressed the need to incorporate some form of collective physical exercise into its activities. 'We had members who liked to jog every morning. Some did so on weekends while others were interested specifically in football. We thought it would be in the association's interest to harness our collective interests for a common purpose', revealed a former sport coordinator of the association. At its inception, members of the association jogged on Wednesday mornings but this arrangement was short-lived because most people preferred football. As the association grew in size, more members demanded the incorporation of football into the association's schedule:

> As you know, everyone here loves football and as the association grew, some people said our group was now large enough to make a team or two. If you have more than 22 members in an association such as ours, then football becomes almost imperative as the sport of choice and that's what we did (NBA member).

Due to popular demand and partly because it was now feasible to organize themselves into two football teams of 11 per side, the association easily resolved to replace jogging with football. Saturday was designated for sports while Wednesday mornings were reserved for clean up operations in the neighbourhood, itself a kind of physical exercise.

The NBA's athletic reputation grew rapidly leading to invitations from athletic associations in town for 'friendly encounters'. Evidence from the NBA archives indicates that invitations came from professional football schools as well as from ordinary 'social' clubs such as the one seen below from the Able Brothers, a now defunct association of younger men (18–25 years) in Old Town:

> Dear Brothers,
> Accept our warmest greetings. We of Able Brothers request for a friendly encounter with the Ntambag Brothers Association. This is due to your constant training. Brothers, you know that one of our objectives as a social group is to keep fit; that is why we thought it is necessary to have a friendly encounter with your association on Saturday the 6th of March 2005 at 7:00am at Big Mankon field (NBA Archives).

Football games with other social and athletic associations in Bamenda permitted the NBA to not only 'keep fit' in their own words, but also to network with local associations in Old Town and other neighbourhoods in Bamenda. Such grassroots networks are critical to every development effort or initiatives, particularly in the light of the NBA's broad objectives detailed below. With time, members of the NBA began to conceptualize football as a tool for development – intended to align sport with the broader developmental objectives of the association as seen in the next section.

9.5 Football and development in Old Town

Although at its conception, the NBA projected itself as a social group comparable to the two female associations in the neighbourhood, it gradually transformed and began to represent itself as a development-oriented association. The NBA, like the two female associations in the neighbourhood and indeed as is the case throughout the sport-in-development community, also perceived itself as a moral agent determined to 'fight against social ills'. It attempted to project a more dignifying image of young people in Old Town through sanitary campaigns intended to rehabilitate the physical environment. The NBA for instance (as noted previously), devoted every Wednesday morning to clean up operations in the neighbourhood such as sweeping the main streets. They were also involved in the fabrication and distribution of garbage cans in public offices and strategic areas without charge, decorating public spaces aimed at giving a fresh look to Old Town, and repairing pot-holes on inner city streets ignored by municipal authorities.

In the past, young men from Old Town were perceived as ruthless and aggressive. It was considered risky to invite them for football anywhere in town. One story illustrates this claim by recounting an incident when a gang of Old Town youth prematurely stopped a football match about three-quarters to the finish time and escaped with the ball because they were being defeated. Another story relates an incident when a group of Old Town youth, certain of imminent defeat during a football match against a visiting team from Ntarikon, stirred up a fight and trashed their opponents in a deliberate show of supremacy. These incidents gave the young men of Old Town such a bad reputation that many athletic associations in town feared to invite or play with them. Many NBA members acknowledged they had witnessed such unruly tendencies while growing up but maintained that they were a new generation engaged in transforming the poor image of their community.

Popular opinion in Bamenda also tended to portray young people in Old Town as prone to violence, robbery, bullying and as peddlers of illegal substances. In the popular imaginary, Old Town embodied in many ways, some of the colonial and postcolonial literary representations of the African town as the site of 'corruption, moral, sexual, and social deviance' in which Africans had lost their souls and their sense of community (Diouf, 1996: 228). This perception was widely held partly because the modern town of Bamenda grew out of Old Town and the latter was perceived, perhaps, in evolutionary terms as the remnant of a forgotten past. Paradoxically, Old Town used to be regarded as a significant cultural centre, and as a focal point for the expectations of modernity during the 1960s and 1970s. It is probable that the positive attributes associated with Old Town declined simultaneously with the pessimism that accompanied the failure of the nation-building project in the 1980s – a failure characterized by sharp economic downturns and political uncertainty. Today, Old Town is perceived as the remnant of a faded dream and its inhabitants, particularly its youth, to paraphrase Comaroff and Comaroff (2005) as 'terrors of the present'.

Young people in Old Town aimed to counter such negative characterizations by encouraging behavioural reforms underscored by discipline and charitable actions such as the donation of food and household items to the sick, needy persons and prisoners. In addition to its frequent sanitary operations in the neighbourhood, the NBA also established a fund to sponsor disadvantaged children in the community – an initiative now perceived as emblematic of its 'development' agenda for Old Town. This unprecedented scheme by a group of inner-city and largely unemployed young men received wide acclaim among community members and beyond. In consequence, community development was re-emphasized as essential in the ideological structure of the NBA with sport as its prime tool. This claim is exemplified by the working relationship established between the NBA and a local elite club in Bamenda. In November 2006 the NBA organized a friendly match with the Veteran's Football Club[14] in Bamenda in celebration of its second anniversary. The NBA used the opportunity of this encounter to showcase its achievements and solicit assistance for future development projects. Marvelled by the activities and projects of the NBA, the veterans promptly donated more than 100,000CFA (US$200) to the association, promising further assistance and the possibility of a working relationship with the young men. This incident enabled many in the association to begin to perceive sport as vital to the association's identity and as a tool for community development.

The fact that many members of the NBA came to perceive sport as an instrument for development provides a basis upon which development actors in the north can engage with local actors (beneficiaries) in the south, predicated on the employment of a bottom-up approach in the pursuit of development objectives. A bottom-up approach presupposes that local priorities and the objectives of prospective beneficiaries should be placed at the top. In the following section I examine some of the disciplinary practices and moral projects carried out by the NBA in the name of sports. I contend that such dispositions emphasize the credibility local associations seek to establish for themselves, particularly in contexts of widespread corruption and moral crisis. Again, such dispositions are critical to any working relationship between local beneficiaries and proponents of sport-in-development.

9.6   Sport, morality and discipline

In Bamenda, like in most of the towns and villages of Cameroon, Saturdays and Sundays were the ideal days for football. The NBA often played on Saturday mornings even though some of its members also played on Sundays because of their membership in other athletic clubs.[15] Every Saturday at 6 a.m., members of the NBA assembled at the Big Mankon football field (owned by the Catholic mission) where they played either amongst themselves or against a guest team. Evidence of the decisive role of sport in the NBA was the fact that two office holders were appointed to manage sport activities in the association. Importantly, members were fined for not participating at football games.

Participation in sport was mandatory for NBA members and everyone was expected to show good conduct and respect for each other during football matches. This rule has contributed to the construction of new sociabilities among NBA members, dispositions that hinge on members' self-discipline, voluntary sponsorship of football events and donation of sport equipment for the common good of the association. The values of discipline and moral practice are not only encouraged but also prescribed as imperative for every member of the association. Take for instance, the critical role of fines in the association as a disciplinary tool. Individuals who fail to comply with regulations governing sport activities are fined. They are fined for absence from sports and sanitation campaigns, lateness at meetings, improper conduct at outdoor activities and unruly behaviour at meetings. Despite the general acceptance of fines as a disciplinary tool, certain members have an uneasy relationship with fines. One of the executive positions in the association is responsible for recording transgressions and the names of defaulters are read out at the end of each meeting. This period is often characterized by shock, uproar and protest from alleged transgressors who tend to deny any knowledge of owing a fine or occasionally, express outrage at how much the amount has been inflated. Most fines are meted out during meetings, mainly for unruly behaviour. An example may illustrate this point better.

An incident stood out during a Sunday meeting when a member, Claude (pseudonym), who incidentally was the day's chairman[16] decided to fine himself following sustained criticisms against him for improper conduct during the previous day's football match against the Brasseries Football Club. At issue was the claim that Claude had unjustifiably and aggressively tackled opponents during the football match at which the NBA was defeated by 8 to 3. Submitting to the torrent of criticisms against him, Claude resolved to fine himself: 'I find the chairman guilty of the accusations and request that he should pay a fine of 1500CFA' [US$5] – a statement that drew thunderous applause amidst laughter and confusion. Although it was fair and indeed remarkable that Claude should fine himself, many considered the amount rather excessive particularly as most members generally oppose heavy fines in the association. Normally, acts of indiscipline were punished with a fine that ranged between 200CFA (US$0.50) and 500CFA (US$1.2) but as far as the records showed, no one had been fined 1500CFA (US$5) for poor conduct during a football match. Claude's inability to pay this fine later strained his relationship with the association from which he was suspended for a couple of months.

NBA members were encouraged to promote sport in the association through material and financial contributions or by soliciting the assistance of donors. Support also came from external sources such as those of the Veteran's club as seen above or from professional footballers as discussed below. Such donations were displayed at regular Sunday meetings where the members appreciated whatever had been donated and expressed gratitude to the donor. This point is illustrated by an event I witnessed at a Sunday meeting during which a member donated a First Aid Box to the association. Although the young men received the gift with customary praise and a thunderous applause, it provoked a debate that seemed to have been simmering for sometime. At issue was the claim that a certain member of the association had promised to donate a First Aid Box to the association but had failed to keep his word even after several months of reminders. This concern was amplified by the fact that a couple of weeks earlier, Elias, another NBA member who owned a small medicine shop in the neighbourhood had donated essential medicines towards the association's First Aid Box. Aaron, who raised the concern then proposed the adoption of a rule that would prevent members from making promises in the association:

> This is not the first time someone has made a promise in this house and failed to honour it. Many people have failed to live up to their promises and it is necessary that we should abolish this habit of making vain promises. Everyone here knows that someone else had

promised to give us a First Aid Box but failed to do so. What prestige does anyone gain by standing in front of us here to make promises which they have no plans whatsoever of honouring? (Aaron, office-holder in the NBA).

Someone who sat opposite Aaron seemed uncomfortable with his suggestion and rose to challenge this. Gerard argued instead that members should be encouraged to fulfil their promises rather than be discouraged or hushed:

Aaron's concerns are genuine, but we should encourage people to honour their word each time they get up and make a promise. What is the point being a member of this group if we cannot feel free to make promises to our fellow brothers? (Gerard, NBA member).

But the matter did not seem to be as straight forward as it appeared. Carlson, the NBA leader supported Aaron's suggestions, citing an example of a member who promised to donate a ream of printing paper to the association but defaulted on his promise. 'Today, Manu is ashamed to come to our meetings' Carlson said.

That's why I think people should express their freedom by donating whatever they have but no one is compelled to do so. But don't come here and tell us you'll bring such and such a thing and in the end you don't show up with it. It is not a good thing. It leaves you embarrassed and compromises your dignity (Carlson, NBA leader).

Just when it appeared the issue had been resolved, Julius, one of the assistant sport coordinators, notorious for his side-comments during meetings, sprung from his seat and suggested that the First Aid Box should be reserved for use at sport events only. Most members resisted this view. They felt that it should be used at any time and for any member of the community in need of basic medical assistance. Consequently, the box was handed over to the charge of an executive member based on the understanding that its use would benefit the entire community.

Clearly, the above example reveals the internal workings of local associations and their relationship to the community. Although the NBA did not see itself as a community organization, it nevertheless tended to act for and on the community's behalf. Members of the neighbourhood also spoke positively of the NBA thereby providing moral support to the association's efforts. Thus, it should be underscored that associations or structures involved in sport-in-development hardly exist as isolated entities but tend to forge relationships within the communities in which they are based. Such relationships tend to be horizontal, informed by a shared history, culture and perhaps aspirations.

Another mechanism by which members were encouraged to promote sports in the association was to sponsor specific football matches amongst themselves or against a guest team. The NBA for instance, claimed the price of 5000CFA (US$15) (donated by a member) after defeating a loosely organized group of young men from Old Town by three goals to one. A few weeks later, Carlson donated 5000CFA as the prize for an intra-associational match pitting the executive members against 'floor members'. Although the executives defeated the floor members, the prize was awarded to the entire association at which point food and drinks were bought for all the players in celebration of sportsmanship.

The salience of football in the association was highlighted by the NBA's attempts to procure football jerseys. Discussions on this issue underscored the tensions between the position of sport in the association and its 'development' objectives. Three trends emerged in the course of the discussions. First, the view favoured by a majority of members that NBA funds should be used to purchase a set of jerseys for the boys; second, the idea that members should contribute afresh towards a special fund for the purchase of jerseys and lastly, to wait indefinitely for a set of jerseys allegedly donated by a prominent Swiss-based Cameroonian footballer whose assistance had been solicited on this issue. For several weeks, members debated these different ideas which eventually dwindled to the first two positions. Whilst a majority, including the president of the association favoured the use of NBA funds for the purchase of jerseys, a small number insisted that the association's savings ought to be used for 'development' activities in the community. Those who opposed the idea for fresh contributions maintained that, contrary to their aspirations, the association had made life difficult for many members by levying too many financial exactions on them. 'Look at the house today,' someone argued during one of the Sunday meetings, 'it is empty because we've taken financial matters to be more important than every other thing' he protested. This point was directed against those who favoured new contributions in addition to the fines some members ought to pay. One of the sports coordinators argued in support of using funds from the NBA coffers:

Since we started this group, we have not bought ourselves anything. Everything we've accomplished has always been based on contributions from our pockets. But now that we have some money in the coffers why don't we use it for the jerseys? How come we cannot do just one thing for ourselves this time?

The debate on this issue was further complicated when a member proposed that whatever funds had been budgeted towards the purchase of jerseys, should be used instead to repair the roof of the meeting venue.

I don't know why we're focusing so much on this jersey issue. I think this association was formed to develop our community and sport was only secondary. I would like to suggest instead that we use the funds in our coffers to buy sheets of zinc to repair the roof of this house. We ought to be concerned that sometimes when it rains, our roof leaks and this disturbs our meetings (NBA member).

Although some members initially considered this perspective cynical, it turned out to be a genuine concern about the perceived dominance of sport (for sport's sake) over the 'development' objectives of the association. With time, some began to argue that sports had become a thorn in the flesh of the association because contrary to their aspirations, sport did not appear to promote the developmental objectives of the association. Criticism against sport began to emerge when some members and the leadership of the association accused the sports coordinators of having strayed from the objectives of the Association. According to critics, the sports coordinators appeared to favour competition and victory over the simple objective of keeping fit. 'The idea was to keep fit, not to compete against each other in such a brutal way' Carlson admonished the coordinators during a Sunday meeting. Another member expressed his outrage over the fact that some NBA players were often replaced during football matches against their will and their positions filled with non-members who were alleged to be better players. Although the NBA allowed for the participation of non-members in its sport activities, this was only permitted when the NBA did not have enough players. The coordinators were accused of having breached this understanding by including non-members who were allegedly reputed to be excellent players simply for the ambition of achieving victory. Enraged by this practice, some members urged the president of the association to suspend the sport coordinators and to school them on the 'real' objectives of the association. This incident highlighted Carlson's warnings about the danger of 'losing focus'. As president of the association, he often reminded the association of his powers to suspend sports activities. He even accused certain individuals of having joined the association simply for their love of football, not because they believed in the association's objectives.

Soon after its first anniversary party in October 2005, the NBA recorded consistent low turn out at Sunday meetings compared to its Saturday football matches. Members alleged that more than 30 persons often attended the football sessions on Saturdays but stayed away from Sunday meetings. Unlike the sport events which attracted most members, a couple of Sunday meetings had recorded less than 10 members in attendance. This apparent preference for sports over the NBA's objectives prompted the president to resort to a drastic measure – the suspension of sports until further notice. During its meeting on Sunday, 20 November 2005, Carlson submitted a motion calling for the suspension of sports from the association. 'It seems to me that people come to this group for their own personal reasons' he declared angrily. Instead of sports, Carlson proposed clean up operations in the neighbourhood aimed at raising consciousness on the objectives of the association. After his remarks, some members of his executive took the floor to support the suspension of sports. Even one of the sport coordinators who had been accused of promoting sports over the association's 'real' objectives, rose to support the decision. 'It seems members have forgotten that the association had a specific objective which is the development of our community. I wish to remind the house that we're a development group and our first objective is to help our community to grow. Sport is meant to support us achieve this objective' he said. Sport was eventually re-introduced in February 2006 following an elaborate meeting during which members debated and agreed on the recreational role of sport and as an instrument for local development.

9.7   Sport, social imaginaries, masculinity and development

Earlier in this chapter, I stated that sport (football) was not included in the NBA at its conception. Football gained popularity as a sport of choice only after the association had grown in membership to over 30. Eventually, it became one of the association's most salient activities, sometimes treated by members as more important than the developmental ambitions of the association. I equally stated that with time, football came to be seen as a tool for development; that is, as a sport activity through which certain development goals could be channelled – fundraising for instance. However, the incorporation of sport into the NBA also led to unintended consequences – in particular, by permitting its members to establish boundaries of discipline and incorporation informed by a determination to transform society. Undeniably, sports provided individuals with an opportunity to identify with the association. As Carpenter (2001) contends, one of the values of sport lies in its capacity to promote social interaction. As in similar youth associations, sport was used in the NBA as a vehicle for the attraction and retention of members (Carpenter, 2001: 283). It also served as a tool of exclusion (Elling and Knoppers, 2005) because non-members of the association were not permitted to play on the NBA's side except on rare occasions. Participation in sport provided an effective medium through which young people built social capital and a support network. This is particularly evident in the current state of socio-economic crisis and uncertainty in Cameroon where institutional support for youth has become tenuous or disappeared completely and the life course has become somewhat destabilized for many young people with less predictable trajectories (Côté, 2002: 118). This claim is especially true for marginalized young men in the poor neighbourhood of Old Town where severe economic conditions challenge the expectations of their manhood – resulting in the protraction of their youth. Against this background, sport provides a basis upon which young people organize social life and create identities. By conceiving sport as a tool for development, however ambiguous, young men in the NBA see themselves as empowered to participate in society as responsible citizens and to give meaning to their lives even if only from the margins.

Through sport, members of the NBA exhibit and grapple with the crisis of their manhood undermined by the economic crisis and the independence and relative success of female associations in the neighbourhood. The fact that many young men were unemployed and tended to depend on others for subsistence led them to resort to the stereotyping of young women in the community, suggestive of their attempts to 'reinvent hegemonic notions of manhood' (Haenfler, 2004: 77). This, they demonstrated by contrasting their physical toughness in sports to the non-involvement of female associations in any form of athletic activities. Thus, sport in the NBA permitted its members to construct a sort of masculinity in opposition to their female peers in the neighbourhood. In many cultures, as in Old Town, sport is considered the 'greatest test of masculinity' (Hess *et al.*, 1988: 574) and the qualities often ascribed to winners irrespective of their sex are those associated with manliness, notably strength, courage, coolness under pressure and self-reliance (Hess *et al.*, 1988: 574). In contrast to the female associations whose members tended to be more economically independent, young men articulated their masculinity by resorting to sport. Messner (2005: 314) contends that men 'created modern sports as an institution that affirms the categorical superiority of male bodies over female bodies...' The fact that young women's associations did not challenge such characterizations contributed in reinforcing claims about the superiority and toughness of young men over their female peers. These identities, although constructed in the domain of sport, were often invoked and articulated in other aspects of social life (e.g. the NBA's dominance in hygiene operations in the neighbourhood). This validates the assumption that identity images expressed in one domain may also help an individual modify his or her self-perceptions in other domains, (Groff and Kleiber, 2001). Indeed, owing to its athletic activities and preoccupation with physically exacting activities in the neighbourhood, the NBA came to position itself as the foremost youth association in Old Town.

Sport in the NBA also permitted the construction of a new social imaginary. This entailed the socialization of members to virtues such as voluntarism, sacrifice and self-discipline. These virtues were apparent not only in the disciplinary sanctions meted out against fellow members but also in the general organization of associational life – e.g. individual donation of sports equipment, medication for the First Aid Box, sponsorship of football encounters *etceteras*. Through sports, young men in the NBA struggled to cope in the face of socio-economic disillusionment as they simultaneously articulated their dreams, aspirations, and expectations of a new moral order where young people in Old Town would regain their dignity and visibility as responsible citizens.

9.8   Conclusion

This chapter shows that the debate on sport-in-development needs to take into account the ways in which local actors (often constructed traditionally as 'beneficiaries') organize and articulate their own goals and limited resources. The example of the NBA demonstrates clearly that there exists groups and associations in developing countries that are not necessarily dependent on external development assistance. The NBA's activities in sport and its sponsorship of disadvantaged children in the community reveals a not-so-unique trend, but nevertheless ambitious disposition of social actors to self-manage their 'development' process without recourse to local government, the state or powerful Western institutions. This does not imply that the NBA would reject prospective assistance from external development sponsors but it remains questionable whose agenda would prevail were such a 'partnership' to emerge.

This chapter also shows that despite the ambiguous role of sport in mobilizing young people in pursuit of group objectives and the construction of identities, it remains a strategic avenue through which sport-in-development initiatives can be implemented. The chapter also shows that indeed, local communities and identities can be shaped and transformed by sport as seen in the ways in which the NBA has instrumentalized sport in the pursuit of development goals (such as providing sponsorship to disadvantaged children).

Through sport, we appreciate the changing ways in which the community of Old Town is imagined – first as a hostile neighbourhood replete with aggressive and unruly youths and later, as a neighbourhood of young people engaged in establishing a new moral order. This validates the claim that sport can indeed contribute to the invention of community and the creation of identities. In other words, sport serves as a mobilizing force through which its practitioners come to perceive themselves as a group apart with a range of common aspirations and shifting boundaries that include and exclude simultaneously.

The donor community can learn from the strengths of local organizations such as the NBA and explore ways in which they can enhance their capacity building. Donors can assist local associations in articulating or fine-tuning their objectives, establish short-term and long term goals and devise mechanisms to measure success and accountability.

This chapter has analysed the potential of youth organizations as channels and partners for local development through sport. It shows that although sport has occupied ambiguous positions in the community of Old Town, it has been instrumentalized in various ways by members of the NBA towards associational ends, namely in pursuit of development. The fact that the association is not elite-driven indicates its determination to define its own agenda and to pursue objectives relevant to the dreams and realities of members and residents. Such actors can benefit from various kinds of aid from donors keen on exploring alternative development strategies and partners, particularly in contexts where local forms of support are either absent or compromised by corruption.

Notes

1 In 1994 for instance, the participation of Cameroon's national football team at the FIFA World Cup Finals in the USA stood in the balance because of a severe economic crisis. Determined to see the 'Indomitable Lions' (Cameroon's national team) participate in the tournament, the government launched an intensive national campaign to raise funds for the Lions to travel to the USA. Unwavering in their support of the national team, Cameroonians irrespective of their ethnicity, political affiliation, age, and religion, donated to the campaign known by its French name as 'Opération Coup de Cœur'.

2 Cameroon's performance during the 1990 tournament saw the African continent rewarded with Africa being allocated three rather than two teams in the FIFA World Cup. Cameroon also went on to win the African Nations Cup three times and won the gold medal in football at the Sydney Olympic Games in 2000.

3 By imagining the nation, I refer to the sort of horizontal comradeship that emerges from the collective support shown to the national team at international tournaments. The nation is imagined through the national team in the sense that Cameroonians irrespective of their ethnicity, class, gender or political persuasion tend to support the team thereby rendering the abstraction of Cameroon (as a nation) real to its citizens.

4 The final of the Cameroon Cup for instance is always a much anticipated national event during which the President of the Republic graces the event with his august presence. 'The fact that he never fails to attend the Cup final is a reminder that the state in general, and the President in particular, take football very seriously' (Vidacs, 2003: 172). In fact, it is popular (and now often expected) of the president to declare a public holiday following the country's victory in crucial competitions such as the African Nations' Cup.

5 In Cameroon for example, the Ministry of Youth and Sport constituted a single ministry until 2004 when an autonomous Ministry of Youth was established, separate from the Ministry of Sport and Physical Education. It is worthy to note that this separation took place despite the blatant lack of infrastructure to house the separate ministries especially at the provincial and divisional levels. Critics have pointed out that the creation of more ministries was intended for political expediency – to satisfy political barons who assisted President Paul Biya to win the presidential election of October 2004.

6 The British Southern Cameroons gained its independence in October 1961 by forming a federated state with the former French colony. The former German colony of Kamerun had been divided between the English and French as mandated territories of the League of Nations in 1919 and subsequently as trustee territories under the UN in 1945, administered as distinct colonies by the British and French.

7 Some of the teams included the Public Works club of Bamenda (PWD Bamenda), the Victoria Area Council Club, the Prisons Club of Buea, and the Power Cam of Victoria. These teams all depended on the colonial administration or on business corporations run by colonial staff.

8 Prominent personalities (such as businessmen, government bureaucrats) tend to sponsor such competitions, sometimes simply for the love of the game, but most especially to win greater visibility and prestige in the community or region they claim to represent.

9 Inter quarter competitions refer to football tournaments organized between various neighbourhoods in a town or village.

10 For instance, prior to his death in 2003, the late Marc-Vivien Foe was involved in the construction of a football academy in the outskirts of Yaounde, Cameroon's capital. Since his death, no private or government initiative has volunteered to complete the construction of the academy, which regrettably has been abandoned to the elements.

11 Europe is now perceived to be saturated as a destination for footballers, and arrangements are being made with the US Soccer Federation for the recruitment of young Cameroonian footballers in Canada, Central America and the USA.

12 'Social clubs' also known as voluntary or self-help associations are sociocultural groupings that cater to the needs of their members by combining a range of activities including "njangi" or rotating savings schemes as well as social support to members in times of need. Social associations are different from charitable groups or NGOs in both objectives and activities.

13 The associations were the Chosen Sisters and the United Sisters. The latter consisted of young women between the ages of 25 and 38 whilst the former had a membership of younger girls between 20 and 26. Both associations had similar activities and represented themselves as "social" groups although some of their activities could also be termed 'development' – by which they implied the material or economic improvement of their living conditions.

14 This informal football club is generally an elite club consisting of government personalities, businessmen, lawyers and upwardly mobile persons. The name 'veteran' is misleading because the club has no association with members of the armed forces or related professions although some military officers are members of the club.

15 For instance, about 15 NBA members were also active members in the Sports Club, a small informal association of young men whose two principal activities involved a savings scheme and regular football matches with friendly associations in Bamenda.

16 Each meeting session was chaired by a member of the association in a rotative pattern, which allowed each person a chance to assume some form of leadership position.

References

Baller, S. (2007) 'Transforming urban landscapes: soccer fields as sites of urban sociability in the agglomeration of Dakar', *African Identities*, 5(2), 217–230.

Carpenter, P. (2001) 'The Importance of a Church Youth Club's Sport Provision to Continued Church Involvement', *Journal of Sport & Social Issues*, 25(3), 283–300.

Clignet, R. and Stark, M. (1974) 'Modernisation and Football in Cameroun', *Journal of Modern African Studies*, 12(3), 409–421.

Comaroff, J. and Comaroff, J. (2005) 'Reflections on Youth, From the Past to the Postcolony', in *Makers and Breakers: Children and Youth in Postcolonial Africa* (eds) De Boeck, F. and Honwana, A. London: James Currey, pp. 19–30.

Côté, J. (2002) 'The Role of Identity Capital in the Transition to Adulthood: The Individualization Thesis Examined', *Journal of Youth Studies*, 5(2), 117–134.

Darby, P., Akindes, G. and Kirwin, M. (2007) 'Football Academies and the Migration of African Football Labor to Europe', *Journal of Sport and Social Issues*, 31(2), 143–161.

Diouf, M. (1996) 'Urban Youth and Senegalese Politics: Dakar 1988–1994', *Public Culture*, 2(2), 225–250.

Elling , A. and Knoppers, A. (2005) 'Sport, Gender and Ethnicity: Practises of Symbolic Inclusion/Exclusion', *Journal of Youth and Adolescence*, 34(3), 257–268.

Groff, D. and Kleiber, D. (2001) 'Exploring the identity formation of youth involved in an adapted sports program', *Therapeutic Recreation Journal*, 35: 318–332.

Haenfler, R. (2004) 'Manhood in Contradiction: The Two Faces of Straight Edge', *Men and Masculinities*, 7(1), 77–99.

Hess, B., Markson, E. and Stein, P. (1988) *Sociology*, 3rd ed. New York: Macmillan Publishing Company.

Kemo Keimbou, D. (2005) 'Games, Body and Culture: Emerging Issues in the Anthropology of Sport and Physical Education in Cameroon (1920–60)', *International Review for the Sociology of Sport*, 40(4), 447–466.

Kuper, S. (2003) *Football Against the Enemy*. London: Orion.

Lawson, H. (2005) 'Empowering people, facilitating community development, and contributing to sustainable development: The social work of sport, exercise, and physical education programs', *Sport, Education and Society*, 10(1), 135–160.

Messner, M. (2005) 'Still a Man's World? Studying Masculinities and Sport', in *Handbook of Studies on Men and Masculinities* (eds) Kimmel, M., Hearn J. and Connell, R. Thousand Oaks, CA: Sage, pp. 313–325.

Ntonfo, A. (1994) *Football Et Politique Du Football Au Cameroun*. Yaounde: Editions du CRAC.

Ntonfo, A. (1998) 'Football et Identité', *Présence Africaine*, 158(5), 119–135.

Nyamnjoh, F. and Page, B. (2002) 'Whiteman Kontri and the enduring allure of modernity among Cameroonian youth', *African Affairs*, 101(405), 607–634.

Sandford, R. Armour, K. and Warmington, P. (2006) 'Re-engaging disaffected youth through physical activity programmes', *British Educational Research Journal*, 32(2), 251–272.

Sarro, R. (1999) Football et mobilisation identitaire: La 'réinvention de tradition' par les jeunes Baga de Guinée, *Politique Africaine*, 74, 153–161.

Sundeen, J. (2001) 'A "Kid's Game"? Little League Baseball and National Identity in Taiwan', *Journal of Sport & Social Issues*, 25(3), 251–265.

Vasili, P. (1995) 'Colonialism and football: the first Nigerian tour to Britain', *Race & Class*, 36(4), 55–67.

Vidacs, B. (2003) 'Football and Identity in Cameroon', in *Cameroon: Politics and Society in Critical Perspectives* (ed.) Gros, J. Lanham, MD: University Press of America, pp. 166–185.

10
Sport as International Aid: Assisting Development or Promoting Under-Development in Sub-Saharan Africa?[1]

Gerard Akindes and Matthew Kirwin

10.1 Introduction

The use of sports as an instrument of development in Africa has gained considerable popularity in the last ten years. Ex-child soldiers in Liberia, children in the slums of Nairobi, marginalized girls in deeply Islamic societies and disabled victims of polio are segments of African society where sport-in-development initiatives have been used in an attempt to empower marginalized groups and enhance general quality of life. Sports and development NGOs have come into vogue, much in the same way that the number of civic NGOs rapidly expanded in the 1990s with the push for 'multipartism' on the African continent.[2]

While considerable potential exists for the use of sport as an instrument of development in Sub Saharan Africa, the long-term impact of a wide range of interventions remains open to question. An important aspect of planning for future interventions is to engage in an objective analysis of the impact of current programmes. In most cases, the literature that examines sport-in-development has tended to focus on the potential of such programmes. This chapter, by contrast, asks if certain aspects of the sport-in-development paradigm have fallen short in the same ways that other international development programmes have failed, or worse contributed to underdevelopment (as Levermore outlines in Chapter 2, particularly section 2.3). Do sport-in-development programmes struggle with sustainability the way that other development initiatives do? Do they exacerbate the exodus of talented people from Africa and does the market for athletes have the exploitative aspects as do other market commodities such as natural resources? Finally what role do African governments play in the success or failure of these programmes? Such wider political considerations must be taken into account in the evaluation process.

Our method of analysis is to focus on the African context and present a comparative examination of several key organizations that have forwarded a sport-in-development agenda. Although there is great variation in sport-in-development programmes on the continent we feel that the issues we raise in the chapter are fairly representative of the region as a whole. This chapter critically examines the sport-in-development initiative broadly defined, focusing specifically on FIFA and football academies, the Meridian Project and sport-in-development NGOs. We argue that the shortcomings of the sport-in-development agenda reflect other problems prevalent in Africa, such as poor governance, economic mismanagement and poverty. Although we critique some aspects of programmes of sport-in-development we do not intend to entirely dismiss the clear potential of these initiatives to contribute effectively to the development process.

In this chapter we begin with a discussion of the contested meaning of aid in development and its relevance to issues of development, specifically within the African context. We look at bi-lateral and multilateral forms of aid and discuss contested meanings of aid. We then move to detail the diversity of actors who are engaged in sport-in-development in Africa. The discussion of actors also highlights the differences between sport plus and plus sport through the use of case studies. Finally we conclude with an assessment of the case studies, which critiques their respective contributions to development in Africa.

10.2   Sport-in-development and international aid

An elucidation of the characteristics of international aid, also referred to as foreign aid or international development aid is necessary when examining aid in the context of sport-in-development programmes. International aid in the traditional sense has been interpreted as the flow of resources from rich countries to developing countries (Riddell, 2007). A range of definitions of development assistance is offered in development literature. Führer, (1994: 24) identifies official development assistance (ODA) as consisting of:

> flows to developing countries and multilateral institutions provided by official agencies, including state and local governments, or by their executive agencies, each transaction of which meets the fol-

lowing test: a) it is administered with the promotion of the economic development and welfare of developing countries as its main objective, and b) it is concessional in character and contains a grant element of at least 25 per cent (calculated at a rate of discount of 10 per cent).

Although recipients continue to be developing countries, over time the types of donors have diversified beyond the OECD Development Assistance Committee (DAC) framework.[3] As identified by the OECD (2007), new approaches pursued by new actors such as private donors, foundations and NGOs have changed the international aid landscape. In addition to the bilateral and multilateral approach of the ODA, NGOs, global programmes, private philanthropy and the private commercial sector are now involved and considered part of international aid. Although the international aid finance system is composed of a wide variety of donors two facts are relevant.

First, historical factors such as cultural linkage between some DAC members and their former colonies in Africa continue to play a significant role in the flow of ODA to Africa. Indeed, as described by Schraeder (1995), throughout the 1980s Francophone Africa annually received approximately 82% of all French ODA allocated to Africa, and in 1989 the top ten African recipients of French foreign were all French colonies. The colonial connection in aid allocation is discussed in Cumming (1996) who noted that British aid to Africa is heavily concentrated on Britain's former colonies. Moreover, notwithstanding the significant French and British ODA contributions in sub-Saharan Africa other sources of ODA are predominantly European. France, the United Kingdom, the EU, and other European countries represent 50% of ODA to Africa in 2005 (OECD, 2007: 38).

Second, the role of agencies such as those under the UN umbrella, remain crucial in determining development agendas and goals. For instance, in the 1970s the UN general Assembly formally adopted the objective that the target of 0.7% of Gross National Income (GNI) for ODA be reached by mid decade (Riddell, 2007). The 0.7% goal continues to be a reference point in evaluating international aid, and the standard was reiterated in March 2002 at the International Conference on Financing for Development in Monterrey, Mexico.

Through its role of agenda setting, the UN leadership has, since 2003, brought greater international prominence to sport-in-development and highlighted the role of recipient governments in providing infrastructures and trained human resources for sport-in-development programmes. In fact The Sport for Development and Peace International Working Group established by the UN expressly acknowledged that the future of sport as a tool for development and peace ultimately depends on national governments (UN, 2006). Without governments providing facilities and training, sport-in-development programmes must make their own provisions. Moreover, as noted by Andreff and Szymanski (2006), limited sport participation is a result of a shortage in facilities and scarcity of qualified coaches, both of which are characteristics of less developed countries. In such context sport-in-development success depends on transferring resources to develop the facilities and human resources The Sport for Development and Peace International Working Group determined prerequisites for sport-in-development programmes. Viewed from this perspective, sports-in-development reflects Darnell's (2007: 561) comment:

> Development through sport operates within two distinctive, yet over-lapping discursive frameworks, sport and play as universal and inte-grative social practices and that of international development as benevolent deliverance of aid, goods and expertise from the northern, 'First World' to the southern, 'Third World'.

Evaluating the sport-in-development paradigm therefore logically leads to an assessment of international aid in sport-in-development programmes. It then follows that cooperation between the 'First' and the 'Third' World, as well as bilateral or multilateral international aid in the form of construction of facilities, donation of equipment, and development of human resources need to be considered when evaluating sport-in-development programmes. National governments play an important role in hosting such programmes as well as serving as the channel through which bilateral and multilateral aid (from both governments and interna-tional governing bodies) moves from donor to recipient. We must examine sport-in-development not only from the specifically labelled sport-in-development NGOs but from other institutional actors and pro-grammes as well.

10.3   Sport and aid providers in Africa

As discussed elsewhere in this publication, there are a wide variety of sport-in-development initiatives and agencies currently operating across Africa. Among the organizations engaged in the process are UN agencies and EU institutions, and also local and international NGOs, international sport governing bodies, continental and local federations, sports leagues, clubs, sport apparel industry corporations such as Nike, Adidas and Puma, and other multinational corporations as well as the engagement of Western governments through their various development agencies and departments. Prior to engaging in the examination of specific case studies, it is important to describe the main characteristics of the organizations acting in the field of sport in development across Africa.

Non-Governmental Organizations

Right to Play in Canada, MYSA in Kenya, and SCORE in South Africa, are more prominent examples of the many sport-in-development NGOs (largely plus sport) that engage in the process. These organizations partner with governmental agencies, international organizations, or philanthropic foundations and fundraisers to deliver and economically sustain their sport-in-development programmes. International and local NGOs are at times both donors and recipients of financial and technical aid. They are involved in a multilateral chain of international aid delivery from indirect aid providers whereby other international and development focused governmental or international agencies grant them resources for specific sport-in-development projects. They also directly convey international aid from their own funds when their sport-in-development programmes are supported by their own fund raising or financial resource generating initiatives. SCORE in South Africa for instance receives funding from the EU while Right to Play is a UN strategic partner in sport-in-development projects. These two organizations function in a multilateral international aid delivery partnership with the EU and the UN. Through their own fund raising structures they contribute through the implementation of their own sport-in-development programmes and also through the allocation of grants to national NGOs. Given their sport-in-development specialization, these organizations represent ideal strategic partners for sport focused multilateral international aid. Besides NGOs, sport leagues and federations benefit from other forms of multilateral international aid for their sport and their own development.

Sport leagues and federations

Professional teams or leagues, global sport governing organizations, FIFA, International Athletic Federation (AIIF), International Basketball Federation (FIBA), UEFA, the IOC and more recently the US National Basketball Association (NBA) are all engaged at some level, with sport-in-development programmes in Africa. In some cases this involves the

supply of financial and technical resources to sport-in-development programmes either directly or through affiliated organizations such as
national federations or associations. Their initiatives generally focus on
elite athlete development in their respective disciplines and in this sense
they may be referred to as sport plus. Nevertheless, while focusing on
elite athletes and sports, the same organizations also channel resources
in social programmes in local schools, and communities and in this
sense can be referred to as engaging in plus-sport activity. The NBA
Without Borders in South Africa for example, is often associated with
social actions such as the sponsorship of health community centres or
the construction of libraries.

Corporate

In addition to governmental and non-profit structures, there are profit-
making organizations that offer some level of aid to African sport.
Multinational sports apparel companies such as Nike, supply clothing
and equipment as well as significant levels of funding to a wide range
of sport-in-development programmes. Puma, as well as Adidas, are
involved in similar actions across Africa, generally through association
with international sports federations. As African national football teams
such as Cameroon and Cote d'Ivoire have gained more prominence on
a global stage, sport outfitters have become more proactive in creating
relations with official sport governing bodies. Most African national
teams have lucrative endorsement deals with sport outfitters and prominent sporting events such as the football World Cup provide great publicity for the companies. In addition to sports apparel corporations, the
development of the concept of corporate social responsibility has led
other private corporations to participate in sport-in-development programmes as direct sponsors of youth sport programmes, but more often,
through their foundations, by association and partnership with sport-
in-development organizations. Nike and Adidas the leading sports
apparel corporate have created special foundations and programmes
such as NikeGo, Sport for Social Change and the Nike Foundation.[4]
Other examples of the corporate social responsibility agenda as pursued
by sports apparel corporations are the Adi Dassler Fund created by
Adidas and the Reebok Human Rights Foundation.

Government departments from 'developed' and 'developing' countries

A further category of sport-in-development activity concerns bilateral
aid as supplied to ministries of youth and sports in a number of African
states, by governmental organizations such as the Conference of the

Youth and Sports Ministers of French-Speaking Countries (CONFEJES) or the Commonwealth Advisory Body on Sport (CABOS). The developed countries of CONFEJES such as France, Canada and Belgium for instance provide training to the developing countries members. Both CONFEJES and CABOS place emphasis on the development aspects of their respective programmes.

Our overview of sport-in-development aid organizations illustrates the diversity in structure and rationale for engagement in the development process in a number of African states. As explored elsewhere in the book, it is often difficult to make a clear distinction between organizations involved in plus sport as opposed to sport plus activity. Nevertheless, those broad distinctions are evident and it points to the diverse array of actors involved in the process. While organizations such as Moving the Goalposts in Kenya follow a holistic development agenda that focuses on the grassroots participation and uses sports as a means to pursue a range of health and social justice objectives, other organizations such as football academies focus on training elite football players (Forde, 2007). Although both target youth and receive aid these two distinct approaches show the wide range of sport-in-development programmes.

Figure 10.1 illustrates the range and diversity of the donors participation in sport-in-development. It also demonstrates that the border

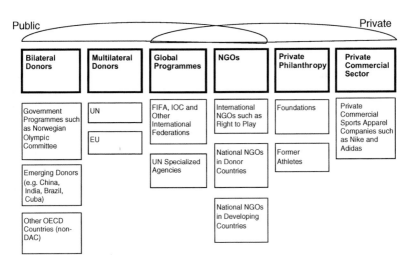

Figure 10.1 International financing of sport-in-development: aid (adapted from the Financing Development: Aid and Beyond (OECD, 2007: 12))

between categories is not rigid, but rather fluid. Indeed, although placed in specific boxes, many organizations such as corporations and NGOs belong to several categories. Nike and Adidas for instance, when considered along with their foundations belong to the private commercial sector as well as private philanthropy.

10.4 Case studies

In the following section we present a diverse set of case studies to illustrate the variation that exists in the field of sport-in-development across the African continent. We focus on FIFA, football academies, UEFA's Meridian Project and a selection of local sport-in-development NGOs. The discussion is followed by an analysis which critiques the contribution generated by each of the respective actors.

10.4.1 FIFA and Africa

The relationship between Africa and FIFA provides insights into how an international sport governing body translates its intervention in development aid in Africa. In the pre-Joao Havelange era there was limited interest in Africa.[5] FIFA was a European dominated organization with limited concern about the rest of the world with the exception of Latin America. Africa and Asia were perceived as peripheral football territories and not considered important for FIFA. Indeed, FIFA Eurocentrism and the power imbalance were explicitly expressed in term of distribution of World Cup host sites.[6] Darby (2002) posits that European matters primarily dominated the first fifty years of FIFA. In fact prior to their independence African nations were not members and therefore did not have the voting weight that they would have after independence. Moreover their continental governing body was very limited with few members who could influence FIFA's agenda.

In Havelange's campaign for election he relied heavily on non-European countries principally those in Africa and in the Caribbean. Havelange's campaign manifesto highlighted a FIFA aid agenda that promised to provide materials (balls, practice equipment and uniforms) to financially challenged associations, infrastructure (construction and improvement of stadia) and the provision of technical and medical teaching to underdeveloped countries (Sugden and Tomlinson, 1998). In exchange for political support, promises were also made to increase the number of African nations involved in the World Cup and to support football development projects in Africa. Although not a football development project, the Under 20 World Cup held in Tunisi 1978 was the first FIFA world competition organized in Africa it pointed to FIFA's intention of creating a more engaged involvement in Africa. Although FIFA's intervention on behalf of Africa may have grown out of 'political payback' rather than an altruistic desire to develop football on the continent, football development programmes including clinics and trainings for coaches, referees and officials have become staple features of FIFA aid to Africa.

Indeed, FIFA involvement in Africa has evolved considerably since the Havelange era. FIFA has launched several programmes for the development of football in Africa and has increasingly become associated with the sport-in-development movement in general. During a tour in Eastern Africa where he inaugurated a football centre, Sepp Blatter, the president of FIFA, stated,

> Africa is my continent.... Football is a school of life and there is a huge pool of talent here in Africa. Although there is obviously no guarantee that every child who takes part in these projects will become a top footballer, I have no doubt that football will make them all better people – and that is something far more important (FIFA, 2005).

Blatter was also vocal in regards to the massive and uncontrolled migration of young African footballers. He made several public statements and supported the passage of several rules and laws to protect African football.

It should also be noted that FIFA desired to present itself as a socially responsible organization. In an attempt to mirror the stated commitment of developed nations to devote 0.7% of their national income to development assistance, FIFA decided to allocate at least 0.7% of its total revenue into football for development activities in reference to the percentage set by the International Conference on Financing for Development in Monterrey (Mexico) in 2002 (FIFA, 2002).

Blatter identified the two focuses of FIFA programmes in Africa as talent and elite football development and social development. These themes are displayed in the various programmes implemented and supported by FIFA in Africa. An overview of the most prominent programmes, the Goal Programme and the Football for Hope programme showcase FIFA involvement in Africa. The different characteristics of these programmes highlight the distinction between sport-plus and plus-sport programmes.

Indeed prior to the Football for Hope programme, in 2001 FIFA was already engaged in a corporate responsibility programme. As an elite football institution FIFA manages the elite focus programme, but delegates the football for development component to Streetfootballworld. Although already supporting the Play Soccer sport-in-development agenda, FIFA's principal engagement could be identified as diversification of its contribution to sport in developing countries.

Goal Programme

The Goal Programme is a sport first initiative whose mission is implemented through a bilateral aid programme between FIFA and its member associations. FIFA (2004) states:

> The aim of the programme is to help promote projects in financially underprivileged associations, providing headquarters, natural and artificial turf pitches, training and education centres and other facilities that are essential to a basic infrastructure. The programme's first aim was reached at the end of 2006 when each member association had its own House of Football.[7]

Of 294 Goal Programmes approved by FIFA, 59 are in Africa, which represent the totality of African football associations and federations. Undeniably, the Goal Programme represents a development programme for national football associations and federations that are presently unable to support themselves. As mentioned by Andreff and Szymanski (2006) about 80% of African football associations are subsidized by national governments. This points to the inability of most African football associations to generate sufficient revenues to build their own headquarters and facilities or even manage day-to-day activities. The Goal Programme objectives address the capacity building of African football, such as training for administrators, coaches, referees, sports medicine and youth football (FIFA, undated). From a football development perspective, the Goal Programme directly subsidizes the infrastructural needs of football associations and federations as a means of assistance to African football associations. The only direct impact of the Goal Programme on the overall national football development in the countries in which it is implemented is better administrative facilities for football associations and federation. Other factors symptomatic of the difficulties of African football as highlighted by Tshimanga Bakadiababu (2001) include the quality of facilities and managerial and organizational weakness of African clubs. Such underlying weaknesses impose limitations on what can be achieved through development programmes such as FIFA's Goal Programme which focus on delivery enhancement.

Football for Hope

Contrary to its direct implication in the design, implementation and financing of the Goal Programme, FIFA's involvement in the Football for Hope programme is of a collaborative nature. In other words the Football for Hope programme, as opposed to the Goal Programme, is not merely a lifeline for financially unviable African football associations. It is rather a programme that works with local and international organizations to implement sport plus projects. FIFA classifies its partners in this programme in two groups, Strategic Alliances and Implementing Partners. The Strategic Alliance is composed of a panel of UN agencies such as UNESCO, the United Nations Development Programme (UNDP), WHO, International Labour Organization (ILO), United Nations Environment Programme (UNEP), and the implementing partners are sport plus and plus sport organizations such as Football Against Racism in Europe, Streetfootballworld and SOS Children's Villages, Play Soccer, Search and Groom and MYSA.

The Strategic Alliance represents a network of agencies already supporting sport-in-development programmes, which extends to development or social organizations that are not specifically sports focused organizations. The strategic alliance is consistent with the UN commitment to support sport-in-development related programmes. Indeed the UN resolutions and decisions adopted by the General Assembly during its fifty ninth session in 2004 establish the framework within which FIFA strategic alliance for Football for Hope is established. The UN resolution:

> Invites governments and international sports bodies to assist developing countries, in particular the least developed countries and small island developing states in their capacity building efforts in sport and physical education.

> Encourages the United Nations to develop strategic partnerships with the range of stakeholders involved in sport, including sports organizations, sports associations and the private sector to assist in implementation (United Nations, 2003).

A combination of factors established the genesis of Football for Hope. The UN resolution and the desire by FIFA to present a more socially conscious image played an important role in the creation of Football for Hope. The president of an NGO that worked frequently with FIFA, posits that after 2004 the commitment of FIFA to the concept of 'corporate social responsibility' led to the establishment of the Football for Hope programme. FIFA (undated) states:

> The Football for Hope movement is the key element of a strategic alliance, led by FIFA in its capacity as a world football's governing body and Streetfootballworld as the driving force behind a global network of non-governmental organizations, developing projects on the ground, in which football is the common denominator.

The Football for Hope programme represents FIFA's commitment to the sport-in-development movement specifically defined by FIFA as football-for-development, suggesting a plus sport focus. Links between the programme and Streetfootballworld is a significant development in terms of the establishment of partnerships to facilitate delivery. One senior development worker interviewed (25th June 2007) when asked about the administration of the organization argued that FIFA has outsourced the administration of Football for Hope to Streetfootballworld. The mechanisms of FIFA's engagement with sport-in-development rely on material and financial support of the implementing partners' organization. The development worker added that FIFA intends to, or in some cases does already, operate with the implementing partners. The implementing partnership is based on a distribution of grants and football material though FIFA business partners such as Adidas, which in this case supplies balls. The same interviewee, whose partnership with FIFA pre-dates the Football for Hope initiative, states:

> FIFA provides financial support and equipment to affiliated organizations like us. But since we have been ahead of the curve we benefited from FIFA grants and equipment donation before the establishment of the Football for Hope programme.

Football for Hope's intended objective, as defined by FIFA, is to respond to a number of social injustices through the medium of football. The social content and agenda of Football for Hope is clearly stated and attempts to implement decentralized development activities. By contrast the Goal Programme is elite oriented and assists national federations and associations in improving infrastructure and capacity building for the development of football. In the context of Africa, when national football federations are responsible for the execution of a sport-in-development programme the potential for successful development is greatly limited. This constraint reflects other problems potentially afflicting sport development and development in general which will be discussed later in the chapter.

10.4.2 Football academies

In the context of limited government resources for sport-in-development, the agenda is often carried out by NGOs or private organizations. Football academies are among the organizations, which could claim their contribution to the development of youth or communities. Although the goals of football academies vary by institution, their core concern is the recruitment of promising young players with the intention of turning them into elite professionals.[8] The following example of the Diambars Institute raises questions about football academies capacities to be sport-in-development actors.

The Diambars Institute is a boarding school that covers all athletic, educational and living cost of the young players. Recruited for football potential and regardless of their literacy, Diambars students benefit from a selective conditioned perspective of sport-in-development. The criteria to access the development potential offered by Diambars is conditioned by the students' talent. Created in Senegal by a group of former and active Europe based football players of African origin, the Diambars Institute launched its first class in 2003, and its leaders endeavoured to create a school for young footballers that promotes self-esteem, self-reliance and offers a traditional curriculum in addition to vocational training (Manzo, 2007). Training a football elite is a clearly stated aim in the institute's statement of purpose which is as follows: 'train, elite footballers and utilize the attractive power of football and the influence of champions as leverage for education' (Diambars Institute, 2003).

The academy relies on funding from a wide range of organizations, one of which is UNESCO. Their role is limited to seminars, public relations campaigns with high profile 'athlete ambassadors', and support for projects with sports as a medium for development such as the Diambars. In this sense it falls into the category of large international organizations such as the WHO, and the United Nations Development Programme (UNDP) and UN who do not generally become directly engaged in sport programmes but promote and encourage sport-in-development programmes and seminars. While the authors' intention here is not to focus on programmes by these institutions, it is noteworthy that sports stars from Africa and elsewhere in the world are often utilized as goodwill ambassadors for public relations campaigns on HIV/AIDS, malaria or other issues affecting development.

Unlike other sport-in-development projects which use a grassroots approach, Diambars is an elite football programme involving substantial investment in facilities, training and equipment as well as support networks for the wider development of young players. In this sense Diambars is undeniably a sport-in-development project being both sport plus and plus sport. Indeed, it provides education to almost 100 young football players. From an economic development perspective the Diambars Institute has the potential to have an impact on the hosting community. The construction of their facilities, recruitment of coaches, teachers and many other administrative and maintenance personnel offers employment opportunities to community members. In this sense, the influence of the organization can be compared with the impact of a small business on a community.

The creation of Diambars is part of a larger trend that has witnessed an explosion in the growth of football academies on the continent. In the relatively small country of Burkina Faso there are now at least twelve football academies. The prospect of a lucrative football career in Europe or elsewhere has attracted many players to academies. By the same token those who run the academies are interested in the profits that can be made from talented players. It is perhaps this phenomenon that points most directly to the ambiguity of sport and development in Africa. It may be argued that football academies have raised the level of African football talent, yet talented players play in foreign leagues, not in domestic leagues. The reason behind underdevelopment of African football at the hands of Western clubs and football academies is four-fold (Darby *et al.*, 2007). First, European clubs find themselves in a position of commodity trading and one consequence of this is that most local African leagues, once vibrant and financially sustainable, are now facing a severe lack of highly skilled players. Such shortcomings negatively affect the potential economic benefits of sporting events, a problem which is discussed in the conclusion to this chapter. Second, elite Europe based players are obligated to play for their respective professional clubs oftentimes to the detriment of national teams. Third, Europe based players lose their unique style of African football in an attempt to mimic the European style of play. Finally, many African players make it to Europe only to get injured, sacked or financially manipulated (Darby *et al.*, 2007).

Football academies in Africa have in some cases, benefited players and opened doors to financial success. However, it is worth noting that these academies have some constraints, not least of which is their exploitative characteristics. For the majority of academies the bottom line is to produce a player who will command a high transfer fee. Nevertheless these profit driven institutions, by means of their socio economic activities, allow us to label them as sport-in-development as well. The Diambars Institute in Senegal showcases the positive socio economic implications of such an organization in a hosting community.

10.4.3   UEFA (Meridian Project)

The Meridian Cup is an initiative, started in 1997, by UEFA and CAF, which aims to promote a cultural exchange between the European and African continents through football. Initiatives include technical courses for referees and youth coaches, development workshops for football administrators and also significant aid in terms of equipment and infrastructure. Furthermore, in September 2006 in collaboration with England's Football Association (FA), The Meridian Project visited Botswana to raise HIV/AIDS awareness.

The bi-annual competition alternatively hosted in Africa and Europe brings the best under 18 national teams from Africa and Europe together to compete. The aid and cooperation agenda of the Meridian Cup is clearly established:

> When it first began the project had three strands: 'Direct Help', in which UEFA aided two national associations selected by CAF over a two-year period; the partnership programme linking executives from different national bodies; and the UEFA-CAF Meridian Cup (UEFA, 2006).

To achieve the development goal, the Meridian Cup includes an educational component consisting of joint training sessions and meetings of coaches from Europe and Africa. The Meridian Project is thus a sport plus example of a catalyst for development of youth football in Africa that focuses essentially on youth elite football. The sport-in-development component of the Meridian Project consists of the donation of football kit and equipment to young footballers in Africa and training of football technicians in Africa. Regrettably the limitations of local leagues bind the capacity of such simple programmes to contribute to the football development of young players. Indeed, local federations infrequently, if at all, sponsor youth football programmes and officials and coaches training. Although supporting affiliated local federations have the administrative capacity to reach a larger audience, they remain constrained by their own inability to implement football for development goals. Lack of financial resources combined with structural limitations handicap their capacity to deliver nationwide programmes for sport and development.

Viewed simply from a perspective of youth football development the Meridian Project, provides an opportunity to youth football players of Africa to face the talent of their European peers. In a context where the young African players emerge from a mass football programme,the Meridian Project would represent an award and recognition of the players' achievement and talent. Unfortunately, most selected players originate from an already elitist youth football system in which academies hand-pick and train the most talented players. In other words, most of the African players are already in the talent pipeline that will eventually bring them to elite status. Consequently, the football competition component of the Meridian Project represents a display of the most talented young African players who will most likely be recruited by European clubs. Like FIFA's Goal Programme, the Meridian Project does provide some experience and training to selected African officials and young players, however, when considered from a broader angle as an aid programme for football development, the value of its impact is debatable. In comparison to the number of young players playing football in many African countries outside of any formal structure, the Meridian Cup effectively transfers resources from UEFA to selected CAF young player but does not affect, structural, technical and material needs of most of young players in Africa.

10.5 Challenges facing indigenous organizations

The increasing focus of sport as a development tool, evident in the activities of international organizations such as the UN as well by governmental and quasi-governmental organizations in donor states has created a flow of resources toward indigenous NGOs. Despite these resources, in Africa economic sustainability remains a challenge and grant funded projects tend to live from grant to grant. In Guinea the PRISM (Pour Renforcer les Interventions en Santé reproductive et MST/ SIDA) girls football programme was at one point successful in its goal,

'Combining Football with HIV/AIDS, Pregnancy Prevention Spells Success for Girls in Upper, Middle Guinea'.[9] It survived and persisted until the end of the grant that financed the implementation of the HIV/ AIDS and pregnancy prevention component of the programme. According to a senior administrator engaged in the health component of the programme, its long-term sustainability is in danger (Bakadi, 2007). The football activity persisted due to the determination of directors who run the programme, but the health component cannot continue. Although sustained for a longer period, the football component is under equally challenging strain. A senior administrator states (interview, 12th December, 2007):

> Once educational material distribution and support provided by the donor during competitions disappeared with the withdrawal of the donor, the girls and their parents lost interest and motivation in the programme. Practice attendance dropped, and competitions became irregular. There was no more incentive for the girls to come out for football. I have to go door to door to invite them to attend practices.

The PRISM case is typical of the challenges confronted by grant-funded programmes. The sudden influx of grant funded material, equipment, and financial rewards such as per diems, raise the standard of the programmes to an unsustainable level once the grant life cycle ends. In essence, PRISM became a victim of the same challenges that all international development programmes face, namely unsustainability.

As another example, the Namibia based sports and development NGO, Mondesa Youth Opportunities (MYO) programme is currently financed by donors mobilized in the US. An administrator of the programme presents it as a development success. Undeniably it supports the education and sports activities of youth in Mondesa. At the same time it could be argued that there is an over-dependence on key individuals in terms of management, fundraising and public relations, and most of the financial resources originate from the US. Here again sustainability is a question (Myres, 2007). The development component depends on external donors who may not remain with the organization after key individuals leave. Until MYO is strong enough to support itself through practices that have been institutionalized, it is only as strong as long as key personnel remain in charge.

10.6 Contextual constraints on the impact of international development and sport

The success of sport-in-development programmes is subject to the general and political environment within which the programme takes place. Sport-in-development suffers from larger political problems, and in some cases merely mirrors wider structural weaknesses in developing societies. In this sense, negative results and challenges that emerge from sport-in-development in Sub-Saharan Africa initiatives are symptoms that represent macro problems prevalent in African countries. The impact of efforts by world sport governing bodies, UN agencies, private organizations, industrialized countries, development agencies or individuals depends on other critical actors, in particular, African governments. Three factors handicap consistent commitment to sport-in-development in relation to African governments. The first factor is the limited awareness of the potential of sport-in-development initiatives on the part of government administrators responsible for youth and sport programmes. A survey conducted by the UN Inter-Agency Task Force on Sport for Development and Peace (2003) underscores the absence of policies related to sport-in-development. The concept of sport-in-development has then, not been defined and established in the overall framework of national sport programmes and policies.

The second factor pertains to the socio economic conditions of most African countries, which typically do not foster a fertile environment for sport. Keimbou (2004) posits that governments monopolize the sports movement in its definition, political orientations, implementation and strategic structure. The political management of sports programmes is still locked in the outdated top-down managerial style that emerged in the days immediately following independence. Unable to adapt or restructure, sports ministries are severely incapacitated and not supported by real financial input. Since the 1980s and the debut of economic crises around the continent, the capacity of governments to intervene effectively in sports has drastically diminished. This is illustrated in the rapid decrease in the budget for sports in Cameroon. The Cameroon Ministry of Youth and Sports budget in 1970 accounted for 5.58% of the national budget, however by 1996 it was 0.06% (Keimbou, 2004). The change in proportion equally indicates the decrease in the budget of the Ministry of Youth and Sports between 1984–1985 and 1994–1995 by almost 50% (Keimbou, 2004). The disengagement of governments under the structural adjustment programmes has affected sports in general, but governmental control remains. In many countries federations rely on the Ministry of Sports money and permission to organize their competitions. The Ministry has the authority to veto the organization of any competition (Loum, 2004). The authority of Ministries combined with the attempt to liberalize sports associations has placed associations and sport-in-development programmes between two sets of expectations. Resource allocation and infrastructure is dictated by ministerial priorities.

Moreover, politics often plays a negative role in sports programmes in Africa. In Burkina Faso, for example, the Federation Burkinabe de Football (FBF) manages the national team. The leaders of the FBF are all prominently placed members of the CDP, which is the ruling party. Due to the economic crisis in Africa, administrative positions that oversee large budgets have become rewards for those who have been politically faithful to the party in power. In other words, a leadership position in the FBF is a political appointment, which is often based on political payback rather than competence. In 2006, the FBF chose a local coach Idrissa 'Saboteur' Traore who was eminently qualified, having coached at high levels in Africa and in Europe. After a tie against Tanzania, Traore was sacked and replaced by a French trainer, Didier Notheaux. There is still a mentality that local African coaches are not competent enough to lead a national team. According to Traore [July 2007], the FBF forced the coach to make selections of players in whom they had financial interests. Some of the players were managed and sponsored by members of the FBF and by placing them in a match of international ramifications these players would have a better chance of signing with European clubs. When Traore refused to select players chosen by the leaders of the FBF, he was sacked.

Sport-in-development also faces major challenges in terms of deteriorating infrastructure. Although capital cities have the privilege of hosting the main national stadia or other sport infrastructure, the pressure of urbanization is progressively destroying many neighbourhood playgrounds that were initially part of all urban planning. Poli (2004: 117) posits that Yopougon[10] does not have any formally dedicated playgrounds available, stating that 'urbanization has had a catastrophic impact on the availability of playgrounds'. Poli's observations in Abidjan are not isolated. The rapidly growing urban population in Africa has put a significant stress on spaces originally reserved for playgrounds.

Organizations such as FIFA, FIBA and UEFA, provide limited assistance for infrastructures with limited resources but with a focus on elite or performance sport. The concentration of these infrastructures in capital cities already hosting the main government stadium or courts does not represent an asset for sport-in-development in rural areas or smaller cities and towns. Although facilities in rural or smaller cities exist, they are simply instances of private initiative with no concern for sport-in-development. In Burkina Faso for example, the best basketball court is actually located within the President Blaise Compoare's personal compound. The court is inaccessible to the public except for three days of the year when the President hosts a basketball tournament.

The previous point leads us to the third contextual limitation, which is that sport programmes are hindered by the political problems frequently found in Africa. Sports in Africa have become highly politicized and as a result such programmes have suffered from mismanagement and patron-clientelism. Elite sport programmes have become a political instrument whereby a victory by a national team in a prestigious tournament gives political capital to the politicians in power. Therefore, priority is generally given to international competitions (mostly football) (Baba Moussa and Herve, 2004). However, with the increasing capability of African countries to rely on foreign based players, there is less and less interest to invest in the development of the local competitions.

Lack of interest in local competitions also effects the degree to which the sports sector contributes to economic activity in the form of the manufacture of sporting goods, sport-related services, infrastructure development and sports events, including supplementary effects from spectators, sponsors, vendors and the media. In the UN's sport and development report (2006), it is argued that the sports sector is an economic engine. The UN's suggestion of sport contributing to economic activity refers mainly to societies in industrialized nations with a sport industry worth several billions of dollars. Although on a much smaller scale one need only witness a major football match in Africa and the economic activity that it engenders. At a recent African Cup of Nations qualification match in Burkina Faso, water and food vendors, parking attendants and other *commercants* descended en masse on the national stadium to take part in the informal economic opportunities that the match offered.[11] Such activities can have a significant impact on local vendors, their families and community and furthermore on the local economy.[12]

Although the example of the international football game in Burkina Faso demonstrates some glimpses of a positive impact of sport on a local economy, the limited number of such events points to the limitations of real potential of sporting events as engines of economic development. Moreover, the economic impact resulting from sports related manufactured goods and services in Africa has not yet been established despite the fact that its potential has been heavily touted by the UN. Another central problem is the imbalance between the funds available for mass sports programmes and elite sports. With all emphasis on elite sports the potential for sustainable development and growth of local non-elite programmes has been severely diminished. Political leaders place a premium on high profile sport victories for the political capital that they engender. Evidence of this practice is to be found in the resources made available to the national football teams. One such example is the recent attempt by the Burkinabe national football team to qualify for the African Cup of Nations. Burkina Faso is one of 38 African countries that played matches in 2006 and 2007 to qualify for the 2008 African Cup of Nations. In April the team travelled for a CAN qualifying match in Mozambique. According to the local newspaper *Le Pays* (2007),

> Expenses for the national team to travel to Mozambique cost 176,000,000 cfa [US $352,000]. 100,000,000 [US$ 200,000] cfa for the minister of sports and 44,319,733 cfa [US$ 88,639] for lodging in Ouagadougou for 2 days, trip to Paris to retrieve players, stop in Harare for friendly match, and the actual match in Maputo.[13]

According to the United Nations Development Program Human Development Index (2005), Burkina Faso is one of the five poorest countries in the world, yet it was able to spend over $300,000 US dollars for a match and its preparation.

Moreover, despite the initiatives of FIFA, there appears to be a disconnect between resources provided to African nations and the results on the ground. Although FIFA has expressed its intent to aid grassroots football and affect positive social change, its initiatives have remained elite-focused. Indeed, known for absorbing a large proportion of sports budget in developing countries, elite sport and more specifically elite football can be considered the economic antinomy of football for development programmes. Baba Moussa (2003) provides several examples of the structural organization of sport in Benin that conflict with sport-in-development, detailing for example that 80% of sports budget are allocated to elite sports, particularly football.

The case of Togo's recent participation in the 2006 World Cup serves as evidence for Baba Moussa's argument. Prior to the World Cup the Togolese team was given US$ 5.6 million by FIFA for their appearance. The players initially refused to play unless they were paid US$ 200,000 per player. With 23 players this translates into a demand of US$ 4.4 million which accounts for 82% of Togo's World Cup appearance fee. Moreover, this does not include the coach's salary, hotel or transport. Furthermore, although Togo consistently ranks among the world's poorest nations, the Togolese government donated US$ 500,000 for 100 Togolese football fans to attend the World Cup (BBC, 2006). These figures point to the emphasis that is placed on elite sports in Africa at the expense of long term investment in grassroots football or development in general.

FIFA's intervention in Africa, regardless of its motivation, has supported the development of African football albeit from the elitist perspective. However, the overall development of football in terms of capacity building, coaches, officials, as well as facilities and infrastructure remains limited. FIFA's contribution is quickly consumed by the national teams' expenses, recruitment of foreign coaches, and nationalist and elite centred African football organizations.

Although important for the development of football in developing nations, FIFA aid, by supporting national federations and associations, encourages governments to focus an inordinate amount of time and resources on elite football. Therefore, without being a direct causal factor of underdevelopment of sport in Africa, it indirectly endorses policies which allocate most of the limited resources available for mass sports. FIFA stokes the fire of elite football and African countries bereft of resources, fan the flames. This clearly raises questions concerning the efficacy of such an approach to development. Football academies are one of the derivatives of the elitist focus of African football.

10.7 Conclusion

As outlined in the introductory chapter, sport-in-development has increasingly been mainstreamed in discourse concerning international development. This chapter has attempted to point to the constraints concerning the use of sports, in particular football, as a development tool within the African continent. In some cases international sports programmes, particularly those involving elite sports programmes, have contributed to the muscle drain and ignored the potential of sport and development programmes that target the masses. In other cases, such as those related to locally based NGOs, positive developments have occurred. Long-term questions remain, however. It is not certain that

African states can intervene to give the support that is needed for sport-in-development to flourish as an aspect of wider development framework in the longer term. By the same token, it is not evident that sport-in-development programmes are sustainable by local means in the longer term either. Sport-in-development programmes must rely on external sources of funding for their operations, which is a constraint that increases their vulnerability. The State Department and USAID in the US and their political agenda are making more and more grants available for sport-in-development programmes. Some of these grants have a one or two year non-renewable implementation plan. This could leave the beneficiaries without substantial resources to sustain their activities. Aid and sport-in-development, although multilateral, relies on local infrastructures which only governments or local rich individuals or private organizations can build.

Ultimately then, the sport-in-development agenda is hampered by broader systemic problems, such as poor governance, patron-clientelism and poverty that are endemic to the region. As such, it is unfair to place blame on the sport-in-development programmes, yet by the same token, the said programmes should adapt their strategies to the existing conditions in order to avoid the undesirable outcomes that are detailed in this chapter. Perhaps the best course is to implement a more inclusive sport-in-development programme that de-emphasizes the success of elite athletes and rather seeks to engage people at the grassroots. This may be difficult, especially in light of the political rewards that await politicians on the occasion of a high-profile victory by the national football team or the success of an ex-patriot in an elite European football league.

The examples of MYO and PRISM also raise the question of sustainability of sport-in-development programmes through NGOs. The models of NGOs financially dependent on external support represent the more vulnerable model of NGOs dedicated to sport and development. However there are opportunities by which to make the sport-in-development paradigm more successful and sustainable. The NGO Play Soccer in Zambia attempts to establish its sustainability through partnership with Agribusiness in Sustainable Natural African Plant Products (ASNAPP) to produce income-generating crops. The study and evaluation of such partnerships may provide a long-term option for sustainability of sport-in-development programmes. However the relatively early stage of most of the programmes, combined with the scarcity of data, limits the capacity to evaluate and assess the economic impact and viability of sport-in-development programmes. A sport-in-development program director with significant experience in Africa posits that due to the lack of resources and organizational know how, long-term evaluation is a challenge. However, she underscores some economic goals and achievements, stating:

> In the countries where we have been the longest such as Ghana and Zambia, we are developing a number of activities that can be income generating and will hopefully add to local poverty reduction but also from a micro level which could be a catalyst for larger socioeconomic development within the community. When these activities are established and ongoing and contribute to help sustain the programme that will be a validation of what we'll be able to accomplish (June, 25 2007).

This statement suggests a potential for an economic impact of sport-in-development programmes in community settings as well as the sustainability challenge practitioners confront. Indeed sport-in-development projects require a network of competencies, initial investments and an economically conducive environment to implement revenue-generating activities capable of impacting the community.

For the reasons addressed in this chapter the long-term impact of sport-in-development remains to be demonstrated. Many programmes have resulted in individual success stories and positive socio economic impact on communities. However, governments' commitment to sport-in-development, the role of international aid in designing, financing and supporting many of the projects in place, and the prevalence of performance sport raise many questions. As a relatively recent addition to the development process, sport-in-development has not yet been fully integrated into most of the sports policies by governments in Sub Saharan African, or other developing regions. Although this situation can be attributed to governments' lack of understanding or awareness of the potential of sport as a development tool, sport-in-development can also be viewed as part of an external agenda with essentially no local design or input. Consequently, despite its potential, sport-in-development is in danger of being evaluated, as any other development programmes, as ultimately ineffective.

The challenge is to identify an alternative approach that would help to overcome this problem. Perhaps by focusing on issues of ownership and partnership, sport-in-development programmes can be more effectual. This can be achieved by engendering a more participatory approach that gives stakeholders more influence. Additionally, although perhaps less likely, a greater emphasis on grassroots rather than elite sports will bring better and more widespread results.

Notes

1 The authors wish to thank Denise Haba, Idrissa 'Saboteur' Traore and Judy McPherson for their useful insights that contributed to this chapter.

2 As democratization swept over the African continent in the 1990s the number of civic minded NGOs expanded greatly. Many of the civic NGOs preceded or coincided with democratization but some of them were created with the goal of gaining access to the external funding that western governments had made available. We argue that the proliferation of sport NGOs is analogous as more external funding has been established more sport focused NGOs have sprouted.

3 The Development Assistance Committee (DAC) has 23 members all industrialized developed countries.

4 'NikeGo' is the only sport apparel corporate visible on the International Platform on Sport and Development web site, http://www.sportanddev. org/en/organisations/sporting-goods-industry/nike-inc.htm.

5 João Havelange was the president of FIFA from 1974 to 1998.

6 Until 1982 only one African team and one Asian team could qualify for the World Cup.

7 Further details of the Goal Programme can be found on FIFA web site section Goal Programme at http://www.fifa.com/aboutfifa/developing/goal-programme/projectstatus.html.

8 For greater details on African football academies see Darby *et al.*, 2007.

9 Johns Hopkins School of Health Center for Communication partner on this project with USAID to implement management sciences health strategic communication.

10 Youpougon is the largest and one of the fastest growing of the 10 communes of the city of Abidjan, the economic capital of Cote d'Ivoire.

11 Observed at Cup of Nations match between Burkina Faso and Tanzania, 16 June 2007.

12 Interview with a former national trainer of Burkina Faso football team, July 2007.

13 Article in Le Pays, Federation Burkinabé De Football L'Heure N'est Pas à la Démission, 20th June 2007, Number 3894.

Bibliography

Andreff, W. and Szymanski, S. (2006) *Handbook on the Economics of Sport.* Cheltenham, UK; Northampton, MA: Edward Elgar.

Baba-Moussa, A.R. (2003) *Sport éducation et sante au Bénin: Un pari manqué?* France: Université du Littoral Cote d'Opale.

Baba-Moussa, A.R. and Herve, N. (2004) *Sport, jeunesse et éducation au Bénin*, in Bouchet, P. and Kaach, M. (eds) *Afrique Francophone et Développement du Sport: Mythe ou Réalité.* Paris: L'Harmattan, pp. 49–63.

Bakadi, G. (2007) 'Sport, Health and Education', paper presented at the *Health, Science and Sport in Africa Conference*, Ohio University, 24 February 2007.

BBC News (2006) 'Togo's fans angry at visa denial', BBC retrieved June 9 2006 from http://news.bbc.co.uk/2/hi/africa/5063716.stm.

Bouchet, P. and Kaach, M. (eds) (2004) *Afrique Francophone et Développement du Sport: Mythe ou Réalité*. Paris: L'Harmattan.

Afriquechos.ch (2006) *Égypte – côte d'Ivoire: La finale en direct sur TF1 ce vendredi 10 février à 17h.* Retrieved 15th May, 2006, from, http://www.afriquechos.ch/spip.php?article1091.

Coalter, F. (2007) 'MYSA: An Evaluation', Unpublished paper presented at the International Studies Association, Conference, Chicago, Illinois.

Cumming, G. (1996) 'British Aid to Africa: A Changing Agenda?', *Third World Quarterly*, 17(3), 487–501.

Darby, P., Akindes, G. and Kirwin, M. (2007) 'Football Academies and the Migration of African Football Labour to Europe', *The Journal of Sport and Social Issues*, 31(2), 143–161.

Darby, P. (2002) *Africa, Football and FIFA: Politics, Colonialism and Resistance*. Frank Cass: London and Portland, OR.

Darnell, S. (2007) 'Playing with Race: Right to Play and the Production of Whiteness in "Development through Sport"', *Sport and Society*, 10 (4), 560–579.

Diambars Institute (2003) *Diambars: The Project, Our Goal.* Retrieved from http://www.diambars.org/index.php?p=rubriques/projet/objectif, accessed 25th January 2007.

FIFA (2002) Make the World a Better Place. Retrieved from http://www.fifa.com/mm/document/afprograms/worldwideprograms/fifa_ffh_en_1851.pdf, accessed 10th December 2007.

FIFA (2004) Goal Program. Retrieved from http://www.fifa.com/aboutfifa/developing/goalprogramme/projectstatus.html, accessed 11th January 2007.

FIFA (2005) 'Joseph S. Blatter in East Africa'. Retrieved from http://www.fifa.com/aboutfifa/federation/insidefifa/news/newsid=101193.html, accessed 25th January 2007.

Forde, S. (2007) 'Doing It Ourselves: Participatory Monitoring and Evaluation in a Girl's Football and Health Project in Kilifi, Kenya, East Africa', paper presented at the *Health, Science and Sport in Africa Conference*, Ohio University, 24th February, 2007.

Führer, H. (1994) *A History of The Development Assistance Committee and the Development Co-Operation Directorate in Dates, Names And Figures.* Paris: OECD.

Keimbou, K. (2004) 'L'Etat du sport au Cameroun. Rhétorique et réalité des politiques sportives en Afrique noire de 1960 à 1996', in Bouchet, P. and Kaach, M. (eds) *Afrique Francophone et Développement du Sport: Mythe ou Réalité*, Paris, L'Harmattan, pp. 13–25.

Loum, F. (2004) 'Evaluation des Politiques Sportives au Sénégal de 1960 à 1998', in Bouchet, P. and Kaach, M. (eds) (2004) *Afrique Francophone et Développement du Sport: Mythe ou Réalité*, Paris, L'Harmattan, pp. 27–47.

Le Pays, 'Federation Burkinabé De Football L'Heure N'est Pas à la Démission', 20th June 2007, Number 3894.

Manzo, K. (2007) 'Learning to Kick: African football Schools as Carriers of Development', *Impumelelo: The Electronic Interdisciplinary Journal of African*

Sports, **2**(1), http://www.ohiou.edu/sportsafrica/JOURNAL/Volume2/learnto-kick.htm

Myres, R. (2007) 'Facilitating Development of the Healthy African Child', paper presented at the *Health, Science and Sport in Africa Conference,* Ohio University, 24th February.

NBA (2005) 'NBA Stars Show Their Love and Support for Africa with Basketball without Borders', (September 2005) retrieved 25th February, 2007, from http://www.nba.com/bwb/africa_release2006.html.

OECD (2007) *Financing Development: Aid and Beyond.* Paris: OECD .

Palan, R. (2000) *Global Political Economy. Contemporary Theory.* London: Routledge.

Poli, R. (2002) *Le football en Côte-D'ivoire: Organisation spatiale et pratiques urbaines.* Neuchâtel: Centre International d'étude du sport.

Poli, R. (2004) *Les migrations internationales des footballeurs trajectoires de joueurs camerounais en Suisse.* Neuchâtel: CIES Centre international d'étude du sport.

Riddell, R. (2007) *Does Foreign Aid Really Work?.* New York and Oxford: Oxford University Press.

Schraeder, P. (1995) 'From Berlin 1884 to 1989: Foreign Assistance and French, American, and Japanese Competition in Francophone Africa', *The Journal of Modern African Studies,* **33**(4), 539–567.

Sugden, J. and Tomlinson, A. (1998) *FIFA and the contest for world football: who rules the peoples' game?.* Cambridge, UK; Malden, MA: Blackwell Publishers.

Tshimanga Bakadiababu, E. (2001). *Le commerce et la traite des footballeurs africains et sud-américains en Europe.* Paris: L'Harmattan.

UEFA (2006) 'Meridian's helping hand', retrieved 25th February 2007 from http://www.uefa.com/competitions/meridiancup/news/kind=1/newsid=49451 8.html.

United Nations (2003) 'Sports as means to promote education, health development and peace', General Assembly Fifty-eighth session, 17 November.

United Nations (2006) *United Nations Report, Report of the Secretary General of the United Nations,* 22 September, 61st Session.

United Nations, Inter-Agency Task Force on Sport for Development and Peace (2003) *Sport for development and peace: Towards achieving the millennium development goals: Report from the united nations inter-agency task force on sport for development and peace.* New York: United Nations.

United Nations Development Program (2005) *Statistics of the Human Development Report* Retrieved 30th November, 2007 from http://hdrstats.undp. org/countries/country_fact_sheets/cty_fs_BFA.html

11
Opportunities, Limitations, Questions

Roger Levermore and Aaron Beacom

Sport-in-development is in its formative years. The use of sport as a development tool reflects efforts to broaden the activities of the development process. This increased usage of a range of sports in a number of development contexts is due to a combination of factors, including the need to find new ways to facilitate and promote developmental goals, especially to areas/communities affected by well documented concerns over the effectiveness of the state (and other mainstream actors) to improve conditions for their citizens (as discussed by Levermore in Chapter 2). The appeal of sport to reach communities, particularly young people, largely excluded from substantive traditional development activity is an argument put forward by many advocates of sport-in-development. For example, Nelson Mandela is frequently referenced as saying:

> Sport has the power to change the world. It has the power to inspire in a way that little else does. It speaks to youth in a language they understand. Sport can create hope, where once there was despair. It is more powerful than governments in breaking down barriers. It laughs in the face of discrimination (quoted for instance by *The Guardian*, 2004 and Sporting Equals, undated).

This adds to ways in which sport is linked to furthering a range of development targets such as the MDGs (outlined in the Preface and Introduction).

11.1 Opportunities and limitations for sport-in-development

Perceptions towards sport, particularly by some of those who are in positions of power, are changing. Those who might have regarded sport suspiciously or dismissed the seriousness of its potential for 'social good' in the past are in some instances being replaced by a generation who see sport in a more positive light. This climate of sport being 'in vogue' is a trend fuelled by its often mutually interdependent relationship with the media and MNCs through sports sponsorship and corporate social responsibility (Smith and Westerbeek, 2007) and by the financial and quasi-political power/influence that sport – and certain sports federations – now possess.

This publication identifies some of the opportunities for this form of development. One benefit, alluded to above, is that sport-in-development is often directed at audiences (such as youth, disabled and women) where traditional development programmes often neglect to address their specific developmental demands. This is particularly the case for young people – a group that the World Bank's 2007 World Development Report, claims is 'neither seen nor heard' in Poverty Reduction Strategies (World Bank, 2007: 235) and as Nicholls discusses in Chapter 7, comprise nearly half the population of the world. Nicholls and Crabbe highlight in their respective chapters the engagement of young people in development activity through schemes like Positive Futures, Goal (in Delhi) and OlympAfrica Youth Ambassador Programme (Lesotho).

In relation to special populations, Beacom (Chapter 5) identifies the potential of disability sport to contribute to the rehabilitation of individuals, in many cases disabled as a result of endemic poverty, political instability and poor health care; the characteristics of underdevelopment. While cultural differences relating to disability present additional challenges to donor-recipient relations in the development process, links to wider debate on the universality of human rights highlights the role of advocacy and social action as part development in relation to people with disabilities.

Furthermore, despite the concerns of gender imaging in sport, a surprising number of sport-in-development initiatives do address women (although Saavedra emphasizes in Chapter 6 that there should be far more focusing on gender). Goal, Moving the Goalposts and Go Sisters are examples of three such programmes that have been addressed by a number of chapters in this publication. Crabbe highlights how Goal is directed towards the empowerment of young women in Delhi. Saavedra notes that the Moving the Goalposts objective is to empower girls through improving literacy, training women in business management and other general capacity-building and education activities. Similarly, Nicholls describes the Go Sisters programme (run by the Sports NGO EduSport Foundation), which aims to provide girls with an education, to highlight the dangers of HIV/AIDS as well as to provide employment skills.

A second perceived benefit is that sport-in-development projects bring together institutions and actors that often have contrasting ideologies (Armstrong, 2002) or positions on development, leading to a deeper critical appreciation of what constitutes effective development. One particularly important issue that arises from this detail are the lessons that donors from developed (Northern) states can learn from the debates/activity taking place in relation to assistance in the Global South. In this case, there is a close link with Crabbe's chapter where he talks at length about the challenging role of peer leaders and their central importance to the delivery of Positive Futures and its diffusion to regions in the Global South. Such an example highlights the potential of the academic community to contribute to the sport-in-development debate through the 'application of theory to practice'. It also relates to comments made in the introductory chapter to the Dreams + Teams programme that requires collaboration to train leaders in both developed and developing states and the capacity for/ importance of knowledge transfer.

The chapters in this book are then concerned with a variety of perspectives on the increased use of sport in the process of international development, particularly in outlining the many 'micro' schemes that exist. The range of case studies incorporated into the chapters, demonstrate how sport might be viewed as a new 'engine' to assist development.

First, specific programmes have introduced sport to alleviate the tension caused by conflict fought along ethnic lines. Many of these emanate from sporting NGOs such as Football4Peace (football coaching to bring Arab and Jewish children together) and Football For Peace, (to 'encourage co-ed football, teach self-responsibility, improve capabilities in conflict resolution and to fight the ethnic divide of the Rwandan population'). This example, also cited by Levermore in Chapter 2, highlights the involvement of relatively recent (BP) and traditional (UNICEF) development actors, in partnering to support this initiative.

This cluster can be broadened to incorporate building social cohesion in societies *not* affected by violent ethnic conflict. This includes tackling exclusion based on race, gender, youth (the Laureus Sport for Good Foundation helps young people overcome a range of issues that help exclude them from society) and poverty (one of Streetfootballworld's objectives, highlighted in Chapter 10 by Akindes and Kirwin, is to incorporate homeless people into mainstream society).

The engagement of sports organizations in development work is not dependent upon traditional resource transfer between donors and recipients. Fokwang's Chapter 9 demonstrates how, on the basis of self-help and without external donors, communities in developing states can become empowered through sports based organizations, to enhance their neighbourhoods and achieve a degree of social cohesion that produces tangible results in terms of quality of life of the inhabitants. His case study of the Ntambag Brothers Association (NBA) highlights one example of where a commitment to self-manage the community development process without recourse to local government, the state or powerful Western institutions, can nevertheless, result in 'community development'. As Fokwang notes, 'this does not imply that the NBA would reject prospective assistance from external development sponsors but it remains questionable whose agenda would prevail were such a "partnership" to emerge'.

Second, sport is used to help in the building of physical, social, and community infrastructures, regarded by many as an essential factor for development to succeed. This can happen as a by-product of building a sporting infrastructure, especially via sport plus schemes (for instance FIFA's Goal programme) and sports events, as identified by Cornelissen, highlighting how some believe that hosting sports events can contribute to reinvigorating the physical infrastructure of a city or region through the building of roads, hotels, job creation *etceteras*. This chapter also notes that developing a sporting infrastructure includes more than building stadia and having access to sports equipment. Deloitte in South Africa advertise that their experience with sports events helps them also develop enterprise and employment for underemployed black communities.

However, it is in the context of capacity-building that sport plays more of a role in building physical and intellectual infrastructures. Plus sport schemes are at the forefront of this activity as the Positive Futures (Chapter 8), MYSA (Chapter 3) and the Playing for Peace programme (that uses basketball to teach children about building community involvement and leadership) demonstrate.

Third, sport has a long history of raising awareness of important issues in a seemingly non-political manner. Educating communities about HIV/Aids dominates the activities of sport-for-development in this field. Projects include the Nike-sponsored Yes to Soccer programme (run by MercyCorps), and Alive and Kicking (which employs local labour forces in countries like Kenya to make durable leather footballs, with HIV/Aids and malaria awareness messages printed on them).

Fourth, many of these educational awareness programmes combine with the first two categories listed in an attempt to *empower* those who are traditionally marginalized. In the context of sport-in-development, girls and young women feature frequently under these schemes, as the examples above highlight. Again, the chapters by Nicholls and Saavedra are particularly adept in discussing this benefit of sport-in-development. Fifth, sport is believed to improve physical and psychological health (World Health Organization, 2003). Whilst the educational/health awareness projects noted above clearly assist health initiatives, this category focuses on more direct schemes, such as programmes that increase physical activity, which the WHO (2003) claims 'improves diets, discourages the use of tobacco, alcohol and drugs, helps reduce violence, enhances functional capacity and promotes social interaction and integration'. This aspect of sport-in-development is also dominated by plus sport NGOs such as Magic Bus. Coalter in this publication illustrates how this programme focuses on improving the health of all children. Sport assists by creating a healthy physical environment, whilst also distracting young people from less healthy pastimes (drugs, gambling *etceteras*). A further example is Right to Play (whose senior officer, Lorna Read, has contributed to the preface in this book), a well-established Toronto-based organization that runs 40 projects in over twenty countries, that includes the improvement of physical health as one of its main objectives. Beacom's reference to medical research on the value of sport in rehabilitation programmes is also noteworthy in this respect.

The sixth category, the use of sport to assist economic development and poverty reduction, has not featured so prominently in this publication. However, Levermore does show in Chapter 2 (2.2) how modernization and neo-liberal perspectives might interpret such macro economic trends in both the sport-in-development movement and the global sports industry in general. Cornelissen also highlights in Chapter 4 that a strong mercantilist ideology drives sports events, identifying four processes behind this.

Some might regard this documenting of the benefits of the sport-in-development and wider sport/development relationship as being superficial, one-dimensional (focusing on sport without an understanding of the societies in which the programmes or events are located (Dunning *et al.*, 1993)) and akin to the functionalist perspectives that over-emphasize the optimistic quality of sport. Willis (2000) and Giulianotti (2004) note that this is often found in much practitioner and academic literature in this field. Similarly, other development perspectives argue that this summary reproduces the dominant understanding of development based around principles of modernization and neo-liberalism. This publication recognizes at the outset that the sport/development relationship requires a range of perspectives through which to assess opportunities and limitations. A starting point for these perspectives is provided by Levermore, who introduces the main (dominant) theories associated with international development to the sport-in-development discussion.

All chapters thereafter explicitly or implicitly analyse specific issues, topics and case studies through a range of theories that broadly speaking, challenge the orthodox functionalist approach to the subject material. Saavedra and Nicholls for instance, employ gender and feminist perspectives in their chapters; postcolonial understanding of sport-in-development is directly or indirectly referred to by Fokwang, Nicholls and Akindes and Kirwin. Fokwang in particular, draws on postcolonialism in focusing on the engagement of Youth Associations in Cameroon to the development process, suggesting that there needs to be considerably more transfers of knowledge from the Global South to the North. Beacom and Saavedra briefly refer to figurational theory when discussing arguments relating to the role of sport in the civilizing process. This informs the debate on the translation and interpretation of sporting forms as they are introduced into different cultural contexts. Furthermore, Crabbe draws on the theoretical work of Pierre Bourdieu and Antonio Gramsci when considering the role of sport in being a 'cultural intermediary' in its role as an agent for social change.

All chapters do then highlight some of the limitations of these development initiatives. Given these concerns, the enthusiasm with which specialist development agencies (such as the UN and WHO), publicly advocate towards sport-in-development is atypical of the response of mainstream development agencies who are generally reluctant to fully support sport-in-development initiatives. This is particularly so with international financial institutions – such as the World Bank, IMF and World Trade Organization – all central to the mainstream development process, whose often formal approach to development is probably a reason for its occasional failure to reach out or appeal to communities in need. This is especially the case in relation to youth audiences. The lack of engagement is recognized by a range of commentators including the ILO, World Bank and the UN. The ILO (2005), for instance, states that, 'in most cases development leaders perceive sports as a recreational tool rather than value-based engine for social changes'. As noted already in the introductory chapter, the UN tacitly admits this, stating in one policy document (2003: 2) that, 'Sport is seen as a by-product of development, not as an engine'.

Similarly, it is suspected that some traditional NGOs regard sport in much the same manner, viewing sporting projects (for development) as amateurish and distracting from the important/main realities and solutions for which funding is required.

11.2 Key concerns

Quite often strategic decisions in sport-in-development are conducted from the top-down (described by Nicholls as being a 'vertical hierarchy'), resulting in those working, and delivering these projects, being excluded from discussions concerning evaluation, good practice and strategic decisions. Similar arguments were presented by Saavedra in Chapter 6 on gender, Crabbe in Chapter 8 (mentors and instructors have little input into the review of Positive Futures) and Beacom in Chapter 5 (people with disabilities need opportunities to participate, compete and lead, manage, administer and develop their sports and sport-in-development initiatives). These comments are not dissimilar to widespread concerns about the largely one way donor-recipient relationship elsewhere in development studies. The issue of such exclusion forms one of the areas that will be considered in detail in the next section (11.2.1).

A further concern that has been raised throughout this publication is the lack of 'objective' measurement of sport/development, particularly the micro level initiatives promoted by sport plus and plus sport NGOs, and the extent to which measurement can be objective. This issue forms the basis of discussion in section 11.2.2. Assessing the issues of exclusion and evaluation leads us to re-visit the characteristics attributed to sport and development (section 11.2.3)

11.2.1 Inclusion and exclusion in sport-in-development

This publication has highlighted the many uses of sport, primarily through analysis of small scale programmes where communities/groups largely portrayed as being marginalized have been targeted in an effort to educate, provide employment and life skills, develop a better health system and infrastructure *etceteras*. As the introductory chapter highlights, the majority of these schemes are focused on young people. Other 'significant' groups targeted are the disabled, girls and women and refugees. As Levermore details in Chapter 2, it is the 'modern' sports of football, volleyball and basketball that provide the focus for most small scale sport-in-development programmes. However, these levels of 'inclusion' belie the extent of potential exclusion inherent within sport-in-development, especially if viewed from a critical perspective. There are two layers to the level of such exclusion.

The first relates simply to sports, communities and regions that currently lie outside of the parameters of the sport-in-development focus. Clearly, as noted above, the sports that are used are almost entirely modern sports. This has led a number of observers to argue that not only is traditional/indigenous sport excluded from the sport/development relationship but this exclusion is resulting in the death of such sports, which has implications for the socio-cultural fabric of the societies affected. As Akindes and Kirwin portray in Chapter 10, this process has been ongoing since colonial times. The travails of indigenous sport is discussed in more detail in section 11.2.3. A close inspection of the book also reveals that almost all the focus on sport/development has been in Sub-Saharan Africa. This is because the vast majority of schemes focus on the region, but more needs to be assessed of the sport/development dynamic in Latin America, Asia, Eastern/Central Europe, North Africa and the Pacific region, not least because of the requirement to understand the cultural nuances in play there that might determine the success or failure of sports events and sport-in-development initiatives. Likewise, there are communities, adults, the elderly, gay (Saavedra points out that there is an implicit message in sport and sport-in-development that participants are hetereosexual) and possibly rural, which are bypassed by the sport-in-development process. Moreover, as the chapters on young people, women and the disabled note, just because programmes are focused on them, this does not mean that they are *included* in creating strategy or evaluation and that the schemes that operate for them do so in the best manner. The same can be said for sport in general, away from the development process, as Saavedra demonstrates in Chapter 6 when asking, 'Why, if women and girls do engage in sport, are they still marginalized or at best a "special case" in the dominant practices, ideologies and organizations concerned with sport?'

Second, many authors in this publication point out that there is a problem with unequal power relations throughout sport and this is also evident in the sport/development relationship. As section 2.3.1 notes, sport can be viewed as a form of resistance, which might occasionally challenge dominant systems and processes, thereby redressing unequal power relations in limited instances. However, far more prevalent is the largely one-way communication process whereby Northern governments, development agencies (based in the US), NGOs, MNCs, higher education institutions, the media and sports federations and teams provide support, information, disseminate news, advice and establish many sport plus and plus sport initiatives. This is inevitably a problem that is concerning from dependency and post-colonial perspectives, especially when programmes and policies are initiated with excessive influence from powerful institutions and actors, which results in a poor understanding of cultural nuances, power imbalances *within* hierarchies and lack of input into policy creation and evaluation by organizations and communities in the Global South. The focus of many of these institutions is often to search for resources and meet the (high) expectations of donors. A corollary of this is exclusion in terms of stereotyping and representation of the poor that takes place through the representation of sport and is something addressed in detail in section 2.3.3. Nicholls (Chapter 7) calls these negative stereotypes 'homogenizing discourses' that continues to portray communities as being materially and often morally poor, disempowered and *needing* development. A working example of this is provided by the Netherlands Catholic Sports Federation, which aims to reduce the 'idleness' of youth in some of their plus-sport schemes (International Platform on Sport and Development, undated).

11.2.2 Evaluation

The relative newness of the movement and its, until now, limited links with the mainstream development community, has resulted in little substantive analysis of how the impact of sport-in-development programmes on recipient communities should be evaluated. However, there has been a 'call' for independent and 'objective' measurement of the power of sport as an agent for social change, especially in programmes that focus on young people, over the past decade. Nicholls addresses this issue in Chapter 7,[1] noting that evidence of the impact of sport participation on empowerment and criminal or delinquent activity among youth is extremely weak. A response is now emerging. Coalter has focused on the issue directly in two recent publications (2006, 2007). He addresses in Chapter 3 of this publication, the need for a complete reappraisal of the evaluation system itself, to ensure that an approach is adopted that works for sport-in-development practitioners, given the inherent instability of the environments within which many initiatives are operating. They must also avoid 'quantitative-led approaches' that Crabbe warns about in Chapter 8. In that sense the somewhat prescriptive performance indicators set out by funding bodies such as Sport England for Crabbe's case study were limiting and there needed to be a more collaborative approach to assessing the impact on young people – including ensuring the voices of young participants, local residents and community groups were heard. In relation to the transferability of the programme to other cultural contexts, particularly in the Global South, this could only take place effectively, if again, such a collaborative and participatory approach were to be adopted. Full participation may provide an arena for grassroots strategists' voices to be heard and provide a forum for their work to be published in the North.

This leads to the suggestion for a 'process-led participatory approach' to evaluation that is integrated into the wider development process and encourages dialogue between different partners. Coalter argues that such an approach can contribute to the promotion of transparency and accountability that is significant not only to funders' interested in the impact of programmes, but also to the sport-in-development organizations – especially in societies where transparency might not be the norm (see also, Munro, 2004).

Alongside this analysis of evaluation strategies in the international environment, the emphasis in the domestic sport policy process, toward target driven policy, has focused the attention of key agencies such as Sport England, on developing strategies to evaluate impact. Most noteworthy, this has led to the creation of the 'Value of Sport Monitor' – a framework that has direct transferability into the wider sport-in-development debate. Clearly it is important to learn from domestic experiences where sport has been used to achieve a range of social and economic objectives and where the issue of evaluation has been addressed in a variety of ways. Crabbe discusses the opportunities and limitations of the initiative Positive Futures, to achieve meaningful social development in a number of community development settings as one example of where domestic experiences can inform debate on international development. Crabbe highlights the difficulty in measuring 'outcomes' in what is essentially a programme aimed at engaging young people in such a way as to build relationships and achieve meaningful social development with projects acting as 'cultural intermediaries, providing gateways between what are often seen as alien and mutually intimidating worlds' (United Kingdom Government Home Office, 2003: 9). Throughout, the focus is on a process based participatory approach to evaluating the influence of the programme on young people that largely answers the call by Coalter for this system of evaluation (a similar ethnographic approach is evident in the work of Fokwang, see Chapter 9).

Other chapters in the book also address the issue of evaluation – but from slightly different perspectives. In the case of Cornelissen (Chapter 4) the complexities and limitations of applying orthodox economic impact models to an evaluation of the effect of international sporting events in development, is explored. She highlights the lack of attention to the social consequences of large-scale events and stresses the need for a multi-dimensional approach to evaluation. Nicholls (Chapter 7) meanwhile, argues that empirical evidence is important in building acceptance and understanding of any concept. She stresses that organizations such as the MYSA and the Zimbabwe Sport and Recreation Commission – both implementing sport-in-development programmes for a number of years, have built up a solid basis of 'evidence' that could benefit the wider debate. At the same time, peer educators (participants in the sense of being instructors of programmes) who are pivotal to the success of programmes and have a practical understanding of how sport development works, need to be directly engaged in the evaluation process. In this sense as the sport-in-development community seeks to enhance the accountability and efficacy of their programmes, the provision of a conduit for youth expertise to contribute to peer-reviewed academic literature could add significant value.

While the sport-in-development community is gradually developing strategies to address the challenge of evaluation, the book argues that other related disciplines must be drawn into the debate. The experiences of the mainstream development community is of particular importance in this respect. The decades of evaluation produced by agencies such as the World Bank should be consulted to seek out its viability for both sport-in-development initiatives as well as the broader economic benefits that are proclaimed for sports events. Yet, they should avoid both the issue of 'tick-box mentality' associated with some measurement processes (evaluation conducted for the sake of evaluation) and the trap of using evaluation to bolster the mainstream understanding of development (Peet, 1991: 4).[2] Crabbe alludes to the pressures that donors have to enhance the results that their evaluation requires in order to entice enough participants to justify the presence of football club coaches, who often lead sports sessions.

Other academic communities can also make a valuable contribution. Beacom notes that there is a substantial body of literature that relates to the capacity of sport to contribute to the rehabilitation process. This predominantly medical literature (see for example, Silver (2003), Anderson (2003), Williams *et al.* (2001) and Dougherty (2001)) as well as the WHO (April 2005) has the capacity to identify tangible benefits, specifically gains made, physiologically and psychologically, through the use of sport. Research in this area has already identified in particular:

• Reducing incidences of rehospitalization
• Reduced reporting of clinical depression
• Improvements in physical competence
• Improvements in self-concept and self-efficacy
• Reduced reporting of loneliness and isolation

Yet there is no evidence that to date such literature has been addressed in the general debate in evaluation of sport-in-development.

Evaluation of sport-in-development is then, a complex process requiring practitioners to adopt a sophisticated nuanced approach that both takes account of cultural sensitivities and produces tangible evidence of impact. Such a multi-dimensional approach will require both 'outcomes' and 'process' based evaluation, the adoption of collaboration with a range of actors involved in the process and a willingness to learn from other disciplinary areas.

11.2.3   Re-thinking the parameters of sport and development

Given the debates outlined in the two preceding sections, there is a need to review the interrelationship of sport and development. As the introductory chapter notes, the phrase development is frequently equated with a dynamic process which is expressed through terms such as 'progress', 'improvement', 'growth' and 'enhancement'. This is subsequently related to physiological processes underpinning the 'development' of individual athletic performance as much as to the social and cultural processes linked with the development of sporting forms. In both cases, development is considered as a linear process. This idea of linear development has carried over into debate as to the characteristics of wider 'human development'. As discussed by Levermore, until relatively recently, the dominant view of social and economic development, was for instance, linked to the idea of *modernization* through *industrialization* and corresponding economic growth. Such ideas fostered the concept of a linear development path, which was quantifiable and which, crucially, could be replicated given the correct pre-conditions. Other perspectives on development that are gaining currency coalesce around a more holistic conception of approaches to enhancing the human condition. These variously relate to the linking of social welfare to economics, replacing concerns about 'standard of living' with a focus on more general well-being and quality of life indicators, environmental health, sustainability, and political freedom (Cowen and Shenton, 1996). Contemporary writers concern themselves with how the agenda for development is defined and attempt to understand the nature of the relationship between donors and recipients.[3] Others see the idea of 'development' as essentially flawed (Norgaard, 1994).

Moving away from the linear perspective of development, a separate body of literature adopts the idea of development as passing through a series of stages, encompassing both destruction and renewal. Development theorists Cowen and Shenton (1996) refer for instance to early writers such as Mills and Burke concerning the 'contribution' of imperialism to development of the human condition. In Burke's writing for instance, the contention was that British imperial intervention in India had led to a regression in Indian society, although there was also a belief in the potential of imperial intervention to ultimately enhance the human condition.[4] Similarly, Frey, (1988) noted how modern (Northern) sports have been welcomed previously in some Global South communities as evidence of 'progression' whilst in others it is seen as the imposition of imperialist values and norms. Fokwang (Chapter 9) lends some credence to this by considering how indigenous sports teams in Cameroon readily borrow European sports teams names and even after development/economic projects (such as the World Bank 'Pipelines' programme).

This argument of development as encompassing destruction and renewal is readily found within the wider context of sport as an aspect of the development process. Levermore in Chapter 2 cites Bale (2004) who refers to the destruction of indigenous forms of sport. As has been the experience in the Global North (Beacom 1998) these old ways of playing evolved from a distinct physical culture that in many respects, is the antipathy of highly specialized athleticism. Similarly, Heinemann (1993: 145) highlighted how, 'Traditional modes of sport – especially dancing in the third world countries – are cultivated in order to sustain and convey a common culture and identity', yet the conservation of traditional sports are often now trivialized as a tourist attraction or as television entertainment. It has largely been superseded by modern (Northern) sport.

While the process of sport development has seen the destruction of some forms of indigenous physical activities, and while there is little evidence of traditional activities forming part of sport-in-development activity, there are strong arguments for taking a closer look at the capacity to engage in development in the context of indigenous sporting forms. Indeed, anecdotal information suggests that the Indian MNC, Tata, supports indigenous forms of sport-in-development. The challenge for the sport-in-development community is however, to avoid the perceived imposition of such 'old ways of playing' in the face of the manifest popularity of international sports such as soccer (Guttmann, 1994). It will require rather, the empowering of communities to take decisions on sporting forms that they engage with.

Given the range of controversies and limitations discussed in this chapter, can sport continue to be regarded seriously as a potential new engine to help promote development initiatives? Some mainstream, traditional development actors are most wary of the claims made by many supporters of sport-in-development, especially when development is viewed in reductionist terms to mean a right to access food and water. How much has changed since Heinemann (1993: 145) commented that:

> Developing countries are faced with various problems such as population surplus, inadequate nutritional resources, low economic growth, lack of jobs, and low educational levels. These problems certainly have greater priority than the attempt to furnish the whole population with the means for developing sport and attaining the sorts of performance levels prevalent in industrial countries.

That does not mean that sport is superfluous but mass sport might be regarded as being of minor significance if Heinemann's 1993 estimates that only 2–5% of the population in Global South societies still hold true.

Where does the right to play sport, or its use in the social development initiatives highlighted throughout this publication and as articulated in the preface, fit within such basic and urgent developmental requirements? Surely, such a debate distracts from what *really* matters in development? Additionally, the long-standing disdain that many policy-makers have had for 'low' culture activities like sport because it lacked *sophistication, intelligence* and was linked to characteristics of male exclusivity, has been supplemented by a growing level of headlines in recent years surrounding greed, corruption, 'unsporting' practices and the use of sport for political and commercial reasons in mainstream (modern) sport. Without a substantial bank of objective evaluation, there are concerns too about the messages being transmitted by sport-in-development initiatives. Are projects, as Crabbe asks in Chapter 8, providing a transient appeal as 'participants search for "highs" rather than helping to build reciprocal forms of cooperation and collectivity?'. Sport schemes can lead to unrealistic dreams and expectations for those participants; Akindes and Kirwin (Chapter 10) remind us that some really hope that it might lead to professional sport and the wealth and lifestyle associated with it.

Why should such a tarnished product be associated as an agent to create positive social change? How long will it be before the adverse headlines result in the decline of sports usage in these schemes? Are there already signs that sport is losing its place as a potential agent for social change? How much will contemporary analyses emulate Frey's (1988: 66) contention that 'in reality, the impact of sport is over played, short-term, and of minor relevance to development'? Even in the UK for instance, where the government continues to adhere to the concept of sport as a tool to achieve social objectives, the November 2007 speech by Purnell, the Secretary of State for Culture Media and Sport, appeared to signal a re-focusing on investment in 'sport for sport's sake'.[5] Just as we are arguing that the sport-in-development movement is at least in part due to 'spillover' from the domestic commitment to development through sport, so a re-defining of sport in the domestic policy agenda may begin to influence how government perceives sport in the context of wider development objectives.

Crabbe in this publication provides one riposte to these arguments. Sport for the youth audience – long neglected by traditional development policies – is attractive because it does not always have a pure image. The 'bad boy' reputation is particularly useful in trying to entice those engaged in potentially anti-social and criminal activities. Moreover, the argument that those in the 'Global South' have more important issues to be concerned with other than sport essentially dehumanizes them. They have as much right as anyone to play sport, whether that is defined as being mainstream or indigenous sport. Akindes and Kirwin also highlight here that athleticism is often crucial to survival in some sub-Saharan African communities, pointing out that games and physical exercise have long been a part of pre-colonial Africa and continues to be a compulsory aspect of many African school curricula. There is a degree of Eurocentrism in reading sport in the ways highlighted above.

11.3   Ideas for future research

In his oblique criticism of the attempts by historians to predict the future, Fisher (1936 preface) comments that 'men wiser and more learned than I have discerned in history a plot, a rhythm, a pre-determined pattern. These harmonies are concealed from me'. While historical determinism has its limitations when charting the development movement and predicting its future trajectory, it is nevertheless helpful to at least identify what appears to be emerging patterns of development assistance, as areas worthy of future research.

11.3.1 Shifts in global relations

Critical literature relating to the development of modern sport (for example, Maguire 1999, Sudgen and Tomlinson 2002) has tended to focus on the unequal power relations between the Global North ('home' of most sporting codes that dominate the international sport environment) and the Global South as recipient first of these 'new' ways of playing and latterly of sport-in-development as a contribution to the development process. Earlier chapters have also referred to discourse concerning player exploitation whereby the flow of talented young players from developing states to developed states, reduces the net pool of talent and contributes to the difficulties faced by Southern states in the international sporting environment. Yet the recent re-alignment of international sport has in a number of contexts, called this into question.

The first relates to the increase in the awarding and hosting of prestigious sports events in countries within the Global South. This includes Formula One motor racing, football tournaments (such as South Africa 2010) and athletics meetings (Olympics in Beijing, 2008 and the Commonwealth Games in Delhi, 2010). This represents a shifting balance in the placement of power in global sport. A particularly apt example is the creation of a new Indian Twenty20 cricket Premier league, which arguably articulates in international cricket this re-alignment of power relations. This highly lucrative league drew enormous sums in the bidding for the eight franchises, with players also attracting contract fees of between $100,000 and $1m to play. Foreign players have been attracted from Australia and New Zealand.[6] This, combined with what BBC Cricket correspondent Bose, presents as a relatively weak International Cricket Council (ICC) with little authority on the international direction of the game, is likely to result in the terms of reference of international cricket competitions being increasingly influenced by the Indian league – a marked inversion of North – South sporting relations.[7] Ultimately, this trend will have implications for the sport/development relationship and is deserving of close scrutiny in future research projects.

11.3.2 International events and the emergence of new actors

Leading on from the shifts in global relations, it is noteworthy to reiterate that the next two so-called 'mega-events' – the 2008 Olympics in Beijing and the 2010 FIFA World Cup in South Africa – are taking place in states outside the Global North. Given the significant body of literature concerning the relationship between major events and the development process, this would suggest that, at least in the short term, states not traditionally known as development donors have an enhanced role to play in the process. The Beijing Organizing Committee for the Olympic Games (BOCOG) news bulletins at the time of writing were regularly making reference to engagement of the 2008 organizers in international dialogue relating to sport and development.[8] The Chinese Foreign Ministry has made a number of statements concerning the responsibility of the Chinese as hosts of the 2008 Games, to engage in the international development process. Foreign Minister, Yang Jiechi, in a recent speech noted that 'the Olympic spirit matches the theme of the times – peace and development – and expresses the common desire of the Chinese people all over the world'. He expressed the belief that the Beijing Olympics would be a success and would benefit 'peace, friendship and cooperation worldwide'.[9] While it remains to be seen the extent to which this is substance or rhetoric, and while in the past, Mao's regime did seek to foster relations with regimes in the Global South through development assistance, it nevertheless demonstrates a significant shift in international development narratives and positions China at the forefront of that process. Indeed it is likely that, in light of the negative coverage of Chinese influence in African development, diplomatic efforts of the hosts will be focused on finding alternative, less politicized development discourses. In view of the aftermath of the Games in Beijing it will be interesting to trace evidence of changing patterns of engagement with sport-in-development. This apparent change in international sporting power relations reflects to some extent wider geo-political change as China expands its sphere of influence to support its domestic growth patterns (*The Economist,* 2008). The capacity to project such 'soft power' through activity such as sport-in-development can however, have implications for the trajectory of the development process.

Similarly, in relation to the 2010 FIFA World Cup, while there is much debate concerning the long term social and economic impact of the event on the cities and regions of South and southern Africa, it is creating a range of new opportunities to link sport development to broader development agendas. As such it is again shifting the centre of gravity of the development process away from the traditional donor states of the Global North.

11.3.3 Breaking down the domestic/international development dichotomy

There is a tendency to discuss international development as dominated by inter-state/transnational transference of resources and not to recognize that key elements of development relate to any situation – intra as well as international. Crabbe's discussion of Positive Futures goes some way to responding to such criticism. The asymmetrical nature of development across states in both the Global South and Global North is noteworthy. In this sense intra-state development assistance is as relevant as inter-state activity. This is evident for instance, in the work of the Australian Sport Commission and their research with aboriginal people who have suffered disproportionately from under-development. It is of interest how the Australian Sport Commission (December 2007) presents the 'value of sport' as, 'Active participation in sport brings with it a multitude of positive values for Indigenous communities', including:

- diverting indigenous people, particularly juveniles, away for antisocial behaviour and the criminal justice system
- inherent health benefits, both physical (reducing the risk of sedentary related conditions like obesity, and mental (promoting healthy well being and reducing depression and anxiety)
- improving the social cohesion between indigenous people and non-indigenous people
- providing active participants with essential life skills like communication , cooperation and leadership, and instil the value of effort
- the promotion of respect, equity, discipline and fair play
- encouraging active participants to pursue excellence, both sporting and personal.

On that basis, a package of sport-in-development programmes and initiatives are being delivered, with a range of objectives now familiar in a number of international development contexts. There is for example, clear evidence of sport plus and plus sport objectives in a programme that: 'aims to increase indigenous participation in structured sport at all levels, build the sporting capacity of indigenous people to organize, manage and deliver sustainable community sport and support talented indigenous sportspeople to achieve their sporting goals' (Australian Sport Commission, December 2007).

11.4   On a final note

In relation to actors involved in the development process, the continuing dominance of the state has implications for the trajectory of sport-in-development in the coming years. The Sport for Development and Peace International Working Group posits that the future of sport as a tool for development and peace ultimately depends on national governments (2006). Yet the prominent role played by the UN and international agencies has yet to resonate at the governmental level. Many governments, in both developed and developing states have yet to be convinced of the potential of sport as a development tool. In spite of the range of other actors engaged in the process, unless and until the relevant government departments (primarily international development departments within developed states and education and community development departments within developing states) engage directly with the sport-in-development agenda, progress will be limited.

As section 11.2.2 points out, this book has focused almost entirely on sport/development within sub-Saharan Africa. As noted earlier in the chapter, this is because the vast majority of schemes focus on that region. Much more work needs to be done on the sport/development dynamic in Latin America, Asia, Eastern/Central Europe, North Africa and the Pacific region, not least because of the requirement to understand the cultural nuances in play there that might determine the success or failure of sports events and sport-in-development initiatives.

Finally, it may be argued that there is value in studying sport-in-development as it can provide a way of articulating the dynamics of the wider development process. Such argument has been presented in other disciplinary contexts. Elias and Dunning (1986) for example, contended that the study of sport provides a window into wider social configurations and so becomes a focal point of study for figurational sociologists (Guilianotti, 2004). Such study should also enable the sport-in-development community to engage with the mainstream development debates, which is after all, a central objective of this publication. The initial efforts of the editors to engage the mainstream development community through conference activity, provided some indication of the challenges inherent in such an endeavour. Nevertheless, as long as sport-in-development remains peripheral to the development movement such scholarly activity is of considerable importance. At the same time, the efficacy of scholarly activity relating to sport-in-development is ultimately dependent upon intellectual inquiry across a number of academic areas. This book has referred variously to the value of international relations theory, mainstream development theory and feminist theory as all contributing to the debate on the direction of sport-in-development. There are others, for example community development theory which, for the past four decades has analysed community relations, and constructed models for community empowerment and policy theory which can contribute to an understanding of the policy process relating to development. The cross-disciplinary nature of the subject requires engagement by a range of academics and practitioners if it is to progress beyond the narrow functionalist field that it has inhabited until now and produce meaningful discourse that can inform the future direction of sport-in-development.

Notes

1 See also Coakley, 2002 who is quoted in the World Development Report, 2007 (World Bank, 2007: 237).
2 Peet identifies that a major problem with measuring development is that it means different things to different people and communities and institutions. Often conventional (Northern) accounting procedures are used and 'solid' economic indicators are sought. This ignores informal aspects (in the wider development context this means informal exchanges, the work of the family (women) and informal education.)
3 One of the most contentious contemporary writers on development is Sen (2001).
4 Engagement of modern sporting forms as a response by the occupying powers to perceived cultural deprivation or indeed cultural regression, has been the subject of exhaustive historical analysis – see for example Mangan (1988), particularly Chapter 5, 'Eton in India'.
5 The Secretary of State for Culture Media and Sport, James Purnell. Speech, 28th November 2007 – 'World Class Community Sport'. In the speech Purnell makes the observation that: '...and yes sport does have all these other [social health and educational] benefits and I'm delighted about that. But they are not the reason we love it. They are not the reason the government is committed to it. Sport is a joy and a passion, not because we can learn about Newton's laws through the movement of a snooker ball, but because of the beauty of sport itself'.
6 While at time of writing, English players under domestic contract are unable to compete in the league, negotiations continue and are likely to result in opening up opportunities for participation in succeeding years.
7 Interview with Mihir Bose, BBC Radio 4 'Today' programme – Friday 14th March 2008.
8 For example, see BOCOG news release (4th January 2008) *Consolidated Strength to make the Olympic and Paralympic Games a Great Success*. http://en.beijing2008.cn/news/official/preparation/n214225780.shtml BOCOG news release (31st October 2007) *Success Stories, Partnerships and Future Activity*. http://en.beijing2008.cn/news/official/ioc/n214186801.shtml.

9 http://en.beijing2008.cn/news/official/preparation/n214203464.shtml
Olympic theme features Foreign Ministry public gathering (2007-11-26)

Bibliography

Anderson, J. (2003) 'Turned into Taxpayers: Paraplegia, Rehabilitation and Sport at Stoke Mandeville', in *Journal of Contemporary History*, **38**(3): 461–475.

Armstrong, G. (2002) 'Talking Up the Game: Football and the Reconstruction of Liberia', *Identities*, **9**(4): 471–494.

Australian Sport Commission (13th December 2007) *Indigenous Sport and Development* http://www.ausport.gov.au/participating/all/indigenous

Bale, J. (2004) 'Three Geographies of African Footballer Migration: Patterns, Problems and Postcoloniality', in *Football in Africa: Conflict, Conciliation and Community* (eds. Gary Armstrong and Richard Giulianotti). Basingstoke and New York: Palgrave Macmillan, pp. 229–246.

Beacom, A. (1998) 'Indigenous Sport and the Search for Belonging', *The Sports Historian*, **18**(2): 34–62.

BOCOG news release (4th January 2008) *Consolidated Strength to make the Olympic and Paralympic Games a Great Success.* http://en.beijing2008.cn/news/official/preparation/n214225780.shtml

BOCOG news release (31st October 2007) *Success Stories, Partnerships and Future Activity.* http://en.beijing2008.cn/news/official/ioc/n214186801.shtml

BOCOG news release (26th November 2007) *Olympic theme features Foreign Ministry public gathering* http://en.beijing2008.cn/news/official/preparation/n214203464.shtml

Coakley, J. (2002) 'Using Sports to Control Deviance and Violence among Youths: Let's Be Critical and Cautious', in Margaret Gatz, Michael A. Messner, and Sandra J. Ball-Rokeach (eds), *Paradoxes of Youth and Sport*. Albany: State University of New York Press, pp. 13–30.

Coalter, F. (2006) *Sport-in-Development: A Monitoring and Evaluation Manual.* London: UK Sport.

Coalter, F. (2007) *A wider social role for sport: who's keeping the score?* London: Routledge.

Cowen, M. and Shenton, R. (1996) *Doctrines of Development*. London: Routledge.

Dougherty, P. (2001) 'Transtibial Amputees from Vietnam War: 28 Year Follow-up', *The Journal of Bone and Joint Surgery*, **83**: 383–389.

Dunning, E., Maguire, J. and Pearton, R. (1993) *The Sports Process: A Comparative and Developmental Approach*. London: Human Kinetics.

Dunning, E. and Rojek, C. (eds) (1992) *Sport and Leisure in the Civilizing Process*. Basingstoke: Macmillan.

The Economist (15th–21st March 2008) 'The Ravenous Dragon: Special Report on China's Thirst for Resources', pp. 3–18.

Elias, N. and Dunning, E. (1986) *Quest for Excitement: Sport and Leisure in the Civilizing Process*. Oxford: Basil Blackwell.

Fisher, H. (1936) *A History of Europe*. London: Edward Arnold & Co.

Frey, J.H. (1988) 'The Internal and External Role of Sport in National Development', *Journal of National Development*, **1**, 65–82.

The Guardian (2004) 'The penny's dropped', 21st August.

Giulianotti, R. (ed.) (2004) *Sport and Modern Social Theorists*. Basingstoke and New York: Palgrave Macmillan.

Guttmann, A. (1994) *Games and Empires*. New York: Columbia University Press.

Heinemann, K. (1993), 'Sport in Developing Countries', in *The Sports Process* (eds. Dunning *et al.*), pp. 139–150.

International Labour Organisation (2005) *ILO's Youth Sport Programme and Common Framework on Sport and Development. Socio and economic insertion and jobs opportunities for the youth,* accessed from http://staging.ilo.org/public/english/universitas/download/events/ba_boll_final.pdf, accessed 21st October 2007.

International Platform on Sport and Development (undated) 'Peace and Sports Programme, Kenya, Sudan and Uganda' accessed: http://www.sportanddev.org/en/projects/kenya/index_675.htm, 6th January, 2008.

Maguire, J. (1999) *Global Sport: Identities, Societies, Civilizations*. Cambridge: Polity Press.

Mangan, J. (1998) *The Games Ethic and Imperialism: Aspects of the diffusion of an ideal*. London: Frank Cass.

Munro, B. (2004) 'Greed vs Good Governance: The fight for corruption-free football in Kenya'. Paper presented at *Play the Game 2005 – Governance in Sport: The Good, The Bad and The Ugly*, Copenhagen, accessed from http://www.playthegame.org

Norgaard, R. (1994) *Development Betrayed: The end of progress and a co-evolutionary revisioning of the future*. London: Routledge.

Peet, R. (1991) *Global Capitalism: Theories of Societal Development*. London and New York: Routledge.

Purnell, J. (28th November 2007) Speech: 'World Class Community Sport' http://www.culture.gov.uk/Reference_library/Minister_Speeches/Ministers_Speech

Sen, A. (2001) *Development as Freedom*. Oxford: Oxford University Press.

Silver, J. (2003) *History of the Treatment of Spinal Injuries*. New York: Kluwer Academic/Springer.

Smith, A.C.T. and Westerbeek, H.M. (2007) 'Sport as a Vehicle for Deploying Corporate Social Responsibility', *Journal of Corporate Citizenship*, **25** (Spring), 43–54.

Sporting Equals (undated) 'About Sporting Equals', accessed: http://www.sportingequals.com/page_landing.asp?section=000100010004, 24th March, 2008.

Sugden, J. and Tomlinson, A. (eds) (2002) *Power Games: A critical sociology of sport*. London: Routledge.

United Kingdom Government Home Office (2003) *Cul-de-sacs and gateways: Understanding the Positive Futures Approach*. London: Home Office.

United Nations (2003) *Sport for Development and Peace: Towards Achieving the Millennium Development Goals*. Washington: United Nations.

Willis, O. (2000) 'Sport and Development: The significance of Mathare Youth Sports Association', *Canadian Journal of Development Studies*, **XXI**(3): 825–849.

World Bank (2007) *World Development Report, 2007: Development and the Next Generation*. Washington: World Bank.

World Health Organization (2003) *Health and Development Through Physical Activity and Sport*. Geneva: World Health Organization.

World Health Organization (14th April 2005) *Disability: Including Prevention, Management and Rehabilitation.* Report to the 58th World Health Assembly. Geneva: WHO.

Williams T. *et al.* (2001) 'Sport and Rehabilitation – Patterns of Initial and Continuing Participation in Wheelchair Basketball in the UK and Germany', in Doll-Tepper *et al., New Horizons in Sport for Athletes with a Disability: Proceedings of the International Vista '99 Conference (Vol2)* Oxford: Meyer & Meyer Sport (UK) Ltd., pp. 603–614.

Index